DESERT STORM AIR WAR

*The Aerial Campaign against Saddam's Iraq
in the 1991 Gulf War*

JIM CORRIGAN

STACKPOLE BOOKS
Guilford, Connecticut

Published by Stackpole Books
An imprint of Globe Pequot
Trade Division of The Rowman & Littlefield Publishing Group, Inc.
4501 Forbes Boulevard, Suite 200, Lanham, Maryland 20706
www.rowman.com

Distributed by NATIONAL BOOK NETWORK

British Library Cataloguing in Publication Information Available

Library of Congress Cataloging-in-Publication Data Available

ISBN 978-0-8117-1776-2 (hardcover)
ISBN 978-0-8117-6589-3 (e-book)

♾️™ The paper used in this publication meets the minimum requirements of American National Standard for Information Sciences—Permanence of Paper for Printed Library Materials, ANSI/ NISO Z39.48-1992.

CONTENTS

AIRPOWER IN THE GROUND WAR

Author's Note

This book uses NATO reporting names for Soviet and Chinese military equipment deployed by Iraq, such as the MiG-25 *Foxbat*.

Mach 1 is the speed of sound, or roughly 765 miles per hour depending on environmental conditions.

A *kill box* is a map square where warplanes may attack ground targets freely and without further authorization.

The *golden BB* is every combat pilot's nightmare—a lucky shot, perhaps even fired blindly—that brings down an aircraft.

Foreword

By Col. Ralph Getchell (Ret.)
Stealth pilot and squadron commander during Operation Desert Storm

To most Americans, mention of the 1991 Gulf War conjures up CNN broadcasts of grainy videos showing high-tech U.S. weaponry in action. Certainly, for the average taxpayer there was a certain satisfaction in seeing the results of the Reagan-era military buildup, which had been intended to counterbalance the Warsaw Pact. The army's M1A1 main battle tank and Bradley Fighting Vehicle, the navy's Tomahawk-equipped fleet, and the air force's stealth aircraft and precision weapons all had their turn in the media spotlight, touting our technological superiority over potential adversaries equipped with Soviet-made hardware.

This modern arsenal was developed to provide our national leaders with the tools necessary to pursue and achieve national objectives. In the summer of 1990, the overarching objective regarding the Iraqi invasion of Kuwait was clearly and concisely stated by President George H. W. Bush in his famous "this shall not stand" speech. In the months of coalition-building that followed, the objectives became more specific: to expel the Iraqi invaders from Kuwait and substantially reduce Iraq's ability to attack neighboring countries in the future.

At first glance, this may have seemed an easy task for the world's greatest military power. The U.S. military by itself certainly had the force structure, but first we had to move many units based in Europe and the Pacific Rim, which supported defense commitments there. U.S. military units on the East Coast were over 6,000 miles from Baghdad. The ability to get an adequate force to the fight would depend on an armada of military and civilian aircraft and ships that could move the kind of forces needed. The Iraqi army at the time was the world's fourth largest, with Russian-made tanks and a huge and widely dispersed support infrastructure.

Much has been written about the new weapons brought on board during the Reagan buildup, but the U.S. success in Desert Storm had its roots in the lessons learned more than twenty years earlier by those who served during the Vietnam conflict. While the U.S. military enjoyed technological superiority then as well, it was applied in a fragmented fashion.

As a lieutenant fresh out of pilot training, I was surprised to learn that the Vietnam air war was actually several campaigns fought simultaneously in a relatively small area. At one point, there were as many as seven different U.S. military entities conducting their own air operations with little or no coordination. For example, Thailand-based fighters of the 7th Air Force conducted air strikes in North Vietnam while Navy 7th Fleet aircraft independently struck nearby targets in their own assigned area. Meanwhile, Guam-based B-52s attacked target sets determined by President Johnson and attack plans developed by Strategic Air Command staffers in Omaha. When forces were tasked to work together, deep-rooted differences in doctrine, terminology, and communications made it extremely difficult for them to operate efficiently and effectively.

Although the problem was obvious, our military was slow to change. As late as 1983, when the United States invaded Grenada to expel Russian-backed Cuban forces, the services still couldn't talk to one another. Congress gave us a push with the Goldwater-Nichols Act of 1986, which directed that the Commanders in Chief (CINCs) of the Unified Commands, historically designated for the European, Pacific, and South American theaters, would report to the president through the secretary of defense rather than through the Joint Chiefs of Staff. The Commander of Central Command had responsibility for the Middle East, North Africa, and Central Asia. This arrangement mitigated much of the interservice rivalry evident during Vietnam by focusing on the needs of the theater warfighter rather than the self-serving biases of the Washington-based service headquarters.

Within each unified command, the CINCs were expected to designate a single joint-force air component commander to control all aircraft operating in the theater, regardless of which service provided the aircraft. Similarly, a single joint-force ground component commander would control all U.S. ground forces engaged in that theater. In 1988, General Norman Schwarzkopf, who had been a battalion commander in Vietnam and in the joint command group for Grenada, was appointed CINC of Central Command (CINCCENT). His air component commander, Lt. Gen. Chuck Horner, had two tours in Vietnam in the F-105 fighter-bomber.

While Schwarzkopf was singularly responsible for Central Command, Horner was "dual hatted" and also served as the commander of Tactical Air Command's 9th Air Force. Ninth Air Force encompassed all TAC aircraft in the Eastern United States and provided combat-ready forces to support wartime operations for European and Central Command. In this assignment, and earlier as the commander of fighter wings at Luke and Nellis Air Force bases, Chuck Horner had a reputation as a no-nonsense leader who always focused on improving practical combat capability. To Horner and other leaders in the fighter community, the keys to growing a force of capable fighter pilots were more training flights, and with greater realism.

As a relatively new pilot flying A-7D Corsair IIs with the Flying Tigers of the 23rd Tactical Fighter Wing, I directly benefited from Gen. Bill Creech's initiative to increase the so-called utilization or "ute" rate, which was the average number of flights flown by each TAC aircraft per month. In some units, this program nearly doubled the amount of training sorties a combat-ready pilot could fly each month. We spent less time training with twenty-five-pound practice bombs and had more opportunities to drop full-scale ordnance. This program not only improved the number of training flights each pilot received, it honed the capability of maintenance units to support the faster tempos of combat conditions. General Creech also instituted the Checkered Flag training program, which required all TAC aircrews to study warplans and operational procedures established by the unified commands for possible combat in their theaters.

With an eye toward the huge Soviet air force massed in Eastern Europe, the services recognized that our forces could succeed in countering these numbers only if we were adept ourselves at conducting large-force operations. Each area command had their own large-force training exercises, but the hub of realistic, large air-combat training was Nellis Air Force Base in Nevada. Nellis is about three hundred miles from Naval Air Station Miramar, home of the navy's Top Gun school. The air force equivalent at Nellis, the Tactical Fighter Weapons Instructor Course, was an intensive six-month deep dive into advanced weapons and tactics. Attendees were the best of the best, selected not only for their stick-and-rudder flying skills but also for their instructional abilities. At the conclusion of the course, graduates returned to their units to serve in crucial Weapons and Tactics officer positions at the wing and squadron level. Chuck Horner was a Weapons School graduate, or "Target Arm," as they were known because of the distinctive flight suit patch they wore on their left shoulders.

The classroom in the sky for the Weapons School was the Nellis Range complex, which consisted of partitioned airspace for fighter training, segregated from most commercial air traffic. The largest chunks of this airspace measured over 120 miles east to west and 60 miles north to south. The western half of the range complex allowed flight at supersonic speeds from just above the sage brush to as high as our jets could fly. Prior to the Gulf War, over 75 percent of the live ordnance expended by the air force annually landed in the Nellis ranges. In addition, the range included an extensive array of captured and simulated surface-to-air missile (SAM) and antiaircraft artillery (AAA) threat radars operated by skilled civilian contract employees. A range telemetry system collected extensive flight data on all aircraft training in the area and displayed flight position and threat "kill" data to training locations at Nellis.

The granddaddy of large air force training in the United States was Red Flag. Combat aviation units from all over the world, including those from the army, marines, and navy, and some foreign countries (notably the French and British) came to Nellis to plan and execute strike package missions that often involved a hundred aircraft, including opposition air. On a daily basis, pilots from the participating units would get together to plan their attacks against the objectives designated by Red Flag staff. The package lead was usually just a captain or major from one of the participating units. Following the mission, as many as 500 aircrew members would gather in the main auditorium to view the telemetry data and threat tapes, to see how they fared against the threats and scored against their targets. These debriefs were often brutally candid. If a flight crew member made a mistake, he was expected to acknowledge it and do better the next time.

This part of the country was not new to large-force training. In the early days of World War II, George Patton began armored combat training in nearby Fort Irwin, California. In 1980, the army stood up the National Training Center there to train its armor officers in large-force tank operations. From Nellis, the air force launched Air Warrior flights that provided a fighter component to the army's large-force program.

The Nellis Range complex was also home to many secrets. Among the best kept was the presence of Tonopah Test Range Airfield in the northwest corner of the complex. Following a four-year tour at Nellis, primarily flying F-16s with the 474th Wing, I was recruited to enter the "black world" and compete for a squadron command with the ambiguously named 4450th Tactical Group, which at the time was secretly flying two operational squadrons of the F-117A stealth aircraft from Tonopah.

With all these advances in technology, organization, and training, by 1990 the air force and its sister services were arguably as ready for combat as they would ever be. But we were slowly losing one of our most important assets: those combat veterans who had been truly battle tested. In the late 1980s, Tactical Air Command announced that fighter pilots could display their experience with a patch on the sleeves of their flight suits. One silver star equaled 500 hours of fighter time, while a gold star on the sleeve indicated the pilot had logged actual combat time, and two gold stars represented over 500 hours of combat time. When the program was first introduced, one could usually spot gold stars on the squadron commanders and a few of the older pilots in each squadron. These pilots knew firsthand what the bullet stream from a 37mm AAA gun looked like and when to start a defensive break against an SA-2 missile. They'd lived with the dry throat and chills that precede the first engagement and learned how to get some sleep before a tough mission. They'd mourned lost comrades who never returned.

On the eve of Desert Storm, combat experience was harder to find. Among the more than sixty stealth pilots with me at Khamis Mushait, Saudi Arabia, only three pilots had gold stars: the wing commander, Col. Al Whitley; his operations deputy, Col. Klaus Klause; and Maj. Greg Feest, who had earned his star over Panama a little more than a year earlier. For the rest of us, January 17, 1991, and the succeeding days would be our chance to earn our gold stars, and a little piece of history.

Col. Ralph Getchell, USAF (Ret.)
Former commander, 415th TFS Nightstalkers

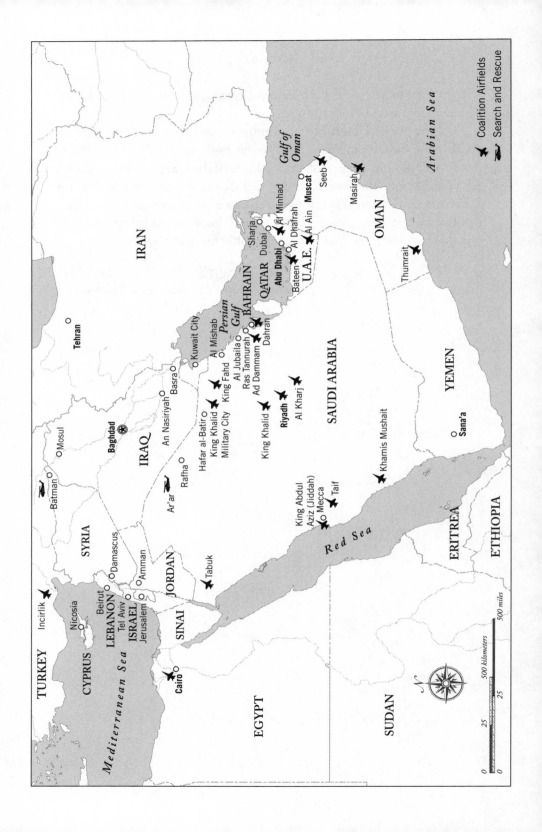

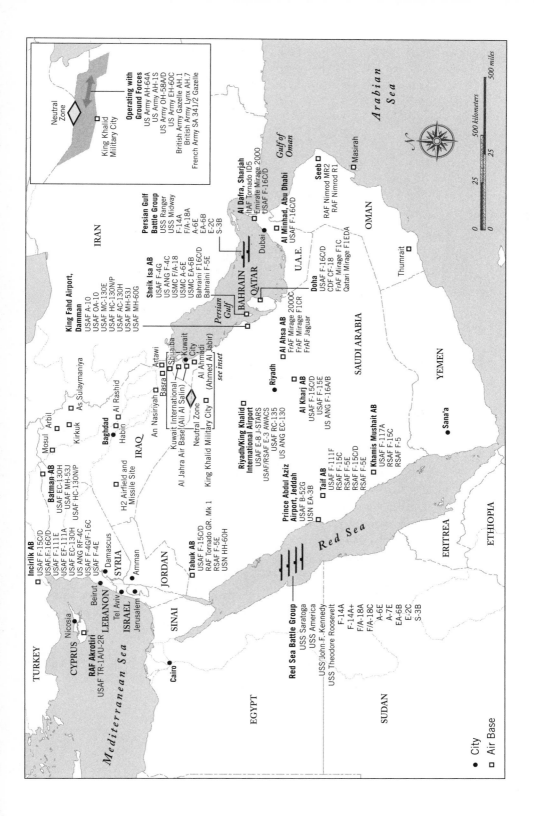

Prologue

WITH HIS BOMBS AWAY, MAJ. JEFF TICE TURNED THE GHOST-GRAY F-16 Fighting Falcon for home. Fresh eruptions bloomed below, adding to the fiery chaos consuming Baghdad's Daura Oil Refinery. Tice was somewhere over the city's outskirts when a shrill tone sounded. An SA-3 was in the air, and as Tice searched the murky sky, he spotted it. The missile was tracking him, closing rapidly.

Tice watched it approach, forcing himself to wait before making his move. With just a few seconds before impact, he yanked his aircraft into a hard break, hoping to make the twenty-foot missile overshoot. His timing was off by a fraction of a second, enough to place him within reach of the blast. He felt the airplane lurch.

"Stroke One took a hit! Stroke One took a hit," called a nearby pilot who witnessed the impact.[1]

Tice saw the instruments on his control panel flicker out, replaced with a growing assortment of warning lights. He craned around to assess the damage. The plane's wings and upper fuselage were pitted with jagged holes, many streaming jet fuel or hydraulic fluid. His sputtering engine trailed oily black smoke.

"Okay, I took a pretty good hit," he radioed. "Okay. Stroke One. I've still got an engine. It's still working."

Half a dozen F-16s from his squadron moved in and clustered around him, and so did a lingering EF-111 Raven radar jammer. The rest of the strike package was already too far south, headed for the tankers circling above Saudi Arabia.

"Unable to roll left very easily. I'm losing fuel like crazy up here," Tice advised. "I'm going to take it as far as I can."

The Saudi border was more than 200 miles away—likely beyond his reach—but the closer he could get before punching out, the better his odds of rescue. He limped along, coaxing the dying aircraft to a higher altitude, while his protectors maintained their defensive ring. After a few moments, a flight of Iraqi MiG-29 Fulcrums tried to sneak up on the slow-moving formation, looking for an easy kill. One of the F-16s turned around and raced to meet them, prompting the MiGs to scatter. The Iraqis had no interest in a dogfight.

More warning lights came on. The oil pressure was dropping and his fuel state had become critical. He asked the distance to the border. Still 160 miles to go, the AWACS operator replied. Too far, Tice knew. The plane's familiar growl soon withered and died, and all that remained was the sound of wind rushing over the canopy.

"Stroke One just completely lost the engine. I got nothing left," he announced. "Okay, I'm on EPU."

The emergency power unit would buy him about ten more minutes of controlled flight. After that, he would be a helpless passenger on a plane plummeting to earth. He continued to nurse the F-16 along as it descended through 26,000 feet. A few minutes later it glided through 20,000, and Tice decided to go. He keyed the microphone a final time.

"That's all I've got, guys. I'm out of here."

He grabbed the ejection handle. Explosive bolts blew off the canopy, and his seat rocketed him upward before falling away. He began to free fall.

"The clouds were coming up fast. I was dropping real fast," he remembered. "Over and over, I kept saying 'The parachute has got to work.'"

After fifteen long seconds, and a plunge of 10,000 feet, the chute finally opened. Tice realized he was going to live, and his thoughts turned to the survival radio in his vest and the possibility of rescue.

Those hopes quickly evaporated.

"As I was falling, some bullets come whizzing at me, and I look down and see muzzle flashes on the ground," he said. "Then I see some guys on the ground shooting at me."

Jeff Tice became a prisoner shortly after his feet touched the ground, on this, the third day of the war. Tice was not the first pilot captured in

Desert Storm, and he certainly wouldn't be the last. Iraq's sprawling air defense network remained largely intact, and quite capable of shooting down aircraft.

For television viewers at home and around the world, the air campaign seemed precise, effortless, and almost risk-free. It looked like a high-tech romp carried out by mysterious stealth fighters and Tomahawk cruise missiles. Viewers saw grainy, black-and-white footage of laser-guided "smart" bombs plunging through doors or down air ducts, and they assumed a new video-game style of warfare had arrived.

Reality was quite different. Coalition aviators fought a well-defended and stubborn enemy. Most pilots flew non-stealthy planes and dropped unguided "dumb" bombs. They came home with battle damage, and in some instances, they didn't come home at all. Subduing Iraq would require more than 100,000 sorties, and they had only six weeks to do it.

By the end of day three, the task still seemed overwhelming.

DESERT SHIELD

CHAPTER 1

Seeds of Crisis

SADDAM HUSSEIN CONSIDERED WAR AN EVERYDAY TOOL OF FOREIGN and domestic policy. Armed conflict, or the threat of it, enhanced his standing in the Persian Gulf and distracted Iraqi citizens from economic hardship. Saddam introduced Iraqis to his wartime way of life shortly after taking power in 1979, when Iraq launched an invasion of Iran. He sought to expand Iraq's coastal access beyond the sliver between Iran and Kuwait and claimed to be protecting his Arab neighbors from the Persian threat.

His invasion faltered, and Iraqi troops soon found themselves fighting to hold their own territory. They dug elaborate defenses and grew skilled at repelling Iranian assaults. Bloody trench warfare, reminiscent of World War I, followed for years. During this time, Saddam used chemical weapons against Iranian soldiers and civilians and initiated the "War of the Cities," in which both sides indiscriminately bombed population centers. He attacked Iranian shipping in the Gulf, sparking the so-called Tanker War.

The threat to world oil supplies drew international attention. President Ronald Reagan authorized Operation Earnest Will, under which U.S. warships escorted Kuwaiti tankers through the Gulf. The move was directed against Iran, which became an American foe in 1979 when Islamic revolutionaries overran the U.S. Embassy in Tehran and took fifty-two hostages.

The Reagan administration tacitly supported Saddam throughout the war, going as far as to share classified satellite imagery of Iranian troop movements. America viewed Saddam as an important counterbalance to

Iran's power in the Gulf and hoped someday to moderate his tyranni-cal nature. The relationship continued, even after a bizarre and alarming incident in 1987.

On the evening of May 17, the USS *Stark* was sailing in interna-tional waters when an Iraqi F-1 Mirage took off and headed out over the Gulf. An AWACS surveillance plane picked up the fighter and reported it. The frigate's crew acknowledged the routine alert and began tracking the Mirage, which appeared to be passing harmlessly at a safe distance. They failed to notice the jet make a sharp turn directly toward them. The Mirage fired two Exocet antiship missiles, which raced toward the *Stark* and slammed into her port side. Thirty-seven crew members died, and the ship narrowly avoided sinking.

The Iraqi government initially blamed the *Stark*'s crew for entering the war zone, a claim U.S. Navy investigators proved untrue. No satisfac-tory explanation followed, and Washington chalked off the attack as a mistake. Saddam still held America's support despite the bloodshed, a fact that was not lost on him.

The stalemate with Iran dragged on until 1988, when both sides accepted a U.N.-sponsored ceasefire. Eight years of warfare had cost roughly a million lives total, yet brought only modest changes in territory. An enormous waste of life and resources, the Iran-Iraq War did yield one significant result: Iraq emerged as a Persian Gulf powerhouse. Saddam's ground forces had swelled to 950,000 men, giving him the fourth largest army in the world. He possessed more than 10,000 tanks and armored fighting vehicles and 3,000 artillery pieces.

His air force ranked as the sixth largest in the world with an esti-mated 750 aircraft, and it was easily the largest in the Gulf region. But fewer than half of these planes were modern combat aircraft. His best pilots flew Soviet-built MiG-29 Fulcrums, or French F-1 Mirages such as the one that attacked the *Stark*. The rest flew older Soviet types—some with technology dating from the 1950s—and Chinese knockoffs of old Soviet designs. Pilot skill and training in the Iraqi air force varied almost as much as its aircraft.

Despite his oversized military, Saddam still seemed relatively benign to American intelligence agencies. The prevailing belief around

Washington was that a war-weary Iraq would rest in the coming years, licking its wounds and attempting an economic recovery.

⸺❦⸺

MacDill Air Force Base
Tampa, Florida
July 1990

United States Central Command, or CENTCOM, bore responsibility for the Persian Gulf and surrounding areas. Its name stemmed from the fact that it lay between the European and Pacific commands, but, unlike those larger and more influential entities, CENTCOM had no troops, tanks, or airplanes to call its own. If America became involved in a Middle East war, pre-assigned units from other commands would be transferred to CENTCOM. During peacetime, it existed only as an administrative headquarters at MacDill.

Since its inception in 1983, CENTCOM—like the entire U.S. military—prepared for World War III with the Soviet Union. In such a war, Red Army divisions would likely dash across the Zagros Mountains in northern Iran to seize the oil fields. CENTCOM's annual war game, code name *Internal Look*, always focused on the Zagros threat. But by 1990 it seemed a dated scenario. The Cold War was ending, the Soviet Union dissolving. CENTCOM needed a new purpose, and its new commander, U.S. Army general H. Norman Schwarzkopf Jr., tried to identify the region's next likely aggressor. Schwarzkopf observed that Saddam Hussein had done nothing to reduce his massive army since the war with Iran.

Internal Look 90 featured a new fictional crisis. Instead of Soviet forces attacking Iran, the war game imagined Iraqi armor flowing across the Arabian Peninsula, as Saddam Hussein made a grab for the Saudi oil supply. It was merely a computer-based exercise in tactics and logistics, since CENTCOM had no actual forces to train, but State Department officials protested. If word leaked of preparations for a war with Iraq, a nominal ally, there could be diplomatic fallout. Schwarzkopf wrote a disclaimer that the war game's enemy was not Saddam Hussein, but rather some future Iraqi regime hostile to U.S. interests, and the exercise was allowed to proceed.

Internal Look's computer war revealed some glaring challenges in airpower, should the scenario ever turn real. America's aging fleet of airborne tankers would be pushed to its limit. The current inventory of laser-guided bombs was too small. And while CENTCOM planners managed to build a rudimentary list of key targets in Iraq, they could find no reliable means of assessing bomb damage. Resolving these problems would take quite a bit of time. As it turned out, CENTCOM had none.

Jeddah, Saudi Arabia
July 31, 1990

Iraq's wartime spending plunged the nation into an economic morass. Saddam had spent billions acquiring high-tech weapons on the world market. He hired a French corporation to blanket his country under an elaborate radar network and lavished funds on his nuclear, biological, and chemical weapons programs. And then there was the cost of his gargantuan army, which could not be drawn down without aggravating the nation's already soaring unemployment rate.

Saddam blamed his neighbors. He had fought Iran on behalf of all Arab nations, he claimed, and now they betrayed him. Iraq filed a formal complaint with the Arab League, accusing Kuwait and the United Arab Emirates (UAE) of intentionally driving down oil prices by exceeding OPEC quotas. Saddam said Kuwait and the UAE were purposely trying to undermine Iraq's recovery, and he would not permit the open act of aggression to continue.

Most Arab League delegates just rolled their eyes. OPEC production almost always exceeded target levels because member nations—including Iraq—cheated on their quotas. The delegates dismissed Saddam's bluster as a negotiating tactic. Iraq's wartime debt totaled $80 billion, and it appeared he was merely creating leverage to have some loans forgiven. The consensus did not change even when he began placing troops near the Kuwaiti border.

The only nation rattled by Saddam's belligerence was the UAE. During the war Iraq had attacked an Emirates offshore drilling rig, an incident Saddam later dismissed as a mistake. Not wishing to chance any more Iraqi "mistakes," the UAE quietly contacted Washington and requested access to American AWACS and tanker planes. The Emirates defense minister said it would enable his fighter jets to patrol their territory more effectively, but President George H. W. Bush's administration knew the true intent was to send Iraq a subtle message. Two KC-135 tankers and a support plane were dispatched to the UAE.

Meanwhile, Saddam's list of grievances against Kuwait continued to grow. He revived a long-standing border disagreement and accused the Kuwaitis of slant-drilling into Iraq's portion of the Rumaila oil field. More tanks and troops appeared along the border, and while Arab observers still believed he was bluffing, they felt it was time for Kuwait to make some concessions. Saudi Arabia offered to host a summit, where negotiators from both countries could hammer out a deal.

The Saudi city of Jeddah, stretching along a coastal plain of the Red Sea, is second in size and importance only to Riyadh, and it offers some relief from the capital's unbearable summer heat. King Fahd was known to reside at his Jeddah palace for at least half of the year. As the month of July 1990 drew to a close, representatives of Iraq and Kuwait met in this modern seaport to discuss their differences.

From the beginning, it did not go well. The Iraqis led off by demanding that Kuwait immediately abandon the disputed border area and pay $2.4 billion for stolen oil. They then insisted that all of Kuwait's low-interest war loans to Iraq, totaling about $10 billion, be forgiven. The tone of the Iraqi delegates was hostile, as if they were delivering an ultimatum. When they finally finished, the sum of Iraqi demands approached $27 billion.

The Kuwaitis listened politely and then tried to negotiate, supposedly the purpose for this gathering. They suggested the border issue be turned over to an international body, which could render a fair and objective resolution. The Iraqis said they would agree, but only if the body held its meetings in Baghdad. When the Kuwaitis replied that the meetings should be held in a neutral location, the Iraqi delegation stood and stormed from the room. The summit was over.

⸺ ∼ ⸺

The Pentagon
Washington, D.C.
August 1, 1990

Satellite imagery made it abundantly clear that Saddam was preparing an attack. Iraqi troops were fanned along the border, outfitted with pontoon bridges and other special equipment that pointed to a real invasion, not just a bluff. From his headquarters in Tampa, Schwarzkopf warned Washington not to believe the assurances still coming from the Middle East. In response he was summoned to the Pentagon.

Inside a secure conference room known as "The Tank," Schwarzkopf briefed Secretary of Defense Dick Cheney and the Joint Chiefs of Staff, including Chairman Colin Powell. Cheney studied the maps and photos before him and asked Schwarzkopf to speculate on Iraq's intentions.

"There's no doubt that this is a military plan. I think they're going to attack," Schwarzkopf said.[1] But at this point even he wasn't predicting a full-scale invasion.

"[I] added that I didn't believe Saddam would grab the entire country," he later recalled. "I anticipated he'd move to positions just south of the 30th parallel, taking Kuwait's part of the Rumaila oil field, as well as Bubiyan Island, which controlled the sea-lane to Iraq's new port, Umm Qasr, and then he would stop."[2]

Cheney's eyes returned to the map of Kuwait, and Schwarzkopf scanned the room, waiting for questions. Eventually he got one.

"Somebody said: 'If that happens, what do we do?' I said not a damn thing. The world will not care. It will be a *fait accompli*."[3]

He wrapped up his ninety-minute presentation with a contingency plan for sending troops to Saudi Arabia should Saddam threaten it, although at the moment that notion seemed pretty far-fetched.

"The meeting ended with no sense of urgency," Schwarzkopf remembered. "In the hierarchy of world crises, this one was still a minor blip."[4]

⸺ ∼ ⸺

Kuwait City, Kuwait
August 2, 1990
0130 Local

Helicopters descended on the city like locusts, their beating blades announcing the invasion. They landed near government buildings and other key facilities, and from each chopper sprang Iraqi Special Forces. On the beaches, where pastel hotel lights bathed the sand, boatloads of commandos came ashore. At Dasman Palace, a fierce gun battle erupted between palace guards and swarming Iraqi marines. The marines failed to capture the emir, who escaped by car, but managed to kill his younger brother.

To city residents, the Iraqis seemed everywhere at once. Yet this was just an advance element. The heavy forces—nearly a thousand tanks and armored personnel carriers (APCs) of the Republican Guard—were still a few hours away. They had flattened the scant Kuwaiti defensive positions and now rolled south unopposed.

History had long pointed to this night. Kuwait, although smaller than New Jersey, held the sixth-largest oil reserves in the world, rivaling those of much larger Iraq. Kuwaitis enjoyed a privileged lifestyle that was the envy of the Middle East. Iraq first made a play for it in 1961, when the emirate gained independence from Britain. Iraq's government asserted an ancient claim to the land, causing UK troops to linger as a deterrent. When the Brits finally departed, an Arab peacekeeping force took over, but Iraq never stopped coveting the wealthy coastal wedge.

By the summer of 1990, Saddam calculated that, at last, the international political scene had left Kuwait ripe for the plucking. The world's sole remaining superpower was distracted by the implosion of its old nemesis, and Saddam knew no regional power would dare oppose him, for they had neither the means nor the will to protect arrogant little Kuwait. And the upside was so very tempting. An annexed Kuwait would yield $20 million a day in additional oil revenues, solving his economic troubles. He expected criticism but assumed the blistering verbal assaults in the United Nations would soon wither, leaving him to keep his prize.

Now Kuwait's tiny air force scrambled to defend its nation, with fighter jets speeding down the runway even as their bases were overrun. The best Kuwaiti pilots had fairly modern French F-1 Mirages, but the majority flew the old A-4 Skyhawk, which was first developed for American aircraft carriers in 1954. Small and nimble, the Skyhawk saw plenty of combat during Vietnam's early years, but by 1967 the navy was withdrawing it from front-line service. Excellent flight characteristics ensured the A-4 a second life, not only in foreign air forces, but also as an adversary plane in training programs like Top Gun.

Three dozen Kuwaiti jets made it into the air, with some dropping ordnance on Iraqi forces before turning for Saudi Arabia and Bahrain. The banished airmen promptly stenciled "Free Kuwait" on their fuselages in English and Arabic and awaited an opportunity for revenge.

CHAPTER 2

Deployment

IN WASHINGTON, NOBODY TALKED ABOUT LIBERATING KUWAIT, AT LEAST not yet. The immediate concern was Saudi Arabia. Saddam's two-day conquest opened a fresh round of questions about his ultimate intentions, since much of the Iraqi armor and infantry continued straight for the Saudi border. If they decided to cross, precious little was in place to stop them. An invasion of Saudi Arabia—America's chief petroleum supplier and closest Gulf ally—now seemed possible, if not likely. At CENTCOM, Schwarzkopf and his staff prepared for the possibility of deployment, marshalling the command's far-flung resources.

At age fifty-three, Lt. Gen. Charles A. Horner was still a fighter jock, and the Ninth Air Force commander routinely flew training sorties in his F-16. Horner had been flying off the South Carolina coast when a priority call came in to his office at Shaw Air Force Base. Schwarzkopf wanted to talk to his Central Command Air Force Component (CENTAF) commander. After a brief conversation on the secure CENTCOM hotline, Horner climbed back into his F-16 for the hour-long flight to Tampa.

Events began to unfold quickly. The president needed options for defending Saudi Arabia, and Schwarzkopf would be flying to Washington the following morning to brief him. The army general was an expert on deploying ground forces but felt less confident with airpower, so he wanted Horner to come along and deliver that portion of the briefing. The CENTAF commander found a spare office and spent the next few hours assembling an air plan.

———

Camp David, Maryland
August 4, 1990

Nestled inside Maryland's thickly wooded Catoctin Mountain Park, Camp David is a twenty-minute helicopter ride from Washington. The Marine VH-3D Sea King that landed on this early Saturday morning contained Defense Secretary Cheney and a contingent that included Powell, Schwarzkopf, and Horner. They proceeded to the main lodge and into a wood-paneled conference room. President Bush and his advisors soon arrived, and the briefing began.

Schwarzkopf outlined the situation in Kuwait and the disposition of Iraqi forces along the Saudi border. From a commander's point of view, the invasion was well executed. Iraqi units had been organized and swift, and if Saddam ordered them into Saudi Arabia they would likely repeat the performance. The Saudis, meanwhile, had a solid air force, but their ground forces were limited in size and ability.

In terms of a U.S. response, Schwarzkopf said a brigade of the 82nd Airborne stood ready. He quickly added that those 4,000 soldiers could not be expected to stop Saddam's tank columns. Mechanized infantry and Apache attack helicopters could do the job, but transporting those units and their equipment to the desert would take at least a month. The earliest available deterrent was airpower.

Horner took his cue and laid out the preliminary air plan. Forty-eight F-15C Eagles from the 1st Tactical Fighter Wing could fly nonstop from Langley Air Force Base, Virginia, and set up a combat air patrol (CAP) over Saudi Arabia. Tankers would escort the Eagles, providing six or seven in-flight refuelings along the way. Once Saudi airspace was secure, the ground-attack aircraft would be cleared to arrive. Horner described squadrons of F-16s and F-111s, and especially A-10 tank killers, descending on the region.

Naval aviation was already available. The USS *Independence* steamed just outside the Persian Gulf with F-14 Tomcats, F/A-18 Hornets, and A-6 Intruders. Meanwhile, the nuclear-powered USS *Dwight D.*

Eisenhower was on the move in the Mediterranean, ready to transit the Suez Canal and enter the Red Sea. These two carrier battle groups were the vanguard of American airpower in the area.

The president was no stranger to carrier operations. In 1944, twenty-year-old navy lieutenant George H. W. Bush was bombing a Japanese-held island when flak ignited the engine of his Grumman TBM Avenger. Bush dropped his bombs and coaxed the Avenger out to sea before bailing. He watched helplessly for four hours as fighters strafed the Japanese gunboats sent out to capture him, until at last a submarine picked him up. In total he flew fifty-eight combat missions during the war, earning several citations.

Bush said little during the meeting, not wishing to influence the debate. When someone asked Schwarzkopf the number of troops necessary to preserve Saudi Arabia, the general replied 100,000, but added that the number would rise if Saddam continued pumping troops into Kuwait. He further noted that he was still talking about defensive operations. An offensive plan to liberate Kuwait would require much more. The notion of Saudi Arabia, an extremely conservative and closed society, hosting hundreds of thousands of U.S. service members—including women—was hard to imagine.

When Bush finally spoke, he expressed a desire not just to hold back Iraq, but to do so with the minimum loss of life. He also talked of the need to build international consensus, a coalition of nations opposed to Saddam's bold aggression. But before any of that could happen, the Saudis would first have to ask for help. Bush turned to Cheney and told him to pay a visit to King Fahd.

Jeddah, Saudi Arabia
August 6, 1990

Late in the evening, a procession of luxury vehicles arrived to carry the Americans from their hotel to the royal palace. The guests were led into a reception room, served tea, and then invited in to see the king. Fahd stood as the delegation entered, and U.S. Ambassador Chas Freeman made the introductions. Cheney extended a greeting from President Bush. Schwarzkopf was given a seat beside the king to show him the latest satellite imagery. By this point, Saddam had pushed more than two dozen divisions to the Saudi border, and there was evidence of patrols sneaking across the border.

As Fahd studied photos of Iraqi tank formations poised to strike, Schwarzkopf offered specifics about the military assistance America was prepared to provide. Clearly, it would be unlike anything the kingdom had ever seen before. Twenty squadrons of aircraft. More than 150,000 soldiers and marines. Loading docks overwhelmed with equipment and supplies.

"If you ask us, we will come," Cheney said. "And when you ask us to go home, we will leave."[1]

A discussion ensued in Arabic, which Ambassador Freeman quietly followed and later translated for the others. The king was polling his counselors, seeking decisive opinions, not useless platitudes. His temper flared when a royal family member hedged, "We must be careful not to rush into a decision." Fahd snapped back, "The Kuwaitis did not rush into a decision, and today they are all guests in our hotels!"

He had heard enough. The king turned to Cheney and said a single word: "Okay."

On the way out of the palace, Schwarzkopf asked Cheney if he should get the forces moving. The defense secretary said yes, so Schwarzkopf turned to Horner.

"Chuck, start them moving."

Within hours, the first squadron of F-15C Eagles departed Langley Air Force Base and headed out over the Atlantic.

* * *

Aerial refueling helped break the monotony of a transatlantic flight. Fuel status was always a concern over water, so the fighters topped off frequently in case they had to divert. East Coast–based tankers escorted them until they were within range of KC-10s stationed in the Azores. The nonstop flight to Saudi Arabia lasted about fifteen hours, making it a test of endurance. Each pilot was issued a couple of sack lunches; a small supply of "go pills," or stimulants; and plenty of "piddle packs" for bladder relief. For entertainment, most relied on the iconic audio player of their generation—the Sony Walkman.

The journey allowed plenty of time to reflect on the prospect of combat, a possibility both exhilarating and terrifying. The deployment's size and pace left open so many questions, including destination. Many squadrons set out across the Atlantic uncertain of their Gulf base assignment. They would learn more along the way, they were told. The first to go, the F-15C pilots out of Langley, wondered if they might find Saudi Arabia already under attack.

"We had a contingency plan to fight our way in if necessary," said Lt. Col. Don Kline, "landing some of our aircraft and keeping others up in the air until we could get some of the earlier ones turned around. We were fully armed, with four AIM-7s, four AIM-9s, and the gun was loaded out."[2]

Kline commanded the 27th Tactical Fighter Squadron, the air force's oldest active fighter unit, which traced its lineage back to the biplanes of World War I. Now, they and their sister squadron, the 71st, were leading the deployment.

"Fortunately, we didn't have to fight our way in when we arrived at Dhahran," Kline continued. "It was a little confused, though. Folks knew we were coming, but we still had to get everybody out of the jets and bedded down. My squadron had one day down on 10 August to recover, and then we were up and operational on 11 August."

Units that followed faced their own challenges. Transiting the ocean at night was mind-numbing, and the inky blackness could cause spatial disorientation. Some flights fought through heavy weather. As a pack of A-10s made a night crossing, one of the pilots, Capt. Greg Henderson, fell ill with a headache and vomiting. His symptoms grew severe, and soon he was struggling just to keep his wings level.

"I couldn't reason, could barely fly, and I thought for sure I was going to pass out," Henderson said. "We were in and out of clouds, and I remember looking down through a hole and seeing a brightly lit ship on the water. I was ready to punch out and let them pick me up."[3]

The other pilots talked it over and decided Henderson was suffering from oxygen deprivation. His symptoms began shortly after his first tanker hookup, so they wondered if fuel vapor might be the culprit. The A-10's refueling port sat directly in front of the cockpit. They told him to increase his mask's oxygen flow to 100 percent and to purge the cockpit air.

"I didn't realize it then but the receptacle seal was bad and fuel was leaking into the cockpit area whenever I took on fuel," Henderson explained. "I was breathing those fumes."

The oxygen helped him feel better, but he was fatigued and sitting in a cockpit full of vomit. The flight lead asked if he wanted to divert to the Azores and get some rest, but Henderson declined. "I said that I wanted to continue, mainly because I was afraid I might miss a war."

Every day more units were joining the deployment: fighter squadrons, hundreds of Military Airlift Command cargo planes, and B-52 bombers. The tanker crews soon had more escort duty than they could handle. America's ample tanker fleet stood at 59 KC-10 Extenders and more than 600 KC-135 Stratotankers. The Extender—a modified McDonnell Douglas DC-10 airliner—was a modern aircraft, while the Stratotanker dated all the way back to the 1950s. The real problem was an aircrew shortage; until more crews could be called to active duty, the number of transatlantic escorts would be limited.

Civilian aircraft would also help move troops and supplies to the Persian Gulf. A Cold War leftover, the Civil Reserve Air Fleet was originally intended to rush army divisions into Western Europe to halt a Soviet invasion. Each year the Pentagon paid lucrative peacetime contracts to participating airlines as an incentive. Now the program was finally paying off, as nearly two-thirds of the 560,000 troops headed to the Gulf would do so in the comfort of a civilian airliner.

CHAPTER 3

Turbulence

AFTER THE MEETING WITH KING FAHD, SCHWARZKOPF DECIDED TO return to Tampa and work the deployment from CENTCOM headquarters. He asked Chuck Horner to stay in Saudi Arabia and oversee the buildup as temporary theater commander. The air force general had packed a bag for just a few days, but, as it turned out, he'd be away for eight months.

Schwarzkopf knew the burden he was placing on Horner. Aside from getting all the incoming American troops dispersed and settled, Horner would need to establish a rapport with their Saudi hosts and the forces of allied nations. The job required political dexterity, and it had to be done under the imminent threat of attack.

As they stood on the tarmac in Jeddah, Schwarzkopf promised to send plenty of logisticians and command staff to help. Then he said he would ask some Pentagon strategists to start developing a strategic air campaign. To an old fighter pilot like Horner, the idea of inviting Pentagon desk jockeys to make combat preparations was a bad one. The usual good humor drained from his face.

"Okay, but we ain't picking the goddamn targets in Washington," Horner blustered.[1]

The flash of anger surprised Schwarzkopf, and he sought to defuse it. "Look, Chuck," he said, "you're my air boss, with final veto authority over everything connected with air." Then he boarded the plane back to the States.

Horner's frustration stretched back to 1965, when he was a green wingman flying F-105 Thunderchiefs over North Vietnam. Gung ho and eager to prove himself, Horner pushed his way through heavy flak and missiles to place his bombs on target. The veteran pilots did too, but they knew something Horner didn't—their efforts were being squandered. America was mismanaging this war, from the top on down.

"They can't even bomb an outhouse without my approval," Lyndon Johnson once bragged of his control over the pilots in Vietnam. Johnson and his defense secretary, Robert McNamara, followed a unique strategy. Rather than destroying the enemy, they were merely trying to dissuade North Vietnam from attacking the South. It was a Cold War tight-wire act.

Operation Rolling Thunder, a forty-three-month bombing campaign of gradually escalating intensity, typified the strategy. Johnson and McNamara ran the show, choosing targets each Tuesday during a White House luncheon. But they didn't stop at target selection. The civilian leaders often specified the number of aircraft to strike a target, the routes of ingress and egress, and sometimes even the weapons to be used. They initially declared airfields and SAM sites off-limits, since a Soviet military advisor might be killed. Pilots were told not to fire on a MiG without visual identification, which made long-range air-to-air missiles useless.

The rules negated America's airpower advantage and placed aviators at undue risk. Young Horner loathed the Washington interference, his hatred intensifying with each lost colleague. Eventually, he and the others began bending the rules. If they were going to risk their lives in combat, it should at least do some good, they reasoned.

"We lied about what we were doing in North Vietnam," Horner admitted many years later. "We lied about what targets we hit. Say my [assigned] target was a ford across a river. If I saw a better target—say, boxcars on a rail siding—I would miss my [assigned] target and somehow my bombs would hit the boxcars." He hated the duplicity, but felt trapped by Washington's style of warfare. "If our leaders had no interest in winning, whatever that was, well, I did; and I was going to try to win, even if they didn't want to or were unwilling to really try."[2]

Now, a quarter of a century later, Horner refused to let it happen again. He would not put another generation of airmen in that impossible position. If an air war was going to be fought in the Gulf, armchair tacticians in Washington must not run it. Schwarzkopf assured him they wouldn't, but Horner remained wary.

—◦—

Ramstein Air Base, West Germany
August 29, 1990
0033 Local

With the deployment in full swing, every base along the routes to Saudi Arabia saw a dramatic rise in traffic. Military Airlift Command pressed nearly all of its jumbo cargo planes into action, calling up reservists and national guardsmen to keep them flying around the clock.

In the darkness at Ramstein, the hulking outline of a C-5 Galaxy turned onto Runway 27. The Galaxy carried 96,000 pounds of rations, spare parts, and medical supplies. For other transport planes, such a load would be far too heavy. The C-141 Starlifter—America's second-largest cargo jet—could not haul it, nor could two C-130 Hercules planes. Yet for the mammoth C-5, this load was relatively light, and its cargo bay remained half empty.

The giant of the sky was not without its problems. C-5s guzzled fuel at an alarming rate, requiring frequent stopovers and aerial refueling. The air force owned 127, but typically one in three was down for maintenance, and sometimes that ratio climbed to one in two.[3] Mechanics who tended the Galaxy's many ailments called it FRED, F[reaking] Ridiculous Economic Disaster.

A generation earlier, the C-5 had also bewildered generals and congressmen, and it nearly drove a major aircraft manufacturer out of business. Their shared dream had been to build the biggest cargo plane possible—a sort of Spruce Goose—to support the troops in Vietnam. The behemoth would carry army vehicles too large and heavy for existing cargo planes. But like Howard Hughes, they soon discovered that extremely large aircraft present design problems all their own. The costly project languished through most of the 1960s.

By June 1968 the first C-5 was ready for a test flight, and there was no doubt manufacturer Lockheed had built a monster. Its tail towered six stories high. Its cargo bay stretched one foot longer than the entire length of the first flight at Kitty Hawk. On each enormous wing hung two TF39 turbofan engines, designed by General Electric just for the C-5. The plane could accommodate six Greyhound buses, or an eight-lane bowling alley.

Test flights revealed its wings weren't strong enough, developing cracks under heavy loading. As Lockheed engineers worked on a fix, cost overruns for the nearly decade-old project reached one billion dollars, prompting a congressional investigation. Lockheed, meanwhile, was losing money not only on the C-5 but also on its new civilian jetliner, the L-1011. The corporation needed government loans just to stay afloat. All parties forged ahead—too much had been invested to give up now—and eventually a trickle of C-5s entered air force service, with more on the way. Disappointment continued, however, as the persistent cracking problem occasionally grounded the fleet.

The C-5 finally showed its potential in the spring of 1972, when a fierce North Vietnamese offensive threatened the South. The Galaxy became a lifeline, shuttling supplies and equipment as battles raged. On one particularly desperate morning, three C-5s swooped in to Da Nang Air Base and began disgorging M48 Patton battle tanks. In less than seven minutes, half a dozen forty-nine-ton tanks came down the ramps and rumbled off into combat. The Galaxy had arrived.

Like its predecessors, the C-5 now departing Ramstein was an older "A" model, and during its two decades of service, this plane had been no stranger to maintenance hangars. Presently it was experiencing a minor fuel leak. Before flying to Dhahran, the crew planned a quick hop to Frankfurt-Rhein-Main Air Base, just sixty miles away, to have the leak repaired. As the Galaxy lumbered down the runway, gradually building up speed, aircraft commander Maj. John Gordon could not have realized the dire situation he faced.

A jet engine's thrust reverser is an important device for landings. When activated, it shunts exhaust forward, helping to slow the aircraft after touchdown. Thrust reversers reduce brake wear and landing distance, but obviously must remain dormant during flight. Unknown to Major Gordon, the thrust reverser of Engine No. 1 had somehow deployed. As three of the Galaxy's engines labored to push it into the air, Engine No. 1 fought them.

The nose wheels lifted from the runway, and the plane became airborne. Immediately it began a port-side roll. Directly ahead stood a grove of tall pine trees. The Galaxy was traveling at 185 miles per hour, less than 100 feet from the ground. Gordon and his crew struggled to comprehend what was happening. The trees loomed larger.

A second-floor troop compartment located directly above the cargo bay was nearly empty for this flight. Just seven officers and enlisted personnel sat sprinkled in rows to the rear of the aircraft. Most were experts of one specialty or another, whose services were needed in Saudi Arabia. Until a few seconds ago, their biggest concern had been finding a way to fall asleep in the narrow, upright seats. Now it was obvious something had gone wrong.

The compartment's only windows were small portholes in the emergency hatches. From her seat, Lt. Cynthia Borecky caught a glimpse of the outside world.

"I could see fire racing by one of those windows as we sheared off the trees," she said.[4] The engines whined desperately and Borecky, a weather officer bound for Riyadh, concluded she was about to die.

The troublesome No. 1 Engine impacted a large tree, sending the Galaxy into a cartwheel. Everyone forward of the wing root perished instantly as the nose plowed straight into the ground. The rest of the plane continued its fiery somersault, shedding pieces as it tumbled through the pine grove and into a grassy field.

"It felt like being in a dryer, the way we were tumbling," said Lt. Col. Fred Arzt, who was in the last row.[5] Arzt commanded the 62nd Services Squadron, with orders to find housing for the growing contingent of troops in Riyadh.

The tail section tore away from the rest of the aircraft, taking Arzt, Borecky, and two other people with it. Passengers sitting forward of the break point continued on with the center portion of the aircraft, and were killed.

Arzt awoke to the acrid smell of burning aviation fuel. He lay on the ceiling of the overturned troop compartment, still belted into his seat.

A voice somewhere outside was calling for help. He crawled from the wreckage.

The plane had cut a neat swath through the pine grove and left a long, blackened gash across the grassy field. A series of blazes along the trail produced a soft orange glow. Some of the fires emitted popping sounds, which the survivors feared was ammunition, but turned out to be only canned goods. Once more, Arzt heard the plea for help.

The voice belonged to S.Sgt. Lorenzo Galvan. A loadmaster who had been sitting in an aft jump seat, Galvan was the only crew member to survive. When he climbed out he found Borecky lying unconscious near the tail. Now he wanted to move her to safety, but with his own injuries, could not do so alone. Arzt hobbled over, and together they carried her away from the flames.

Rescuers found just one other survivor, M.Sgt. Dwight Pettit of Arzt's unit. At daybreak, they began the grisly task of recovering the remains of thirteen people who died in the crash.[6] They erected a tent over a gnarled lump that was once the cockpit, where their hardest work awaited. Ramstein's C-5 tragedy was a reminder that deployments carried risk even before the shooting started. It would not be the last crash.

* * *

The first few days in Saudi Arabia were the worst, when the probability of attack was greatest. Saddam's likely invasion route would be the Saudi coastal highway, which passed through sprawling oil fields on the way to Dhahran. Lightly armed American troops positioned along the road referred to themselves as speed bumps. They'd be unable to stop the Iraqi armor, and neither would the few aircraft available to support them.

As each day passed, Chuck Horner breathed a little easier. A steady stream of soldiers and marines landed at Saudi airports and trundled off into the desert. Formations of incoming fighter jets passed overhead like migrating geese. For the first time in fifteen years, an American aircraft carrier was venturing into the confining waters of the Persian Gulf.

At Diego Garcia, a remote island in the Indian Ocean, a convoy of Maritime Prepositioning Ships left port. The cargo ships were an old Pentagon insurance policy. They held enough tanks, artillery, and supplies to outfit an entire marine brigade. Shortly after the convoy departed Diego Garcia, a squadron of B-52s arrived. Each heavy bomber could deliver thirty-five tons of ordnance on advancing Iraqi columns.

In Washington, conversations had already shifted from saving Saudi Arabia to liberating Kuwait. Intelligence showed Iraqi troops were digging in along the Saudi border, constructing elaborate fortifications like those from the Iran-Iraq War. Saddam officially annexed Kuwait, declaring it the "19th Province of Iraq," and he appeared content to sit still and protect his gains.

George Bush, meanwhile, was anything but still. The crisis summoned from Bush a resolve rarely seen during his many years in Washington. He relished the clarity of this situation. Bush had labored through countless Cold War quandaries as ambassador, director of the CIA, and vice president. But now the Soviet rival had receded, and Saddam Hussein presented him with an obvious course of action.

It was wanton aggression, Bush said, the kind reminiscent of the dictators who sparked World War II. There was no place for such behavior in the new world order, Bush proclaimed. For the most part, the world agreed. Thirty-eight nations offered to send combat or support troops, while a dozen more kicked in monetary support. The United Nations passed a series of resolutions endorsing the coalition and condemning Iraq. Behind the scenes, U.S. officials coaxed some reluctant countries with debt forgiveness and generous trade concessions. Still, no one doubted that George Bush had forged an impressive alliance to liberate Kuwait.

At the Pentagon, the view extended beyond Kuwait to Saddam himself. The crisis was seen as a priceless opportunity to bring stability to the Persian Gulf by knocking down its biggest bully.

"I won't be happy until I see his tanks destroyed," said Colin Powell in a meeting.[7] The Joint Chiefs chairman, himself a Vietnam veteran, typically counseled against the use of military force. But not in this instance. "I want to leave their tanks as smoking kilometer fence posts all the way back to Baghdad," he emphasized.

Beneath Powell's office, deep in a basement warren of workstations, a team of air force strategists was busy designing a comprehensive air plan against Iraq. The planning cell, known as Checkmate, had formed in the 1970s to analyze a potential air war between NATO and Soviet forces. Checkmate planners typically spent their days running complex computer simulations of battles that would never be fought. Now Checkmate had the chance to develop a real air campaign, and they envisioned a radical plan.

Conventional wisdom called for heavy airstrikes on an enemy's frontline defenses, and then striking incrementally deeper until his capital was flattened. Checkmate instead focused on what they called the enemy's "centers of gravity." They wanted to strike Iraq everywhere, and all at once. The team—now brimming with enthusiasm—boarded a flight for Riyadh, where they would present their unorthodox plan to the theater air commander, Lt. Gen. Charles A. Horner.

CHAPTER 4

Instant Thunder

CHECKMATE'S LEADER, COL. JOHN WARDEN III, MORE CLOSELY RESEMbled a college professor than a combat pilot. Yet in Vietnam he had been a forward air controller, circling low over smoky battlefields in a propeller-driven airplane, guiding fighter-bombers to their targets. More than once, Warden's little OV-10 Bronco returned to base perforated by enemy ground fire.

But Vietnam was long ago, and, in the intervening years Warden transformed himself into an air force scholar and a leading airpower theorist. The reputation was a blessing and a curse. Warden walked the halls of the Pentagon revered as a deep thinker who would help lead the military into the twenty-first century. Elsewhere in the air force, he was derided as a preening intellectual, someone lacking the common sense and fortitude to command men. His last overseas assignment, as a wing commander in Germany, lasted just six months before a hard-nosed general sent him home.

Chuck Horner's bitter experience during Operation Rolling Thunder and other Vietnam-era fiascos left him biased against "airpower airheads," as he called them. Theorists always promised better results than could reasonably be expected, he believed, and risked people's lives on harebrained schemes. Horner had no interest in hearing the Checkmate plan, but his bosses were adamant. Powell and Schwarzkopf both received Checkmate's briefing in the United States, and now they wanted his opinion. So Horner fidgeted inside a small conference room at the Royal Saudi Air Force Headquarters, while outside the urgent business of the deployment went on without him.

Warden and his staff knew they would be playing to a tough room, so they arrived with a goodwill gift: a case of toiletries and other small comforts not readily available in-theater. Horner dismissed the care package with a wave of his hand. The briefing began.

"This is not Rolling Thunder," Warden said grandly. "It is Instant Thunder."[1]

Where Rolling Thunder sought to cripple the enemy gradually—nearly four years, as it turned out—Instant Thunder would do so immediately, he said. In just six days.

Horner sat stone-faced.

Warden's slide projector clicked and a bull's-eye with five rings appeared. These were the Iraqi "centers of gravity," he explained, using a term coined by nineteenth-century Prussian military theorist Carl von Clausewitz. The outer ring represented Iraq's hard military shell—the tanks and troops and artillery. The inner rings supported it. They were the weapons factories, oil refineries, electrical grid, and transportation system. The bull's-eye's center represented Saddam and his generals, and the communications network they used to command their forces.

Instant Thunder's around-the-clock airstrikes would largely bypass Iraq's thick outer shell, focusing instead on its soft interior rings. After six days, Baghdad would be crippled and dark, with no phones, computers, or radios. Any military leaders still alive would be cut off from their field commanders in Kuwait and southern Iraq. The military command-and-control system would be paralyzed. Hungry front-line soldiers, meanwhile, would be watching for supply trucks that weren't coming. Iraq would crumble from the inside out.

As Warden showed slides with bold predictions like "Strategic Air Defense: Destroyed" and "National Leadership: Incapacitated," Horner grew impatient. The whole thing sounded like the same dreamy academic nonsense he'd heard coming out of Washington his entire career. He asked about the Republican Guard divisions arrayed along the border. What if they began moving south once the war started? Warden frowned and said he thought it unlikely; reconnaissance showed the Iraqi tanks were dug into revetments. Warden returned to his lecture.

"At every question I asked that dealt with the Iraqi ground forces, he would dismiss my concerns as unimportant," Horner later complained.

The briefing continued, and subordinates noticed the two men becoming visibly aggravated. Horner kept harping on the ground forces, and each time Warden implored him to look at the bigger picture of a strategic air campaign.

"We could be looking out the window right now and see the Iraqi tanks come into Riyadh," Horner finally shouted.

"You are being overly pessimistic about those tanks," Warden shot back.

The room fell quiet. Officers stared at the table or squirmed in their seats. Warden realized he'd gone too far and apologized. He tried to explain himself. The Iraqis knew an invasion of Saudi Arabia would over-tax their already limited supply lines, and they also knew it would place them squarely in the crosshairs of coalition airpower. In his opinion, the tanks weren't coming.

"Apology accepted," Horner replied icily. He declared the meeting over, then turned to several Checkmate members and invited them to remain in Riyadh as part of the planning staff. Their knowledge of Iraq's infrastructure and air defense network would be welcome, he said. No invitation was extended to John Warden. Once more, he was sent home.

Seeb Air Base
Muscat, Oman
September 30, 1990

The F-15E Strike Eagle was America's newest air-to-ground attack jet, such a recent arrival that, when the crisis broke, a single Strike Eagle squadron was up and running. The rest were still transitioning from old F-4 Phantoms and other soon-to-be-retired aircraft.

The operational squadron—the 336th Rocketeers out of Seymour Johnson Air Force Base, North Carolina—had wondered if they would be going to the Gulf, since they were still learning the aircraft and refining tactics. But almost immediately the orders came. If Iraqi columns did invade Saudi

Arabia, the F-15E would be the perfect plane to stop them. By August 12, two dozen Strike Eagles were aligned neatly on the shimmering concrete of Seeb Air Base in Oman. There was little to do in the desert except fly training sorties, and since war seemed imminent, the Rocketeers trained a lot.

On this blazing Sunday morning, as Maj. Pete Hook took off on yet another practice mission, he was in an exceptional mood. The previous night Hook had arranged a phone call home, and he was still buoyant from chatting with his wife and three young children. In the Strike Eagle's back seat, serving as weapon systems officer (WSO or "wizzo") was Capt. Jim "Boo Boo" Poulet, a lighthearted Californian who dabbled in the French language of his ancestors. Both men were in their mid-thirties and enjoying the benefits of successful flying careers, as evidenced by their selection for the air force's newest strike aircraft.

The McDonnell Douglas design team who in 1969 laid out the original F-15 Eagle could scarcely have imagined a ground-attack variant of their plane. The F-15 they knew was an air superiority thoroughbred, created solely for the purpose of shooting down Soviet MiGs.

For all of Vietnam's painful lessons, the one that stung aviators most was the decline of America's dogfighting supremacy. During the Korean War, U.S. fighters shot down seven MiGs for every jet they lost. In Vietnam, the ratio slipped to two kills for every loss. Part of the problem was inadequate pilot training, so the services created intensive programs such as Red Flag and Top Gun. But, clearly, American aircraft design also needed improvement.

The previous generation of fighters had sought to fill nearly every combat role—air superiority, deep strike, close air support—and as a result excelled at none. Bloated multitaskers, they could not keep up with the smaller, lighter MiGs. By 1969, air force officers at the Pentagon were clamoring for a pure air-to-air fighter. They urged manufacturers to pare away all other design considerations, using the mantra "not a pound for air-to-ground." The F-15 Eagle met their criteria, and the air force ordered it by the hundreds.

McDonnell Douglas knew it had a winner and spent years refining the plane's pedigree. When the C-model first flew in 1978, it represented the pinnacle of dogfighting performance, with a state-of-the-art radar that spotted enemy fighters from astonishing distances. The U.S. Air Force was delighted, and so were the air forces of Israel, Japan, and Saudi Arabia, who also acquired the Eagle. Over the years, regardless of the flag it flew under, the F-15 achieved absolute success, tallying more than 100 kills without suffering a single combat loss.

In the early 1980s, a new generation of McDonnell Douglas engineers toyed with the idea of a ground-attack F-15, in effect turning the high-flying thoroughbred into a mud-slogging draft horse. Horrified Pentagon officers refused to back the project, but the engineers persisted. They added a back seat and stuffed it with air-to-ground avionics. Advanced engines and a reinforced airframe ensured the new plane could carry heavy bomb loads. Form-fitting external fuel tanks would permit raids deep into enemy territory, without sacrificing too much maneuverability. The Strike Eagle would hug the landscape to avoid radar detection, so they gave it an olive paint scheme.

Test exercises suggested the F-15E could fight its way into a target area without fighter escort, then drop its payload and fight back out. At last, the air force was sold. Strike Eagles began rolling off the assembly line in 1988, and handpicked aviators entered a training program at Luke Air Force Base in Arizona. Dogfight-centric F-15C jocks scoffed at the bastardized version of their airplane, calling it the Mud Hen. Strike Eagle crews, meanwhile, referred to the eggshell-colored F-15C as the Albino.

Pilots with low-flying ground-attack credentials had first crack at the new airplane, and Peter Hook made an ideal candidate. He had spent more than a decade in F-4 Phantom cockpits, including a stint as an exchange pilot with the Royal Air Force, where treetop maneuvering was a way of life. But Strike Eagles were also supposed to be air-to-air fighters, and many of the converted F-4, F-111, and A-10 pilots were new to that realm. It was one of the disciplines they practiced in the Omani desert. On today's mission Hook and his wingman, Capt. Steve Sanders, planned to intercept a flight of British Jaguars, who would be simulating an attack on Seeb Air Base.

The pair of Strike Eagles loitered in a brilliant blue sky of unlimited visibility. Flying in this part of the world was incredible, with its flat and sparsely populated landscape. Broiling heat and blowing sand made extra work for the maintenance crews, but to an aviator the desolate environment was liberating. Most would remember these training sorties as the most carefree and enjoyable flights of their lives.

Sanders' backseater, Capt. Rick Henson, spotted two inbound bogeys on his radar and called them out. The Brits were coming in fast and low, just as expected. Hook ordered a pincer maneuver, and the F-15Es split in opposite directions. They would circle around and rejoin behind the Jaguars.

Henson was watching the pincer develop on his radar when suddenly the scope went dark. His air-to-air radar was dead—more work for the maintenance guys—and the timing couldn't be worse. He called out the problem, and Hook instructed the second Strike Eagle to break off the maneuver and go into a holding pattern. The flight lead said he and Poulet would handle the intercept alone.

Hook completed his half of the pincer and rolled in behind the bogeys. He called tally ho, meaning he had visual contact, and a few seconds later radioed that the engagement was underway. It seemed the lone Strike Eagle was in perfect position for a kill, but unknown to Hook, the Brits had a surprise waiting. Trailing far behind was a third Jaguar, ready to pounce.

He saw the trap too late. The trailing Jaguar was closing fast on his six o'clock position. Hook knew he was in trouble and decided on a sharp U-turn to face his attacker. He rolled the plane onto its back and pulled down toward the ground. The vertical U-turn would put him nose-to-nose with the Jaguar.

Hook had misjudged the altitude needed to complete the maneuver. At the bottom of the turn, his plane no longer inverted, he saw the desert floor rising up to meet him. He yanked hard on the stick, desperately trying to bring the nose up. It wasn't enough. The Strike Eagle's twin engines scorched a black exhaust trail into the sand, and then its tail plowed in, triggering an explosion.

Far away in their holding pattern, Steve Sanders and Rick Henson wondered why the radios suddenly went silent. Hook was a pro who always stayed in constant communication with his wingman.

"Without knowing anything is wrong, I have a bad feeling, like when the hair on the back of your neck stands up," Henson said. "I didn't know what it was. I tried to call Pete a couple of times and can't get an answer."[2]

The emergency frequency came alive with calls of a downed aircraft, but it wasn't clear who crashed or if there were survivors. Once Sanders and Henson passed over the crash site they knew no one could have survived the impact. Among the few recognizable parts they saw was the shattered wing of a Strike Eagle.

* * *

Across the theater, more accidents followed. An RF-4C—a reconnaissance version of the F-4 Phantom—crashed near Abu Dhabi on October 8, killing both crewmen. They had been practicing low-level tactics when the pilot lost his situational awareness and flew into the ground. In the North Arabian Sea, two marine UH-1N Huey helicopters practicing night rescues crashed, apparently after colliding, killing eight. A day later, the two-man crew of an F-111F Aardvark died while attempting a low-level run over a Saudi bomb range. Chuck Horner ordered a halt to all air force training missions to review flight safety procedures.

Horner and his wing commanders determined that the pilots were training too hard. They wanted razor skills for combat, and as a result were becoming reckless. The fearsome reputation of Iraq's air defense network didn't help. Maps hung in every squadron headquarters showing radar sites, missile batteries, and antiaircraft gun emplacements. The only way to defeat such an extensive system was to fly beneath it, so pilots were pushing their machines to frighteningly low altitudes. Horner ordered a training deck of 500 feet for air force training sorties, which he felt was low enough for a Mach 2 jet.

But Horner couldn't stop the British from going lower, as they loved to do. RAF pilots routinely flew at 100 feet or less, a feat the Americans regarded as insane since the slightest distraction could mean instant death. Long-standing RAF strategy exploited Europe's rolling valleys for stealth and surprise. Specialty weapons such as the JP233 bomblet dispenser required pilots to swoop along heavily defended runways at just 180 feet. Yet the ground-hugging tactics came with a cost. On November 13, a Jaguar crashed during ultra-low-level training, killing the pilot. British squadrons refused to change, accepting occasional losses as an unfortunate byproduct of their trade.

CHAPTER 5

Black Hole

BEFORE IRAQ INVADED KUWAIT, BUSTER GLOSSON WAS CONTEMPLATING the end of his air force career. The brigadier general felt retirement was being foisted upon him. Glosson's confident, outspoken manner had always earned him trouble, but this time it seemed his natural charm and leadership ability could not bail him out.

The latest affront came during a stint as a legislative liaison in the Pentagon, where he said some things best left unspoken. As punishment, Glosson was tossed into obscurity, reassigned as the air force representative aboard the USS *LaSalle*, an administrative command ship in the Persian Gulf. The prematurely gray general planned to finish out this backwater tour and then retire to his native North Carolina.

A phone call from Riyadh changed everything. Chuck Horner knew Glosson, who had flown F-4s at the tail end of Vietnam, and considered him brash but practical, a man who could get things done. If you asked Glosson a question, you got a straight answer, precisely the type of personality Horner needed to lead the air planning staff and develop a comprehensive air strategy against Iraq.

Glosson left the *LaSalle* without even bothering to pack. In Riyadh, he commandeered a conference room near Horner's office and began assembling his planning cell. People called the mysterious room the Black Hole, with its closed doors that warned away anyone lacking the highest security clearance. Horner deemed the nickname appropriate for a different reason. He said every time a bright, young officer arrived from the United States, after a few days that person vanished, pulled by Glosson into the Black Hole.

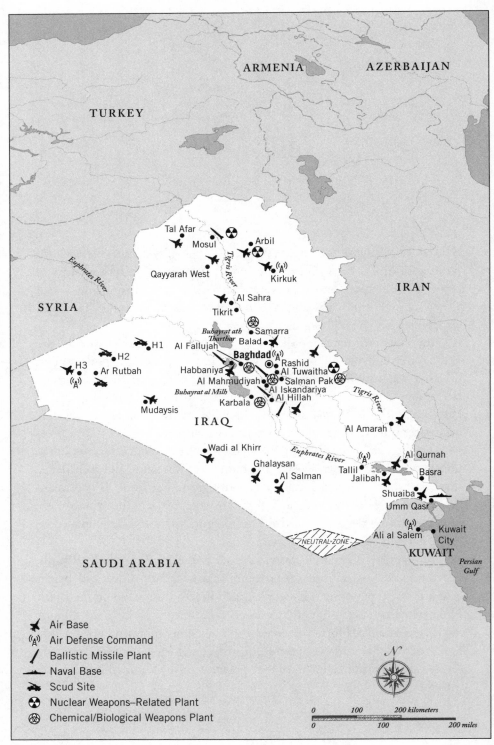

ARMENIA   AZERBAIJAN

TURKEY

Euphrates River

SYRIA

IRAN

Tal Afar
Mosul ☢   Arbil ☢
Qayyarah West   Kirkuk (A)
                  Al Sahra
                  Tikrit
        Buhayrat ath   Samarra ⚙
        Tharthar   Balad
H1   Al Fallujah   Baghdad ◎ (A) Rashid
H2   Habbaniya ⚙   Al Tuwaitha ☢
H3 Ar Rutbah   Al Mahmudiyah ⚙   Salman Pak ☢
(A)   Al Iskandariya
A   Buhayrat al Milh   Karbala ⚙ Al Hillah
Mudaysis   Tigris River

IRAQ   Al Amarah

Wadi al Khirr   Al Qurnah
                 Euphrates River
Ghalaysan   Tallil (A) Jalibah Basra
Al Salman   Shuaiba
                    Umm Qasr
                        (A) Kuwait
NEUTRAL ZONE   Ali al Salem City

SAUDI ARABIA   KUWAIT   Persian
                                    Gulf

N

✈ Air Base
(A) Air Defense Command
/ Ballistic Missile Plant
⚓ Naval Base
🚜 Scud Site
☢ Nuclear Weapons–Related Plant
⚙ Chemical/Biological Weapons Plant

0   100   200 kilometers
0   100   200 miles

Principal Targets in Iraq

The team read through a copy of Instant Thunder left behind by John Warden and were intrigued. Warden's plan proposed using new technology—particularly stealth jets and laser-guided bombs—to create chaos within Iraq, leaving its army deaf and blind. Some elements of Instant Thunder were either incomplete or overly optimistic. "As for the estimate of finishing the campaign in six to nine days, they were smoking dope on that one," Glosson recalled, with his typical verve. "I needed an air campaign plan for a full fifteen rounds, not two or three ending up with just giving Saddam a bloody nose."[1]

In the coming months, Glosson's team would expand Instant Thunder and take it in entirely new directions. Checkmate originally identified eighty-four Iraqi targets. By December the target list stood at 237, and counting. While Warden had argued that airpower alone would force Saddam out of Kuwait, the Black Hole assumed a ground war would be necessary. They made plans to "prepare the battlefield" beforehand and to assist coalition troops with close air support once the shooting started.

Although he was banished from the theater, John Warden continued to help. From his Pentagon warren, he analyzed raw intelligence data and ran computer simulations of proposed airstrikes. Warden's protégé, Lt. Col. Dave Deptula, had been one of the Checkmate members to stay behind in Riyadh. Now mentor and protégé spoke by telephone almost daily, giving Warden direct input into the planning process. Deptula's easygoing nature and sharp mind made him a natural second-in-command for the Black Hole. He had a knack for handling Buster Glosson's outsized personality, and, unlike Glosson, he had tact. Whenever a Checkmate report needed to go to Horner for review, Deptula first removed Warden's name to avoid friction.

* * *

Long before his forces set foot in Kuwait, Saddam planned to take hostages. The wealthy emirate attracted many foreign workers, business professionals, and tourists—including roughly three thousand Americans. Iraqi security officers began rounding them up, detaining foreign nationals in their hotel rooms or placing them on buses to Baghdad. Of all the unfortunate men, women, and children who became Saddam's pawns, perhaps the unluckiest were the 350 passengers of a British Airways 747 that happened to be making a refueling stop at Kuwait International Airport when the invasion occurred.

When the coalition began to gel in August, Iraq announced that 10,000 Westerners would become "human shields" at strategic sites in Kuwait and Iraq. The ploy backfired, and Saddam backpedaled in the face of international outrage, first by releasing all women and children in September, and then by hinting in November that the remaining detainees would soon be set free "if peace continued in the area."

His reassurances appeared to exclude the twenty-seven Americans still holed up at the embassy in Kuwait City. Iraqi troops surrounded the compound, but did not enter. The embassy standoff vexed Schwarzkopf, who was now back in Saudi Arabia. As commander in chief, he was responsible for the safety of the diplomats trapped inside, and he doubted the Iraqis would continue their restraint once the war began. Any rescue attempt would likely be bloody, for the Iraqis had turned Kuwait City into a fortress. Still, he might have to try.

The dilemma resembled the 1979 Iran hostage crisis, when Islamic revolutionaries stormed the embassy in Tehran and took fifty-two Americans prisoner. President Jimmy Carter authorized a rescue attempt, Operation Eagle Claw, in April 1980. The elaborate two-night plan called for the establishment of two remote staging areas—both inside Iran. Helicopters and support planes would leapfrog across desolate terrain to Desert One and Desert Two, then mount a large-scale helicopter insertion of special operations forces into Tehran. As Delta Force operators rescued the hostages, U.S. Army Rangers would seize a nearby airstrip for incoming air force C-141 Starlifters. Orbiting AC-130 gunships would provide close air support, while navy and marine jets gave cover.[2]

Eagle Claw disintegrated almost as soon as it began. Several helicopters malfunctioned on the first night after flying through a sandstorm, forcing the crews to abandon their mission, and in one case, their aircraft. The Desert One site proved less secluded than believed. When an Iranian bus driver bumbled onto the scene, he and his passengers were taken captive. Then the final blow came. In the pitch-black desert night, with pilots squinting for reference points through propeller-churned sand, a low-hovering marine helicopter collided with an idling C-130 tanker plane. A hellish explosion lit the night sky, killing eight service members and spraying nearby aircraft with shrapnel. The next day, Iranian television broadcast images of charred aircraft, as bus passengers described the pandemonium they witnessed before the Americans fled. It was a boon for the revolutionaries, and a humiliation to the United States.

Schwarzkopf desperately hoped to avoid another Eagle Claw. At least Operation Pacific Wind, the plan to rescue the embassy staff in Kuwait, faced fewer logistical challenges. Instead of two nights, it could be carried out in just a few hours.

Pacific Wind would test American advances in stealth and precision. Four radar-evading F-117 Nighthawks would lead the way, using laser-guided bombs to knock out city power plants and destroy a hotel housing Iraqi officers. F-15E Strike Eagles would pound dozens of anti-aircraft batteries, cutting open a swath for special operations helicopters. As Delta Force teams rescued the diplomats, more Strike Eagles would streak down three boulevards, scattering cluster bombs to suppress the Iraqi response. Navy F-14 Tomcats would provide air cover, while jamming aircraft scrambled Iraqi radar and communications.

Back in the United States, pilots and special operators rehearsed the plan using a mock-up of the embassy compound and surrounding buildings. They tested their tactics and equipment, leaving no detail unexplored. Back in 1980, Eagle Claw investigators blamed its failure on a lack of planning and coordination between the armed services. Individual units knew their own specific jobs but had failed to come together as a cohesive force. This time would be different.

The Eagle Claw debacle occurred in the lingering shadow of Vietnam, with services that were underfunded and demoralized. The U.S. military remolded itself in the 1980s, aided by Reagan-era spending and Defense Department restructuring. The soldiers and aviators who would carry out Pacific Wind were better trained, and they carried superior weapons and equipment. Their generals knew how to minimize risk and maximize the odds of success. Still, the ugly memory of Eagle Claw weighed on everyone.

"If the choice was to let the Iraqis start executing our people or taking the risk to get them out, I would have been all in favor of Pacific Wind," said Buster Glosson. "But it was definitely a high-risk mission."[3]

An F-15E pilot offered a more sobering assessment. "We knew of at least seventy-two AAA pieces within a mile and one-quarter stretch of beach by the embassy—and that didn't include the stuff with the armored divisions in the area," he said. "I estimated we would have lost nine out of twelve of our airplanes and probably half the helicopters."[4]

Schwarzkopf had an even larger concern. He worried the rescue attempt might touch off the war prematurely, forcing major revisions to his plans. In early November the commander in chief had persuaded Washington to send him an additional 200,000 ground troops, but it would be mid-January until the last of those reinforcements arrived.

Saddam solved the problem for him. On December 6, he announced the release of all detainees in Iraq and Kuwait, including the embassy holdouts. The diplomats received safe passage to Baghdad and boarded flights out of the theater. Pacific Wind was shelved, much to the relief of everyone involved.

Royal Saudi Air Force Headquarters
Riyadh, Saudi Arabia
January 16, 1991

Operation Desert Shield, the campaign to defend Saudi Arabia, was over, about to be replaced by Desert Storm, an offensive operation to liberate Kuwait. Desert Storm would be fought by air, sea, and land in pursuit of a secondary purpose: eviscerating the Iraqi war machine. A third and largely unspoken goal was the downfall of Saddam Hussein. The coalition had no intention of going to Baghdad and removing him from power, but if he happened to perish in an airstrike, or fall victim to a popular uprising after losing his military grip on Iraq, no one would be disappointed.

In late November, the United Nations Security Council sanctioned the use of force if Iraq failed to withdraw by January 15, 1991. Saddam responded that he would never surrender Kuwait, adding that, if attacked, he would not hesitate to use weapons of mass destruction. As the deadline neared, the Bush administration gave him one more chance with a round of high-level talks in Switzerland. Saddam viewed the offer as further evidence of American hesitancy and weakness. When Secretary of State James Baker met with Iraqi Foreign Minister Tariq Aziz in Geneva, nothing significant happened.

The Black Hole was ready for war. Its four-phase plan would first establish air superiority over Kuwait and Iraq, freeing the coalition's fighter-bombers to execute the second phase, a strategic campaign against Iraqi leadership, communications, and war-making infrastructure. The planes would then turn to Iraq's ground forces, striking tanks, artillery, and troop concentrations. Once airstrikes reduced the Iraqi army by 50 percent, the ground war would begin, with aircraft transitioning into their final phase: close air support.

The basement of the Royal Saudi Air Force Headquarters was now TACC, the Tactical Air Control Center, a buzzing bunker of computers, telephones, large-screen monitors, and hastily constructed plywood cubicles. TACC officers came from every service, every allied nation, and every aircraft type. They handled the air campaign's countless details, turning the Black Hole's target list into actual missions, and assigning those missions to squadrons across the theater. They published the daily Air Tasking Order (ATO), a ponderous twenty-four-hour game plan listing every flight, tanker rendezvous, and mission call sign. The ATO was sent electronically to air bases and hand-delivered to aircraft carriers in the Persian Gulf and Red Sea.

On the eve of war, Schwarzkopf visited TACC to pump up the troops and get a final briefing. H-Hour was set for 0300 on January 17. Everything was in place. The weather was good. The squadrons were ready. TACC previously distributed the ATO for the first three days, like a football team scripting its opening plays before a big game. The Iraqis, of course, were on high alert, their long-range radars peering deep into Saudi Arabia. During the past two weeks, waves of coalition aircraft had dashed to the border and then turned around. The ploy was meant to gauge Iraq's response and to desensitize its radar operators.

Schwarzkopf walked into the Black Hole flanked by Horner and Glosson. He commended everyone on their hard work and then turned to the enormous map of Iraq and Kuwait hanging on the wall. Dave Deptula, who had been with the plan since its earliest stages at Checkmate, began walking him through the opening salvos. As Deptula spoke, he pointed to clusters of target pins. The first two phases—air superiority and strategic bombing—would begin simultaneously, as air-to-air fighters escorted the ground-attack planes to their targets, dealing with Iraqi interceptors along the way. During the war's initial five hours, coalition aircraft would be dropping nearly 40,000,000 pounds of ordnance on targets across Iraq.

Schwarzkopf scowled at the map. Where were the B-52 strikes on the Republican Guard, he asked. Saddam's three fiercest divisions sat in reserve in southern Iraq, surprisingly free of target pins. Schwarzkopf was counting on airstrikes to hold the Republican Guard in place until he was ready to deal with them. He wanted B-52s harassing them from the first moment, and he thought the air planners understood that.[5]

Chuck Horner cleared his throat and replied that the heavy bombers would indeed move in, once the Republican Guard air defenses were defanged by F-16s. Sending the subsonic B-52s over untouched SAM batteries would be far too risky, Horner explained.

The commander in chief turned crimson. He said he'd been lied to, that he'd been assured of immediate airstrikes on the Republican Guard. Horner tried to prevent a public scene, suggesting they go to his office and sort it out. Schwarzkopf didn't budge. He wanted those B-52 strikes, not excuses, and he wanted them from the outset.

"Well, then how many B-52s are you willing to lose in order to do this," Glosson asked.[6] The sarcasm bordered on insubordination.

Schwarzkopf seemed too angry for words. His eyes blazed with contempt. When he finally spoke to the air force generals, it was in a low growl. If they couldn't follow his orders, he warned, he'd find people who could. He stormed from the room. Horner gave chase.

Glosson turned to his shocked, disheartened team. Junior officers rarely witnessed such open conflict between the higher ranks. He reminded them that Schwarzkopf was under tremendous pressure. Their plan was a good one, he said, and this episode would be soon forgotten, washed away by success. Privately, Glosson blamed himself for the blowup. He'd developed a good working rapport with Schwarzkopf in recent months, and he wondered now if his trumpeting of airpower may have left the commander with unrealistic expectations.

In Horner's office Schwarzkopf continued to vent, repeating again that his entire ground strategy hinged on keeping the Republican Guard immobilized. Meanwhile, in the Black Hole, Glosson and Deptula worked frantically on a fix. The ATOs for the first three days were already published, but they'd built in some flexibility. They pushed up the first Republican Guard strikes for H+18 hours. The F-16s would have that long to make it safe for the heavy bombers. In the meantime, RF-4C reconnaissance jets would overfly the area, confirming that nobody down there was on the move.

DESERT STORM

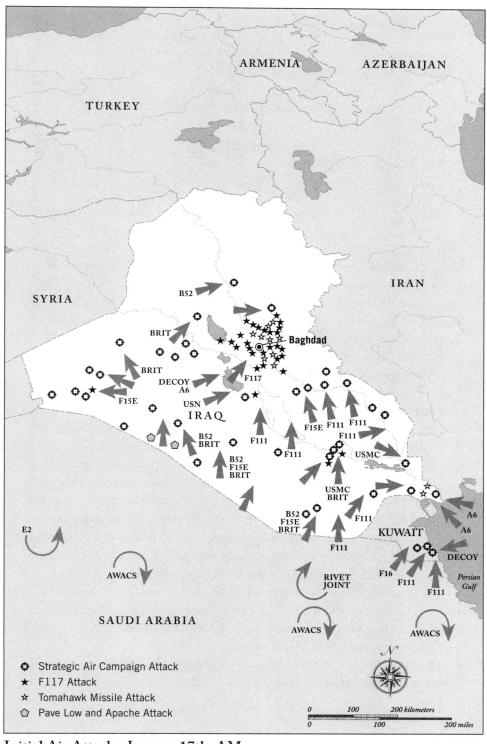

Initial Air Attacks, January 17th, AM

CHAPTER 6

Leading Edge

FIVE MONTHS OF PLANNING AND TRAINING WERE ABOUT TO CULMINATE. The desert deployment had begun at the height of summer, when only night offered a respite from the sun's heat. Now it was winter in the desert, with ashen days and bitter nights. Stinging sand blew through the camps, adding to the gloom and desolation. With war just hours away, those aviators scheduled for the opening missions began their ritual preflight preparations. The rest waited and wondered.

Any pilot who studied the history of air warfare, and many did, could take comfort in some recent developments. America's last major conflict was nearly two decades distant, but significant events since then pointed to a positive outcome. The first occurred in Lebanon's Bekaa Valley in June 1982. Syria had established an extensive SAM network along the valley, which Israel viewed as a potential threat and decided to attack.

The two-day campaign began with Israeli drones buzzing through the seventy-five-mile valley, inducing the Syrians to light up their radars. Israeli F-4 Phantoms then raced in with radar-homing missiles. Syria scrambled nearly a hundred fighters—mostly aging MiGs and Su-20s—but as the Syrian pilots arrived over the valley, they found they had no communications. Their radios were being jammed. As the Syrian jets milled around in disarray, dozens of Israeli F-15s and F-16s descended on them, downing twenty-nine in just a few hours. The next day, when the F-4s returned to destroy the last two SAM sites, Israeli fighters scored another thirty-five kills without suffering a single loss.

The significance of the Bekaa Valley Turkey Shoot was not lost on the superpowers. For many years previous, both sides wondered if modern

U.S. aircraft could survive against a Soviet-style SAM network. The miniature air war in Bekaa Valley offered the first hint. With clever tactics, they could not only survive but also achieve total victory.

A second encouraging episode from history occurred in 1986 when Libyan dictator Muammar Gaddafi's support of terrorism provoked an American response. After a Berlin nightclub bombing killed a U.S. service member, Ronald Reagan authorized a retaliatory strike against Libyan airfields and terrorist training camps. Libya's sophisticated air defenses were expected to make the raid a challenge, as Gaddafi fielded a variety of French and Soviet weapons systems, all tied into an extensive radar network.

On the evening of April 14, 1986, twenty-one F-111s left their bases in England on a seven-hour flight to Libya. As they drew near, nearly three dozen navy and marine aircraft launched from carriers in the Gulf of Sidra. The precision raid took just twelve minutes. As A-7 Corsairs and F/A-18 Hornets suppressed the defenses with antiradar missiles, low-flying F-111s and A-6s sped toward five targets in Tripoli and Benghazi. They destroyed barracks, parked aircraft, and one of Gaddafi's residences. Operation El Dorado Canyon was a success, reinforcing the notion that Soviet-style air defenses could be defeated. But the mission ended with a stark reminder of their potency. As the strike package egressed Libyan airspace, a coastal SAM battery brought down an F-111, killing both crewmen.

Losses were inevitable, especially in a massive campaign like Desert Storm, and the Black Hole team wondered how many aircrews they were sending to their deaths. The planners spoke about it frequently, and always in hushed tones. Optimistic assessments went as low as 100 aircraft lost, while the group's pessimists predicted 300 or more.

As H-Hour approached, Horner and Glosson took their seats in the TACC. The command center normally resembled a newsroom, with ringing telephones and fervid conversation. Now the TACC was quiet, smothered in tension like a hospital waiting room. In a whisper, Glosson asked his boss how many planes he thought they would lose. Horner took a scrap of paper and scribbled "42." Glosson felt encouraged; it was the lowest number he'd seen yet. Later, Horner would admit that when he wrote it, he had been thinking of air force planes only.

—◆—

Barksdale Air Force Base
Bossier City, Louisiana
January 16, 1991
0636 Local

More than half a day before hostilities were set to begin in the Persian Gulf, seven B-52G Stratofortresses departed their home in northwest Louisiana on a highly classified mission. The morning was rain-soaked and dreary, and within minutes the seven BUFFs—Big Ugly Fat F[ellows]—vanished into the overcast sky. Soon even the heavy drone of their turbofan engines faded, and they were gone. The BUFF crews were not due back for at least thirty-five hours, and when they finally did return they could boast of flying the longest combat sortie in history, not to mention the first sortie of Desert Storm. And the weapons they would fire represented yet another first.

The B-52 was nearly as old as the air force itself. When Congress granted independence to the U.S. Army Air Forces in 1947, Boeing's designs for an ultra-long-range bomber were already on the drawing board. The idea was to build an aircraft that could carry American firepower anywhere on the globe, without the need for friendly air bases. It was a tall order, and Boeing engineers suffered through several long years of rejected design proposals.

The plane that finally emerged, the B-52B, was still a work in progress when it entered service in 1955. During the next eight years, Boeing rolled out a half-dozen improved models, proving that the B-52's true strength was its ability to evolve and adapt. Originally envisioned as a nuclear bomber, the Stratofortress instead carried huge payloads of conventional bombs over Southeast Asia, terrorizing enemy soldiers in a way no other aircraft could. (A young Norman Schwarzkopf witnessed the B-52's psychological impact in that war; he wanted Republican Guard troops to experience the same fear in this one.)

Surface-to-air missiles nearly forced the Stratofortress into early retirement, as thirty-one B-52s were lost over Vietnam. The air force pursued supersonic bombers, but those sleek, nimble planes lacked the same payload and range. Cruise missile technology helped the B-52, since it could launch the self-guided weapon before entering SAM range. Nuclear-tipped cruise missiles joined the Stratofortress arsenal in 1960, but their guidance systems were too crude for conventional warheads, where pinpoint accuracy mattered. The 1980s brought GPS navigation, and suddenly a cruise missile could find its way to a specific building, not just the city.

The seven B-52Gs departing Louisiana were some of the oldest machines in air force inventory, but they carried one of the newest weapons: the AGM-86C Conventional Air-Launched Cruise Missile (CALCM). This twenty-foot winged torpedo contained a half-ton warhead and traveled below radar level near the speed of sound. Any ground-defense system would be hard-pressed to shoot down such a small, low, fast projectile. Each B-52 could carry up to twenty missiles.

Their marathon mission was not essential—the coalition already had plenty of firepower in the Gulf. Rather, the Louisiana BUFFs were finally putting the air force's "global reach" theory into practice. And although they were the first to fly in Desert Storm, others would fire the opening shots. By the time the B-52s launched their high-tech weapons, the war would be well underway.

The U.S. Navy owned cruise missiles, too. In fact, the two services had collaborated on missile development since the 1970s. But the navy had far more riding on Desert Storm missile performance than the air force did. Tomahawk Land Attack Missiles (TLAMs) were said to extend a vessel's firing range dramatically, and the navy deployed them aboard battleships, destroyers, cruisers, and submarines. Some officers believed the Tomahawk might revolutionize naval warfare, just as the aircraft carrier had done half a century earlier. They would soon find out, as scores of Tomahawks were ready to burst from their launch tubes and rocket off into the night.

No one doubted cruise missiles more than Colin Powell. The Joint Chiefs chairman loathed high risk, and these unproven, automated weapons seemed off-the-chart risky. "Any target you intend to destroy with the TLAM, put a fighter on it to make sure the target's destroyed," he reportedly told Schwarzkopf.[1]

King Khalid Royal Saudi Air Force Base
Khamis Mushait, Saudi Arabia
January 17, 1991
0026 Local

The air force's investment in stealth technology would also be tested. Two squadrons of pilots were about to risk their lives on the F-117 Nighthawk, a plane designed to elude radar. If the technology failed, they would not be coming home.

The single-seat Nighthawk was remarkably vulnerable. Like a bat it flew only in the dark, spending daylight hours nestled in the cavelike safety of a hangar. The F-117 was unable to defend itself, for it carried no weapons other than the two bombs in its bay, and subsonic speed left no hope of outrunning a pursuer. The Nighthawk survived with guile, darkness, and a peculiar airframe covered in radar-absorbent skin.

For nearly a decade, the air force denied its very existence. Fifty-six black jets stayed cloistered at Tonopah Test Range in the Nevada desert, where strict rules forbade the opening of hangar doors during daytime. Range officers kept track of Soviet spy satellites, ensuring each jet was tucked away whenever one passed overhead. And even after the Pentagon finally acknowledged the stealth plane's existence in 1988, it remained shrouded in mystery. For Desert Storm, the Nighthawks quietly migrated from Nevada to a heavily guarded air base in the remote south of Saudi Arabia, where they holed up inside hardened aircraft shelters.

The men who flew the F-117 were handpicked for their calm demeanor and devotion to accuracy. There were no brash hotheads in these squadrons because the Nighthawk required icy composure. The plane was actually easy to fly, and media reports of the "Wobblin' Goblin" were grossly exaggerated. Rather, a pilot's patience was tested during mission planning and execution, for in the stealth world these tasks were far more intricate than usual. F-117 missions demanded near-perfect timing, with acceptable deviations measured in seconds, not minutes. And since each plane flew solo, and under communications blackout, a healthy self-reliance also helped.

The Nighthawk's cockpit canopy resembled a glass pyramid, with the pilot's head situated near the peak. The fuselage was just as angular and faceted, designed to bounce radar waves in harmless directions rather than back to their sender. From above, the plane looked like an arrowhead chiseled from obsidian. Its profile—with sharply swept angles and three long, stalky landing-strut legs—evoked comparisons with an insect's carapace. The radar-absorbent material clinging to every surface demanded constant care, since the smallest bit of exposed metal could boost the plane's radar signature. After sealing up an exterior maintenance panel, a stealth technician always needed to re-grout its screw heads with black resin.

The stealth concept worked well enough in Nevada and Southern California, where pilots flew training missions undetected by air traffic controllers. It also succeeded during America's 1989 invasion of Panama, where the F-117 made its combat debut. But Iraq represented an entirely different radar environment, one thick with Soviet missile systems, and operators who would react to the faintest, fleeting return on their scopes. The Nighthawk's final exam was at hand. On opening night, they would leave in waves of ten. Since Baghdad was nearly 1,000 miles away, the first wave needed to take off two and a half hours before H-Hour. They would meet their tankers and refuel in silence before crossing the Iraqi border.

A fighter pilot suiting up for a mission typically listened to heavy metal or other adrenaline-laced music, but stealth pilots—or Bandits, as they called themselves—preferred mellow tunes. Their job required a slow heartbeat and a steady hand, so they cultivated inner calm. Within the air force, the Bandits were seen as elitist and insular, a reputation bred from the secrecy that surrounded them. Now they would prove the enormous stealth investment had been worth it, or die trying.

"We were taken out to our jets from the crew area by shuttle bus," one remembered, "and as each pilot was dropped off at his shelter, he shook hands with all the others. In the back of our minds, we all wondered who would return and who would not. After all, we had been told to expect two or three F-117s to go down on the first night."[2]

At the pre-appointed second, ten shadowy figures moved in unison at Khamis Mushait.

Chapter 7

First In

Task Force Normandy thundered through the darkness, hugging the gently undulating landscape as they entered Iraq. A smattering of ground fire presented no threat to the helicopters; nervous Iraqi conscripts were shooting blindly at the noise. The eight U.S. Army Apaches were split into two teams—Red and White—with each team following a U.S. Air Force special operations Pave Low helicopter.

The Pave Lows, which were beefed-up descendants of the Vietnam-era Jolly Green Giant, possessed sophisticated navigation equipment. The trailing Apaches bristled with Hellfire missiles, Hydra rockets, and 30mm chain guns. Their targets, code-named Nebraska and Oklahoma, were early warning radar stations in the western desert, and Task Force Normandy hoped to destroy them before any warning could be sent to Baghdad. The helicopters were opening a radar-free corridor for coalition warplanes, like a surgeon applying local anesthetic before plunging in the scalpel.

The Apache gunship, like stealth planes and cruise missiles, was expensive, sophisticated, and unproven. Its development stretched back more than two decades, beginning with the AH-56 Cheyenne, a troubled forerunner that never entered service. But the Cheyenne's failures became valuable knowledge and experience for the Apache program, which produced a flying prototype in 1975. Seven more years of testing and refinement would pass before the army finally felt it had a winner, and in 1982 the Hughes AH-64 Apache went into production. During its early years of service, the helicopter became notorious for a temperamental nature, breaking down frequently and demanding intricate repairs. For Desert

Storm some 274 Apaches—nearly half the fleet—were in Saudi Arabia, where the harsh environment was not expected to improve its reputation.

Teams Red and White each pushed to within seven miles of their targets, which sat twenty miles apart. The Pave Lows slowed to a hover and dropped bundles of green glow sticks for the Apaches to use as navigation markers, then turned around and headed for the safety of Saudi Arabia. The mission now belonged to the shooters.

The Apache crews felt confident when they saw the radar complexes calm and drenched in floodlight, like any other night. They lined up four abreast and hovered, waiting for the stroke of 0238. Hundreds of miles south, formations of F-15E Strike Eagles and EF-111 Ravens orbited in tanker tracks. To the northeast, F-117 Nighthawks circled undetected over Baghdad. In the Persian Gulf and Red Sea, navy ships had already launched their first salvos of cruise missiles. The Tomahawks could not be recalled. The war was about to begin.

Both compounds suddenly went dark; somebody was suspicious. The Apache gunners eyed their targets through pale-green forward-looking infrared (FLIR). For weeks they had studied models of the compounds and practiced on old Saudi vehicles in the desert. An alternate plan called for Special Forces to storm the radar complexes, but Schwarzkopf chose immediate and total destruction by the Apaches. As the final thirty seconds ticked off, each gunner steadied the Hellfire laser designator on his first target.

"Party in ten," the White Team leader called out, breaking silence.

Small figures scurried around the compounds.

Hellfire missiles streaked toward the electric generators at each site, producing brilliant white explosions. Radar dishes, command vans, and radio antennas went next, followed by barracks and antiaircraft pits. When the missiles and rockets were gone, they switched to 30mm fire. As each gunner peered through his helmet-mounted display, the helicopter's belly-mounted chain gun mimicked his head movements.

They raked the few buildings that still stood, including an ammo locker originally thought to be a latrine. A spectacular eruption crowned the four-minute attack. They had expended 27 Hellfires, 100 rockets, and 4,000 rounds of ammunition. Nothing remained but flaming ruins and crumpled bodies. The Apaches withdrew, and before they reached the border, a wave of coalition jets passed overhead. The scalpel was making its first cut.

Baghdad, Iraq
January 17, 1991
0255 Local

Lieutenant Colonel Ralph Getchell had to remind himself to relax his arms. The Nighthawk's pyramid canopy always tricked him, making him forget how much elbow room the cockpit had. He took a deep breath and tried to let the tension drain from his muscles. Getchell commanded one of just two F-117 squadrons in existence, and now here he was, high over Baghdad, leading the initial stealth raid of the war. He and his Bandits would try to knock out the city's communications, the first step in severing Saddam from his military.

Clearly, stealth technology worked. Getchell and his pilots were cruising unnoticed over one of the most lethal air defenses in the world. Yet exposure could come in an instant. "Stealthiness" was equal parts art and science, with no guarantees. A small mechanical glitch, or the simple mistake of flipping a wrong switch and extending an antenna, could be deadly. The Bandits knew from experience that some Nighthawks could actually be stealthier than others, depending on atmospheric conditions, and the types of radars they were up against.

Nobody knew what to expect on this first stealth mission, so Getchell and his men decided to get a little help. They arranged for an EF-111 Raven to slip through the radar-free corridor opened by the Apaches and dash as far as possible toward Baghdad. At precisely two minutes before H-Hour, the Raven would activate its powerful jamming equipment, drawing the attention of Baghdad's radar operators. The Bandits hoped this distraction might provide an extra edge as they guided their bombs on target.

Laser-guided bombs were nothing new, although Desert Storm would introduce them to the American public. The weapons owed their existence to the Vietnam War, and in particular to a sturdy steel bridge near Thanh Hoa nicknamed the Dragon's Jaw. In April 1965, a seventy-nine-ship strike package attacked the bridge, dropping 1,200 conventional bombs, but when the smoke cleared it still stood. The bridge became a symbol of North Vietnamese resolve, and an American obsession. U.S. aircraft went on to fly nearly 900 Dragon's Jaw sorties, suffering eleven losses to MiGs and antiaircraft fire. Yet the defiant bridge remained, blackened but intact, supporting the flow of reinforcements and supplies.[1]

On May 13, 1972, a flight of F-4s appeared over Thanh Hoa. The lead Phantoms filled the sky with chaff to scramble enemy radars, while the rest descended on the bridge with laser-guided bombs. Moments later, the western span of Dragon's Jaw splashed into the muddy river, announcing a new era in aerial warfare. A dozen smart bombs had accomplished something thousands of unguided "dumb" bombs could not.

The two Paveways inside Getchell's bomb bay closely resembled those early ancestors: standard 2,000-pound bombs outfitted with laser seekers and movable flight fins. As long as Getchell illuminated or "painted" his target, the bomb's seeker would follow his infrared beam, while the flight fins made constant corrections to stay on target.

Smart bombs often missed their mark. If a seeker lost its lock, or the bomb was released outside its glide parameters—represented by an imaginary cone over the target, which pilots called the "basket"—the result would be a miss. Good weather was important because fog and clouds scattered the laser beam. Occasionally smart bombs simply "went stupid" and dropped to the ground like typical gravity bombs. Yet for all their shortcomings, smart bombs were a dramatic leap forward. During 1972 and 1973, nearly half of the laser-guided bombs dropped on Hanoi scored direct hits. In previous years, unguided bombs barely cracked the 5 percent threshold.

The Bandits, armed with modern smart bombs and the benefit of stealth, were poised to make history.

* * *

Three EF-111 Ravens surged toward Baghdad at just 400 feet. These unarmed jammers were some of the first non-stealthy jets to enter Iraq.

The mission was so risky that the EF-111 squadron commander sent a trio of planes, reasoning that at least one would survive long enough to jam for the Nighthawks. As the EF-111s moved deeper into the desert, they spotted an Iraqi patrol. The fighters were cruising south with their wing lights on, apparently unaware a war had just started. The Ravens slid beneath them undetected.

A few minutes later, AWACS advised that the patrol had suddenly turned around, but their intentions were unclear. The Iraqi jets might be pursuing the Ravens, or just returning to base, or fleeing the onrushing swarms of coalition fighters. The EF-111 flight leader decided not to take any chances. "Touchdown," he radioed. Instantly, a wingman broke formation and rocketed skyward. If the Iraqis really were in pursuit, he would serve as bait.

The other two Ravens pressed on toward Baghdad, eventually drawing within seventy miles of the city. They were still beyond ideal jamming range, but the clock showed two minutes before H-Hour. It was time. They fired up the electronic gear.

* * *

Ralph Getchell knew the instant the Ravens started jamming. "I'm arcing in from the east at fifteen thousand feet, looking down at the city," he said. "And this does not look like a city that's hunkered down and ready to be bombed. It's lit up like Las Vegas out there. Then, all of a sudden, every gun in the place goes off. I didn't know there were that many bullets in all the world."[2]

Ever since the U.N. deadline passed, Baghdad's defenders watched and waited for hints of an attack. The jamming was proof enough. They opened fire in unison, transforming the skyline into a swirling maelstrom. Streams of glowing green tracers mingled with auburn bursts and silver flashes. Every rooftop seemed to have a weapon. The pulsing barrage quickened and intensified, spraying successive patterns of molten shrapnel for any aircraft that dared approach.

As he watched the fireworks, Getchell grimaced under his mask. The request for jamming had cost his pilots one free pass over the city. Now their initial bombing run was going to be a white-knuckled ride through some of the thickest flak imaginable. "In retrospect, it was the dumbest thing we could have done," he admitted.

The black jets always flew solo, taking separate and unpredictable routes into the target area. Coordination by radio was not an option. Stealth planes avoided midair collisions through precise timing. Nobody, not even the all-seeing AWACS controllers tracked them, meaning no Nighthawk could deviate from its assigned flightpath or schedule. As the cauldron of fire boiled outside their windows, the pilots flew straight and level toward the first targets, concentrating only on the clock and their cockpit video displays.

At exactly 0300, a GBU-27 Paveway III dropped by Capt. Paul Dolson slammed into the twelve-story International Communications Center in downtown Baghdad. Roughly half of all Iraqi military traffic passed through this facility, as well as most telephone lines out of the country. Black Hole planners called it the AT&T building. The bunker-busting GBU-27 crashed through its lower floors and destroyed vital telecommunications equipment. One minute later, Maj. Jerry Leatherman took aim at the upper floors, releasing a pair of GBU-10s. The AT&T building became a burning shell. The Nighthawks struck other key targets in the city, but none ranked higher than this.

In Riyadh, Chuck Horner and Buster Glosson agonized in the stifling silence of the TACC. On one wall, a massive radar display showed coalition aircraft converging on points all across Iraq. The level of resistance those planes would face depended largely on F-117 strikes, and at this very moment the Bandits were, hopefully, eliminating key pieces of Iraq's air defense network. Major Blake Bourland was hitting the Sector Operations Center in Tallil; Capt. Marcel Kerdavid would take down the Al Khark communications tower, a difficult target that was studded with microwave relay antennas.

"If Iraqi telecommunications were destroyed, the air superiority battle became manageable," Horner explained. "Blind the enemy air defense system, and isolate the elements from the brain, and it is no longer a 'system' but individual weapons operating in the dark."[3]

Horner knew the F-117s would be unable to report until they returned to Saudi Arabia, an interminable wait. Then he remembered that

CNN was currently airing a live feed out of Baghdad—a reporter crouching by a hotel window as the camera panned the dark sky for movement. Live video coverage of a war was yet another technological first. Horner realized the CNN feed almost certainly passed through the AT&T building on its way back to the United States for broadcast. He sent an officer upstairs to his third-floor office to turn on the television.

At 0302, the officer called down with the news: CNN just lost its live feed out of Baghdad. A cheer went up across the TACC. The allies were in business.

CHAPTER 8

Attack of the Machines

THE F-117 RAID ON BAGHDAD WENT OFF BETTER THAN EXPECTED. Getchell and his men dropped seventeen Paveway bombs, scoring thirteen hits. Their targets included radio relay towers, military command bunkers, and a fortified palace outside the city where they hoped Saddam Hussein might be staying.

Success with Paveways came as no surprise, given the refinements to laser-guidance since Vietnam. Bandits routinely flirted with 100 percent accuracy in training, lasing targets as small as a garden shed, but of course perfection could not be expected in actual combat. The success of stealth technology was more significant, since it answered a question that haunted every Nighthawk pilot: Can they see me? But the real surprise wouldn't reveal itself until hours later, when the black jets finally began landing at Khamis Mushait.

Before the mission, Ralph Getchell steeled himself to the likelihood that he was going to lose a pilot, maybe two. With so many unknowns it seemed foolish to hope for a better outcome. Even if all of their intricate plans and high technology worked flawlessly, there was still the "golden BB"—that lucky shot that brought down an aircraft. Getchell worried about the effect on his squadron, which had only a few combat veterans. How they might react to a loss, he just couldn't tell.

They all came back. Despite passing through the flak barrage of approximately two thousand antiaircraft guns, every jet returned without a scratch. Their relief turned to elation when the next wave of Nighthawks came back undamaged, and then the wave after that. The Bandits had made it through the first night unscathed, and they had dealt solid blows to Iraq's command-and-control network.

* * *

The next aircraft to visit Baghdad had no pilots. Tomahawk cruise missiles sent from ships in the Persian Gulf and Red Sea took center stage minutes after the F-117s departed. Each Tomahawk had begun its journey by bursting from a pressurized tube and climbing into the night sky with a fiery rocket plume. Stubby wings and tail fins popped out, and a turbofan engine propelled the missile along a preprogrammed course at 100 to 300 feet of altitude.

The Tomahawk used gyroscopes to navigate over water, but over land it switched to a system called TERCOM, for "terrain contour matching." In TERCOM mode, the missile compared detailed maps in its memory with features of the ground passing beneath it. Tomahawks that launched from the Red Sea would have no difficulty following the choppy terrain of western Iraq, but the country's southeastern desert was a different story. Any missile coming in from the Persian Gulf would surely get lost over that flat, featureless moonscape.

Tomahawk programmers saw just one solution. They proposed flying the missiles north along the Zagros Mountains before making a left turn toward Baghdad. The problem was that the Zagros Mountains ran along the Iran-Iraq border—in western Iran. The Iranians were hostile to the United States but neutral in the current conflict. Washington had no desire to antagonize them, or let an errant Tomahawk fall into their hands. But the mountain chain was the only reliable TERCOM route to Baghdad, so scores of twenty-foot cruise missiles went speeding over remote stretches of western Iran before entering Iraq. If the Iranians noticed the airspace violation, they chose not to complain about it.

Navy ships launched 122 Tomahawks during the war's opening hours, striking targets such as Baath Party headquarters, a Scud missile plant, and another presidential palace. Baghdad's gunners kept up their fusillade, not realizing this new wave of attackers traveled well below the rooftops. A British photojournalist standing on the balcony of his room at the al-Rashid Hotel watched in dismay as a Tomahawk streaked past him, continued down the boulevard, and slammed into the Ministry of Defense.

Some Tomahawks carried a special payload to knock out power plants. Rather than a 1,000-pound explosive warhead, the top-secret Kit-2 Tomahawk contained tightly wound spools of carbon filament. The Kit-2 released its nonlethal cargo while passing over an electrical plant. As the poker-chip spools drifted to earth, they unraveled into long strands, a bit like Christmas tinsel, which short-circuited transformers and switching stations.

Kit-2 was conceived after an embarrassing incident several years earlier, as the navy conducted exercises off the California coastline. The drill called for a number of aircraft to use chaff against simulated enemy missiles, a common tactic, but in this instance the metallic strips were caught in high winds. Rather than wafting harmlessly into the sea, the filaments stayed aloft and drifted ninety miles eastward, at last making landfall over Orange County. The chaff strips that settled on power lines caused significant damage, leaving several neighborhoods in blackout. A sheepish navy apology and payments to the affected power companies ended the affair, except in the minds of weapons developers. They realized that floating metal filaments could instantly disable a power station without destroying it.

Thousands of wriggling carbon snakes now descended on five generating plants around Baghdad, creating showers of sparks and sizzling blue arcs before the system seized. Block by block, Baghdad went dim, lit only by burning government buildings and the staccato flash of artillery.

* * *

Baghdad's sixty SAM batteries remained silent. The F-117 pilots did observe a few unguided missiles corkscrewing through the air, but most operators showed greater discipline, waiting patiently for non-stealthy aircraft they could lock up and kill. Until then, they kept their tracking radars in standby.

The wait was short. With Tomahawk blasts still echoing across the city, and blackouts rolling through the streets, Baghdad's defenders received an alert: Early warning radars in the south and west were picking up large formations of aircraft. The missile operators fired up their tracking radars and started sweeping the skies. Waves of approaching planes glowed brightly on their scopes and could be locked up with ease. Smoky white columns from scores of SAM launches soon joined the spectacle over the city.

Since the earliest days of Desert Shield, coalition planners had worried about Iraq's SAM arsenal. The threat existed not just in Baghdad, but at strategic points throughout Iraq and Kuwait. Saddam possessed a variety of Soviet missiles, including the SA-6 Gainful, which sat on a mobile launcher and could turn up virtually anywhere. Other mobile threats included the French-built Roland missile and a small number of American HAWK (Homing All the Way Killer) systems captured during the invasion of Kuwait. Saddam's most potent missiles could climb as high as 45,000 feet, moving at two to three times the speed of sound.

In Riyadh, the task known as Suppression of Enemy Air Defenses, or SEAD, belonged to a guru named Larry "Poobah" Henry. Brigadier General Henry was a SEAD pioneer. During Vietnam he flew as an F-4 Phantom weapon systems officer, and he later commanded a wing of F-4G Wild Weasels, which were Phantoms that had been converted into radar hunters. Wild Weasels protected other aircraft by ferreting out and destroying enemy air defenses.

While attending the National War College in 1982, Henry became fascinated with Israel's raid earlier that year on Syrian SAM sites in the Bekaa Valley. He particularly admired the crafty use of drones to trick the Syrians into lighting up their tracking radars. In the fall of 1990, sitting at his desk in Riyadh, Henry imagined a similar spoof for the Iraqis, but on a much grander scale. His vision would grow into a joint air force and navy operation, officially code-named Scathe Mean, but the officers who worked with Henry used a different name: Poobah's Party.

At 0348 local, the party got underway. The warplanes that Iraqi radars spotted coming in from the west were actually navy decoy drones launched by A-6 Intruders. The 400-pound decoys were essentially long-range gliders that appeared on radar as large strike aircraft. The Iraqis launched a volley of missiles. As the decoys reached the end of their sixty-mile glide path, they fell off the radar scopes, convincing jubilant SAM operators that they'd scored numerous kills. In fact, they'd only exposed themselves to counterattack. Behind the decoys lurked navy and marine F/A-18 Hornets armed with AGM-88 High-speed Anti-Radar Missiles (HARMs).

Meanwhile, thirty-seven BQM-74C jet-powered target drones approached Baghdad from the south, most traveling in flights of three. One trio of drones was intercepted and destroyed by Iraqi fighters, but the rest reached Baghdad, where they assumed menacing orbits. The air force Wild Weasels that arrived behind the drones found a glut of active radar sites. Together the Hornets and Weasels launched roughly seventy-five HARMs, nearly half of which were believed to have struck their mark.[1] Iraqi radars began blinking off, in order to survive.

The SEAD team knew their Poobah Party spoof had a short shelf life—warnings would spread quickly through Iraq's air defense network—so they threw mini parties during the same time period at Kuwait City, Basra, and heavily defended military bases in western Iraq. These smaller affairs achieved similar success.

After a disastrous first night, the Iraqis learned to use their radars in quick bursts, usually just a few seconds at a time, since lengthy sweeps risked drawing a HARM. Eventually, they realized that the American radio call for a HARM launch was "Magnum," and radar operators who heard this call immediately went off the air. By the end of the war, many coalition aviators were making bogus "Magnum" calls as an easy way to shut down ground threats.

Hostile Airspace
Anbar Province
Western Iraq

Deception and technology were permitting deep strikes inside Iraq, so far without a single loss. But the high-tech strategy placed a heavy burden on the specialty aircraft that supported it, like Wild Weasels and EF-111

Ravens. No electronic warfare jet was in shorter supply than the Raven. The air force had two dozen jammers in the theater, or two-thirds of its fleet, and they were besieged with requests. Most strike aircraft carried underwing jamming pods, but those devices lacked the overwhelming power radiated by an EF-111 or the navy's EA-6B Prowler.

With the war still less than an hour old, an EF-111 piloted by Capt. Jim Denton led a large package of F-15E Strike Eagles through western Iraq. The Strike Eagles were tasked with knocking out Saddam's launch pads before he could begin lobbing Scud missiles at Israel, something he vowed to do if attacked. On Denton's right sat his electronic warfare officer, Capt. Brent Brandon, who prepared to activate the Raven's three tons of jamming equipment.

Most of the high-tech gear was stowed in a compartment that had once been a bomb bay, for the Raven began its life as a first-rate striker. Long-nosed F-111 Aardvarks flew more than 4,000 combat missions over Vietnam, losing just six planes. Built by General Dynamics, the F-111 was a low-level comet featuring variable-geometry "swing wings" and a revolutionary terrain-following radar. The Aardvark carried four times as many bombs as an F-4 Phantom, and it breezed through weather that grounded most aircraft.

Smart design and Mach 2.5 speed ensured the F-111 a long service life, and in the late 1970s the air force converted forty-two Aardvarks into jammers. Engineers fitted the plane's weapons bay with electronic modules and receivers and added a bulbous, tail-mounted pod crammed with antennas. The plane's electrical and cooling systems needed upgrades to handle the enormous power that would surge through it. Officially named the Raven, the EF-111 almost immediately acquired a more stylish nickname: Spark-Vark.

Brent Brandon studied the large video display before him. When the jamming system showed ready, he began flipping switches, and the megawatts flowed. "The hair comes up on the back of your neck, and the jet starts to crackle with all this electronic energy," he said. "It literally feels electric."[2]

The Strike Eagles commenced their runs on the Scud sites, which were scattered around a pair of sprawling air bases known as H-2 and

H-3. The Iraqi air force had several combat air patrols (CAPs) in the area, and two flights of F-15C Eagles hunted them from high overhead. Within minutes, the Spark-Vark crew saw a bright red cone appear in the distance at about seven thousand feet. F-15C pilot Capt. Robert "Cheese" Graeter was tracking an Iraqi F-1 Mirage and had just destroyed it with a Sparrow missile.

Seconds later, Denton and Brandon realized they had a problem. Another Mirage, possibly from the same flight as Graeter's victim, had discovered them. An urgent tone warned them that the Iraqi was acquiring a missile lock. The unarmed Raven, cruising at 5,000 feet, made an easy target. Denton accelerated for the deck in a tight left-hand turn. Brandon looked over his shoulder just in time to see the Iraqi jet shoot. "Missile launch, right side! Break right," he yelled.

"So at this point I'm completely blind, at four hundred feet, at night, and I've got a missile coming toward me," Denton recalled.

He pulled his plane hard right in a desperate attempt to outmaneuver the missile. Both men grunted against the weight of five gravities (5 Gs) produced by the turn. The missile flashed past. It was a short-lived victory, for the Iraqi was descending to their altitude and closing rapidly. His next missile would be much more difficult to evade.

From high above, Robert Graeter spotted what appeared to be an Iraqi Mirage, like the one he'd just killed, but speeding along the ground. Graeter had no idea why the Iraqi jet was flying so low, or that it was in hot pursuit of another aircraft. He nosed downward for a closer look.

An Eagle in the fray completely changed the nature of the engagement. The Mirage pilot was absorbed in the chase when suddenly he saw an alpha predator appear overhead. He recognized his own vulnerability and instinctively broke to escape. But the Raven had led him all the way down to 400 feet, much too low for his escape maneuver. The Mirage failed to clear a shallow ridgeline, instead skidding across its crest in fiery brilliance.

"We saw the fireball just spit out in front of us," Brandon said. "It slid and hit in front of us at about our right two o'clock."

Graeter, who was still unaware of the Raven's presence, watched in puzzlement as the Iraqi plane disintegrated. "I could see the burning jet tumbling and cartwheeling across the desert floor," he said. "There was an overcast, so the light from the explosions bounced off the cloud deck—it was pretty surreal."[3]

His arrival had startled the Iraqi pilot, causing the crash, so Graeter was credited with a maneuvering kill.

CHAPTER 9

Bogeys and Bandits

JUST MINUTES AFTER CROSSING INTO IRAQ, CAPT. JON KELK, AN F-15C pilot, picked up an unknown radar contact about thirty-five miles away. At nearly the same instant, he heard a tone indicating the other plane's radar had picked him up. They were like two distant figures walking toward each other on a lonely road. The first step was figuring out the other guy's identity.

Identification was an age-old problem. From radar's very beginning, users struggled to label the featureless blips on their scopes: Was the contact friendly or hostile? British scientists addressed the problem early in World War II with the first IFF (Identify Friend or Foe) system. Allied airplanes began carrying transponders that could reply to an electronic query. Any aircraft failing to respond to the IFF query could be considered suspect. It was like asking someone for a password, and not getting it.

Fifty years later, identification systems were more advanced but still imperfect. The IFF interrogator on Kelk's F-15C challenged the bogey. The other plane failed to squawk the correct code, making it appear hostile—a bandit. But Kelk wanted to be certain. With so many coalition jets swirling through the air, the risk of a "blue-on-blue" shootdown was high.

"We had a thing called a Mode 4 rollover, where all the Mode 4 IFF codes changed at 0300 hours," Kelk explained. "But what if a guy was doing other things then? What if he was trying to evade, drop bombs, forgot to change the code, or move the switch? I didn't want to shoot down a guy just because he had forgotten to flick a switch, so I wanted to get an additional confirmation from AWACS."[1]

Three E-3 Sentry airborne warning and control jets orbited high above Saudi Arabia, their massive Doppler radars painting a comprehensive picture of the developing air war. AWACS ran the show, and in most instances a pilot would get AWACS clearance before firing an air-to-air missile. But before Kelk could obtain confirmation, the opposing plane became aggressive.

"The bandit climbed from about seven thousand feet to seventeen thousand feet, and was clearly maneuvering in relation to me when I eventually took the shot," he said. "I was in an advantageous position at thirty thousand feet because I could increase the range of my weapons against the lower-flying MiG."

Kelk released bundles of chaff to confuse any inbound missiles, but it soon became apparent he was in the clear. His Sparrow missile detonated ten miles away, and, even from that distance, he knew he had a kill.

"It was nothing like the red glowing fireballs that you hear about," he said. "It was a bright purplish-white color that lasted three to five seconds. Then it was dark again."

Intelligence officers later identified Kelk's bandit as a MiG-29 Fulcrum, and they believed the deceased pilot to be Capt. Omar Goben, a highly decorated veteran of the Iran-Iraq War with three kills on his record.

Hostile Airspace
Southeast of Baghdad
0320 Local

Captain Steve Tate was leading his F-15C flight on an escort mission, taking some F-4G Wild Weasels to Baghdad for Poobah's Party. Tate marveled at the chaotic activity of this first night. The coalition had 700 planes in the air, headed in all directions with their lights off and mingling with an unknown number of Iraqi jets. Even with the watchful eyes of AWACS, there was bound to be some confusion. Tate focused on keeping his situational awareness. Upon reaching the city's outskirts, he set up a combat air patrol.

"I split my four-ship into two counter-rotating CAPs, oriented toward two different threat axes," Tate explained.[2] He and his wingman, Capt. Bo Merlack, assumed a medium-altitude orbit, while the other pair of Eagles went high. By varying height and direction, the F-15Cs could scan more airspace with their advanced radars. As they patrolled, the Eagle pilots witnessed the opening raids on Baghdad.

"There was AAA everywhere," Tate said. "SAMs were being shot and friendly airplanes filled the dark skies. Bombs were dropping everywhere, and the Wild Weasels were shooting their HARMs at all the SAM sites."

An AWACS operator called out a flight of bandits, but before the Eagles could move to engage, the Iraqis scurried back to base and landed. Then came a bogey call, meaning AWACS could not confirm the contact's identity. Tate and Merlack sped off to the southeast, only to discover that they had intercepted an F-111 Aardvark.

By now, both Eagles were carrying empty drop tanks, which they jettisoned to reduce drag. On their way back to the patrol area, they received notice of yet another bogey, this one heading west at 8,000 feet.

"I was talking to AWACS about who this guy was, and what he was, but they did not have a good idea," Tate said.[3] The plane, which was not squawking friendly codes, appeared to be on an intercept course with the other pair of Eagles in his flight. All the evidence pointed to a bandit, and the rules of engagement said he was clear to fire. Tate decided to take the shot.

As his thumb hovered over the weapon-release button, he kept his eyes fixed inside the cockpit. A natural temptation was to watch the missile come off the rail, but at night it could cause temporary flash blindness, so he forced himself to stare at the radar screen. The bandit was twelve miles away, seemingly unaware of him. Tate punched the button.

"Fox One," he called, indicating the launch of an AIM-7 Sparrow radar-guided missile.

The Sparrow roared to life, spitting an orange flame so bright it startled his wingman. Bo Merlack was some distance away and had heard the Fox One call, but he thought for an instant an Iraqi missile had been fired at him.[4] But before Merlack could flinch, the Sparrow was gone, closing on the bandit at four times the speed of sound.

The launch betrayed Tate's position in the sky so he turned to a new heading, carefully holding the radar lock that guided the Sparrow. By now, the Iraqi pilot likely knew he was in trouble but had only milliseconds to react. During the Vietnam War, early Sparrows performed so miserably that pilots often fired their full complement of four at once, hoping at least one missile would reach its target. The modern Sparrow needed no backup. Its solid-state electronic brain kept a dogged pursuit.

"The missile hit the Mirage at four nautical miles off my nose. We saw the huge fireball," Tate said.

The burst expelled white-hot fragments like an exploding pyrotechnics shell, and then flaming chunks of wreckage began drifting to the desert floor. He and Merlack lingered in the area, waiting to see if the activity might attract more Iraqi planes. Beneath them a jagged wedge of fuselage continued to burn. Five minutes later, with their radars still clean and fuel gauges getting low, the Eagles headed south to pick up a tanker before landing at Dhahran.

* * *

Vietnam convinced the air force that dominance of the skies required a dedicated dogfighter, not some multirole fighter-bomber, so the F-15C Eagle was built strictly for air superiority. The navy went in the opposite direction after Vietnam, instead looking for a versatile aircraft that could fill air-to-air and ground-attack roles.

Manufacturer Northrop offered its YF-17 prototype, which the air force had just rejected in favor of the General Dynamics YF-16. The twin-engine YF-17 would need a redesign for sea duty, so Northrop partnered with McDonnell Douglas, an experienced player in naval aviation. Together they strengthened the plane's undercarriage, widened its landing gear, and gave it folding wings to save deck space. The companies initially planned two variants—an F-18 fighter and an A-18 striker—but eventually merged all necessary elements into a single aircraft. The navy was delighted and the F/A-18 Hornet entered service in 1984.

The manufacturers touted their sleek new jet as an electronic wonder. With its cockpit full of multifunction displays, a Hornet could switch between dogfight and ground-attack modes in a heartbeat, they said.

Supposedly, the plane was so powerful and nimble it could tangle with enemy fighters while toting a full bombload. Desert Storm would, at last, put those claims to the test.

On the frenetic flight deck of USS *Saratoga*, half a dozen F/A-18C Hornets crept to the catapults. These planes of VFA-81 Squadron, known as the Sunliners, would form the trailing edge of a large strike package, which included aircraft from USS *John F. Kennedy*, also in the Red Sea. Each Hornet carried a heavy load: four 2,000-pound bombs, a centerline drop tank for the long flight across Saudi Arabia, and a complement of air-to-air missiles.

Their mission did not start well. The Sunliners had barely formed up after launching from *Saratoga* when they began to encounter technical glitches. One plane turned back with radio problems, while another pilot aborted after discovering he could not draw fuel from his drop tank. It seemed a bad omen, given the Hornet's record-setting reliability. The four remaining Sunliners pressed across the Arabian Peninsula. High above, an E-2C Hawkeye—a smaller, carrier-launched sibling of AWACS—monitored their progress.

Their target was a stoutly defended air base known as H-3. The base took its name from an old oil-pipeline pumping station, which originally had a rough airstrip for bringing in maintenance workers. Following the Arab-Israeli war of 1973, Iraq decided to expand some of the landing strips into military airfields. Since then, H-2 and H-3 had grown into sprawling bases with numerous runways, each surrounded by clusters of hardened aircraft shelters and countless air defense batteries.

As leading elements of the strike package approached H-3, Hawkeye and AWACS operators began calling out bandits. The Iraqis were beginning to realize just how heavily they were outmatched but refused to yield the skies. A pair of MiG-29s moved to intercept the attackers, apparently unaware that a flight of Eagles was flying cover. The F-15Cs swooped in, adding two more kills to their growing tally.

At thirty miles out, the Sunliners were setting up for their bombing runs when the E-2C made another bandit call. Two contacts, which turned out to be MiG-21 Fishbeds, were coming head-on at supersonic speeds.

"It all happened very quickly," said Lt. Cdr. Mark Fox. "I switched back to air-to-air and got a lock on one of them. I had the MiG on the right while the second Hornet in our formation—Lieutenant [Nick] Mongillo—took the MiG on the left. The other two Hornets had also acquired radar locks."[5]

In an earlier era of jet combat, the MiG-21 was a holy terror. During the month of December 1966, a North Vietnamese Fishbed squadron shot down fourteen F-105 Thunderchiefs without a single loss. The agile, straight-lined plane also gave fits to F-4 pilots, downing more than three dozen Phantoms during the war. It remained in production as late as 1985, with the final versions including enough upgrades to make them serviceable fighters.

A favorite North Vietnamese tactic was to rush head-on at a strike package—inducing the American pilots to jettison their bombs—and then dash away to safety before a dogfight could develop. Now, a quarter of a century later, the Iraqis appeared to be stealing a page from the Communist playbook. However, since then American missile and radar-acquisition technology had improved considerably.

"I shot a Sidewinder first," said Fox. "It was a smokeless missile, and I thought at first that I had wasted it because I couldn't see it tracking toward the MiG. I fired a Sparrow. The Sidewinder hit, though, followed by the Sparrow. The first missile actually did the job, and the Sparrow flew into the fireball."

His wingman, Nick Mongillo, opted right away for a Sparrow, releasing it in concert with Fox's first shot. The trailing MiG was traveling at Mach 1.2 near his leader's left wing when the missile arrived. It vanished in a sudden, fiery burst. The entire engagement lasted forty seconds. Fox and Mongillo had reacted so quickly that the onrushing Fishbeds never maneuvered, and they exploded in formation.

There was no time to reflect on the sudden violence. The Hornets formed up and executed their bombing raid on H-3 just as planned. During their egress, the navy aviators stole a distant glimpse of the MiG crash sites—two columns of oily smoke. The engagement made a strong case for multirole fighters, although Lieutenant Commander Fox conceded it was less than definitive.

"If the MiGs had got behind us, we would have had no choice but to honor their threat," he said. "You can't do that with eight-thousand pounds of bombs. We would have had to jettison our ordnance to face them, and that would have served their purpose in stopping our strike. They failed; we succeeded."[6]

CHAPTER 10

Luck Runs Out

THE AIR CAMPAIGN WAS OFF TO AN INCREDIBLE START. STEALTH AND cruise missile technology proved effective in combat. Clever tactics such as the Apache radar-station raid and Poobah's Party dealt early blows to the Iraqi air defense system. And advanced aircraft such as the F-15C Eagle and F/A-18 Hornet were fulfilling the roles for which they had been designed. In Riyadh and Washington, moods swung like a pendulum between joy and foreboding. Everyone knew the coalition's remarkably good fortune couldn't last forever. Statistically, something had to go wrong soon.

The first bit of bad news came from USS *Saratoga*: An F/A-18 was missing. The vanished Hornet had been a participant in Poobah's Party, armed with HARM missiles to destroy Iraqi radars. Its pilot, Lt. Cdr. Michael Scott Speicher, was widely regarded as one of the finest in VFA-81—the Sunliners—the same squadron that had just enjoyed so much success during the H-3 raid. As those four jets landed on *Saratoga*, their commanding officer was below decks in the squadron ready room, cobbling together details of the disappearance. Every passing hour made it less likely that the missing jet had diverted to a backup airfield.

Commander Mike Anderson, the Sunliner skipper, thought back to the previous day when Speicher came to him, pleading for a bigger role in the mission. "Spike" was scheduled as an airborne spare, meaning he'd go to Baghdad only if another plane was forced to turn around. If all the strikers were fully operational, then Speicher would be the one turning around. The idea gnawed at him, and he begged to be made a scheduled shooter. Anderson, who was leading the strike, granted his wish. The younger pilot left wearing a broad grin.

Scott Speicher was the son of a World War II fighter pilot, and he had been in airplanes since the age of five. Now thirty-three, he was the navy's ideal specimen, a real-life version of the fighter jocks from *Top Gun*, only better than those Hollywood caricatures. Speicher was the father of two small children, a humble man who taught Sunday school to kindergartners. He had captained the swim team at Florida State University, where he met his wife, and graduated with dual business degrees before joining the navy. He spent three years as a Hornet flight instructor before joining VFA-81 last year. The Sunliners immediately warmed to his sharp wit and quick smile, and his steady hands in the cockpit.[1]

After a final briefing in the ready room, Spike and his roommate, Lt. Cdr. Tony Albano, crawled into their bunks for some rack time before the overnight mission. Neither could sleep. By 0100, they were in their flight gear, ascending *Saratoga*'s decks toward their jets. Scores of crewmen scurried about the noisy flight deck, preparing forty aircraft for launch. Speicher and Albano stood in a cramped cabin with a few other Sunliners, holding their helmets and cracking stupid jokes to cover their nerves. Each man awaited the signal to step out into the flight deck's maelstrom when his jet was ready.

"See you back on deck in a couple of hours," Albano told his roommate.[2]

The carrier began flinging planes into the air, and in twenty minutes they were all aloft and forming up to meet the refueling tankers in Saudi airspace. The tankers were busy, so each pilot felt added pressure to get his gas quickly and clear out for the next guy. At the Iraqi border they spotted some scattered AAA fire. The Hornets were cruising at assigned altitudes between 25,000 and 30,000 feet, with lights out, their formation loosening as they pushed toward Baghdad. Every plane had a different target area to cover, so they needed to fan out.

Two hours into the mission, a glowing orb appeared on the horizon. It throbbed in the darkness with mesmerizing intensity, and at first some aviators mistook it for an optical illusion, or a natural phenomenon like the northern lights. Then it dawned on them that they were looking at the antiaircraft barrage over Baghdad, still fifty miles away. Their radar warning receivers began chirping. Iraqi radar operators were falling for the spoof, furiously tracking Poobah's decoys. Each Hornet carried three HARMs, and they would soon be within firing range.

Commander Anderson, the strike leader, was sweeping for airborne threats when he spotted a contact climbing up from a nearby airfield. Logic said it was an Iraqi fighter, and as the plane zoomed skyward Anderson knew for sure. The pilot—in his zeal to engage the attackers—was using his afterburner, which scorched the night sky like a giant blowtorch. No coalition aviator would give away his position so carelessly.

"I could see the afterburner flame, and it was an extremely long, yellow [flame], which I had seen before on a MiG-25," Anderson said. "No question what you have in front of you when you see that."[3]

Despite his certainty, he could not shoot. The rules of engagement called for AWACS confirmation. He keyed his radio.

"I've got a fast-mover, on my nose, he's hot. Confirm bandit?"

"Negative," the AWACS operator replied. "Negative bandit. Confirm bogey."

Anderson analyzed his sudden dilemma. He knew he had an Iraqi fighter, but until the controller concurred, he could not fire. The MiG-25 Foxbat was a lightning-fast Mach 3 interceptor, armed with the oversized AA-6 missile. He couldn't let the Iraqi roam unguarded while his Hornets went about their work of engaging ground targets.

The jet streaked toward him, trailing its long, amber tail. Anderson locked it up with his radar, and immediately the plane broke into a defensive turn.

"Confirm bandit," he demanded of AWACS.

"Negative bandit. Declare bogey."

Now the Iraqi jet was arcing counterclockwise, trying to get behind Anderson. They fell into tight circles, spiraling around each other, each pilot seeking the advantage.

"Confirm bandit!" Anderson yelled.

"Negative. Bogey," the operator came back. "Negative. Bogey."

The pulsing AWACS radar wasn't picking up the Iraqi jet, possibly because of an electronic blind spot called Doppler notch. The controller had no choice but to deny Anderson's request for confirmation. It was bizarre. Both men were doing their jobs properly, yet not reaching the desired outcome. The coalition's strict rules of engagement, designed to prevent friendly shootdowns, were working against them because of a technical glitch.

The Iraqi pilot, meanwhile, realized his mistake and came out of afterburner. The blowtorch vanished into darkness. Then he disengaged and sped off to the west, quickly sliding from Anderson's scope. Pilots who overheard the radio conversation searched frantically with their radars but found nothing. The MiG seemed to have bugged out, so they proceeded with the task of launching their HARMs.

Hornets from a sister squadron, VFA-83, lagged farther back in the loose formation, coming in behind the Sunliners. Lieutenant Commander Dave Renaud heard Anderson's transmissions about the bandit. Renaud checked his radar but saw no sign of the MiG. The action was getting heavy, with HARM launches, AAA bursts, and urgent warnings of SAMs in the air. A brilliant flash caught Renaud's attention.

"I see a big explosion off to my right," he said out loud, so it would be recorded on the plane's mission tape. Later, intelligence officers could determine his location, and get a general fix on the explosion if they wished. Renaud was five to ten miles away from the blast, but he could still see a mass of glittering debris plunge downward. He suspected an F-15C had just bagged the MiG-25 or perhaps another Iraqi plane. By noting the explosion, Renaud was giving confirmation of the kill. He figured he was doing a favor for some hotshot Eagle driver.

When the Hornets expended their HARMs, they turned back toward Saudi airspace and the tankers. No fighter was easy on jet fuel but the F/A-18 guzzled it, so their tanks were getting dry. Near the border, Anderson took a Sunliner roll call. Everyone but Speicher answered. It was strange but not terribly alarming. They figured Spike probably ran too low on fuel and diverted to a Saudi air base.

Then they realized that nobody heard his voice once during the entire raid. This too was unusual, but not conclusive. Pilots were told to stay off the air as much as possible to minimize the chatter. Perhaps he simply had nothing to report. Or maybe a radio problem had forced him to abort the mission entirely, and he was waiting for them back aboard *Saratoga*. At least that's what they hoped.

A couple of hours later, Dave Renaud walked into the ship's intelligence center for his mission debrief. He described every detail in his memory, including the big burst that looked like an exploding aircraft. The intel officer asked a few questions about it, and then paused.

"You know, Speicher did not come back," the officer said. He sent Renaud below decks to speak with the Sunliner skipper.

Anderson pulled the videotape from Renaud's plane and cued up the moment when he witnessed the explosion off to his right. They watched it again and again. The video, which only showed a forward view of the night sky, was still useful because it contained instrument readings from the Hornet's heads-up display. They used the flight data to calculate Renaud's position in central Iraq, and from that they estimated the blast's location. Renaud drew a circle on his mission map. Beside it he wrote a single word in bold letters: SPIKE.

A circle on a map wasn't nearly enough to launch a rescue mission. Before sending helicopters and support planes deep into enemy territory, the special operations commander in charge of combat search and rescue (CSAR) would want details. He'd want a more precise location, and evidence that the explosion was actually the missing Hornet. Most of all, he'd want some indication that Speicher was still alive. As hard as it was for Renaud to admit, the blast did not seem "survivable." None of the pilots wanted to risk lives if Spike was already dead, but they couldn't help thinking he ejected. He might be out there, wandering the desert, injured and searching for water.

Twelve hours later, Secretary of Defense Dick Cheney stepped to a Washington podium. "There's been a single American aircraft lost. It involves a single casualty." He stopped and looked to Colin Powell. "I don't know that we want to identify the aircraft, do we?"

Powell didn't see a problem. "It was an F-18," he said.

Reporters asked Cheney to define "casualty." Did he mean an injury or a death?

"A death," he said.

Cheney's announcement echoed through *Saratoga* like a thunderclap. Spike was dead. The pilots set aside any further thoughts of a rescue operation. Clearly the Pentagon had evidence of the fatality, or they would not have announced it. Declaring Speicher dead absolved Saddam of any responsibility for him. Red Cross workers would not be looking for him during their POW inspections, and nobody would expect to see him during the postwar prisoner exchange.

The loss of their friend meant more than sorrow for the *Saratoga* pilots. It also drove home the unpleasant truth of their own mortality. The F/A-18 offered tremendous speed, agility, and sophisticated avionics, but not invincibility. A full-scale air war was underway, one that seemed likely to last for weeks and possibly months. Each man would return to Iraq again and again, and even if he performed his job flawlessly, the golden BB might be waiting. Combat aviators are trained to avoid dwelling on factors beyond their control, since it is a counterproductive use of time and energy. For Speicher's colleagues, maintaining that mental discipline just became a little bit harder. "Spike, he's better than me and he got it," one pilot kept thinking. "That means I can get it."[4]

The Pentagon had no hard evidence of Speicher's death, just supposition. A key factor was the handful of eyewitness accounts by Renaud and other pilots in the area. None saw a parachute, or deemed the explosion survivable, but of course such observations fell far short of proof, especially at night.

After the war, the Pentagon stated that Speicher was lost to a SAM, but the *Saratoga* pilots were skeptical. The explosion occurred over a remote area, about a hundred miles west of Baghdad, well beyond the city's SAM umbrella. If the Defense Department analysts had that wrong, maybe their assessment of Spike's fate was also in error. The Speicher family complained about the military's apparent disinterest in finding the crash site. Journalists began digging into the story. Before long, Pentagon staffers were fielding congressional inquiries about a mounting MIA controversy.

In December 1993, a senior military officer from Qatar was hunting in western Iraq when he came across the wreckage of an American jet. He took photos of the crash site and forwarded them to the U.S. Embassy. His pictures showed a crumpled F/A-18 with *Saratoga* markings. The canopy lay some distance from the crash site, suggesting Speicher ejected.

Two years lapsed as the Saddam Hussein regime hemmed about access. When navy investigators finally arrived, they found a plane robbed of its avionics, and no human bones in the area.

The investigators were able to determine some facts. Speicher's plane had been at 28,000 feet, traveling at 620 miles per hour, when it suffered massive damage from an air-to-air missile, possibly an AA-6 missile fired by a MiG-25. Speicher initiated the ejection sequence. His canopy flew away and the ejection seat left the aircraft. At that point, the trail of facts went cold. They could not locate the ejection seat on the ground.

Local Iraqis came forward with a flight suit said to be discovered in the area. The flight suit, which appeared to have been cut off the wearer, was the same type and size as Speicher's suit, with Velcro in the correct places for affixing his patches. (Aviators remove insignia and personal items before a combat sortie.) The suit showed evidence of brief exposure to intense heat, such as from a cockpit fire, but lacked any weathering, suggesting it spent little time in the open desert. In 2001 the CIA concluded that "Speicher was either captured alive or his remains were recovered and brought to Baghdad."[5] Saddam's regime continued to deny any knowledge of him.

More years passed and eventually American forces were back in Iraq. Troops occupying Anbar Province routinely asked local residents about the pilot who went down in the area so long ago, and in 2009 they received a credible tip. A man recalled that in 1991 some Bedouins buried a body they found in the vicinity of the crash site. He led a group of marines to the grave, which yielded skeletal remains, including a jawbone. Dental records confirmed that, at last, Michael Scott Speicher had been found. Whether he died during the ejection, or succumbed later from injuries or the elements, was never established.

CHAPTER 11

Low Level

A DOZEN BRITISH TORNADOS TOPPED OFF THEIR TANKS AND DESCENDED to just 200 feet before crossing into Iraqi airspace. Desert Storm, or Operation Granby as the British called it, was just a few hours old. The jets carried large drop tanks, which was not uncommon in the far-flung Gulf theater. But between the plump wing tanks was a weapon unique to the Tornado. A pair of long cylinders, roughly the size and shape of cruise missiles, clung to each airplane's belly. The Tornados were headed for Tallil Air Base in southeast Iraq.

The coalition planned to neutralize Iraq's air force by grounding it. As the Speicher shootdown illustrated, roving enemy fighters were unpredictable. A capable Iraqi pilot posed a greater threat than the fiercest ground defenses, but only if he could get into the air. The Royal Air Force specialized in denying an enemy the use of his runways. For decades, they practiced low-level dashes into enemy territory—then presumed to be Eastern Europe—to sprinkle runway-cratering bomblets and then thunder away.

As the Tornados closed on target, they aligned their flight paths to Tallil's 10,000-foot parallel runways. The aircrews knew they would have a single shot, for the JP233 Low-Altitude Airfield Attack System required one steady pass down the length of the runway. A pilot needed to ignore all distractions, including Tallil's thick air defenses, keeping his wings straight and level as the JP233 dispensed its destructive cargo. With the concrete runways now unfolding before them, the pilots nudged their aircraft down to 180 feet. Torrents of neon tracers told them the Iraqis were alerted.

"You're flying as low as you dare, but high enough to get the weapons off," explained Flt. Lt. Jerry Gegg, a navigator in the back seat of one of the Tornados. "It's absolutely terrifying. There's no other word for it."[1]

As Gegg and his pilot streaked down the runway, the two JP233 dispensers beneath them spat out a total of sixty bomblets. Each of these submunitions held a one-two punch. On impact, a shaped charge produced a molten stream of metal, which cut through the concrete and carved out an underground chamber. The bomblet's second charge followed its mate into the hole and then detonated, creating a deep, high-rimmed crater.

The damage from each blast would require extensive repairs, but the JP233 was not finished yet. The dispensers also tossed out hundreds of anti-personnel mines to deter workers. Once the five-pound mines stopped rolling, they extended tiny spring-loaded legs and stood upright. They sat there, spread across the runways like an army of metallic spiders.

The Tornados finished their runs and disappeared from Tallil as quickly as they came. On the way home they climbed to tanker altitude and refueled once more. The mission was a success but the flak had been worse than imagined. They felt lucky to have escaped without injury.

Muharraq Airfield
Bahrain International Airport
January 17, 1991
0700 Local

Dawn broke, removing the safety of night, but the airstrikes continued without pause. Coalition planners wanted to keep Iraq under pressure around the clock. They had no shortage of available airpower—warplanes were shoehorned into facilities all across the Gulf, making for some odd routines. In the winter sky over Bahrain's northern tip, fighter jets and civilian airliners mingled as if it were normal. The haggard men who returned after lengthy missions trudged not to barracks or tents, but airport hotel rooms.

Pilot John Peters and navigator Adrian John Nichol, both flight lieutenants, had been in Bahrain since early December, sharing a room at the Sheraton. At age twenty-nine, Peters was already a ten-year RAF veteran. Nichol was a year younger. He had served for a few years as an electronics technician before earning his commission as a navigator. Now they were lifting off on their first combat sortie, soaring across the cobalt Gulf water. They were the second Tornado in a four-ship flight, tasked with a low-level daylight raid on an air base near Basra, not far from Kuwait.

The four Tornados climbed to the tanker tracks in Saudi airspace, where they topped off, and then plunged low before crossing the border. They accelerated to 600 miles per hour, and after twenty minutes they reached the initial point for beginning their attack. They carried thousand-pound bombs, destined for targets inside Ar Rumaylah Air Base.

The Tornado was designed as a multirole aircraft, with variants built for dogfighting, ground attack, and reconnaissance. Low-level bombing was its true forte. In many respects the Tornado owed its existence to a similar plane, the F-111 Aardvark, and in fact the RAF nearly purchased the F-111 from General Dynamics in the 1960s. Instead, the British teamed up with Italy and West Germany to build their own plane, forming a consortium called Panavia.

Panavia's engineers adopted many F-111 innovations, including its variable-sweep wings, which they placed on a smaller airframe. Production began in 1976, and within five years the Tornado was flying for all three air forces. Panavia found one other buyer, Saudi Arabia, which rarely turned down the opportunity to acquire a new fighter. Desert Storm was the Tornado's combat debut.

As the four jets approached Ar Rumaylah, dozens of gun batteries opened up. In daylight, the gunners had better opportunity to score a hit, and within seconds the air filled with high-explosive AAA rounds. Some of Iraq's Soviet-built guns fired up to 4,000 rounds per minute.

"No aircraft has any real defense against visually aimed antiaircraft fire," said Nichol, "apart from trying to dodge it or put your head down in the cockpit and try and make yourself as small as possible."[2] Shrapnel peppered their aircraft. "At the time we didn't know we were being hit because we were concentrating on the task of trying to get the weapons on the target," he explained.

The metal storm was too fierce, buffeting the plane and making an accurate drop impossible. Their thoughts turned to escape.

"After our attack failed we were running back home when suddenly we were hit by a heat-seeking missile—a SAM 7 or a SAM 14," Nichol said. "It knocked the aircraft sideways and almost out of the sky—we were within a few feet of hitting the ground. I can still visualize the missile hitting home and the aircraft tumbling around the sky with absolute clarity."

Shoulder-fired missiles like the SA-7 Grail and SA-14 Gremlin were too limited to threaten high-flying aircraft, but down low they could inflict serious damage. Peters regained limited control of the plane and tried to keep a heading for Saudi Arabia. The stick felt sluggish. Nichol looked over his shoulder and felt panic. Flames were licking the aft fuselage.

"We were desperately trying to go through the drills that might get us back into a controlled situation and give us enough systems and power to get back to the Saudi border," he said. "But it wasn't to be—the aircraft was on fire and the flames were marching steadily to where I was sitting in the rear cockpit."

He told Peters it was time to go and then reached for the yellow-and-black ejection handle. The canopy disappeared and their seats rocketed upward at 200 miles per hour.

"You've gone from a burning aircraft to silence and floating down in a parachute and finding yourself sitting deep behind enemy lines," he said. "I think we were on the ground for about three hours. We were trying to make our way to one of the search-and-rescue points, where perhaps some Special Forces would be waiting, or a helicopter could come in and rescue us. But this was the first day of the war and it was unlikely that was going to happen immediately."

An Iraqi patrol found them and carted them off to Baghdad. Saddam had his first prisoners of war.

Anbar Province
Western Iraq
January 17, 1991
2200 Local

More *Saratoga* planes were headed for H-3, where hours earlier a pair of Hornets had splashed two MiGs before carrying out their bomb runs. The H-2 and H-3 air bases were high-priority targets. They supported not only fighter jets but also Scud missile launchers, and the Bush administration feared Saddam would keep his threat to launch Scuds at Israel.

H-2 and H-3 occupied vast expanses of desert. They boasted secondary airfields, fuel dumps, hardened aircraft shelters, and thick rings of air defenses. In the coming weeks, nearly every type of coalition striker would visit these complexes, from high-tech F-117 stealth planes to the U.S. Navy's venerable A-6 Intruder, a Vietnam-era attack jet that was inching toward retirement. A flight of four low-flying Intruders now closed on H-3.

The Intruder crews had overcome a major hurdle just to get this far—a winter storm arrived that afternoon and was now sweeping through the Gulf, making a mess of air operations. The all-weather A-6 still flew. Southeast Asia's fiercest monsoons didn't ground it, and neither would a winter storm. The hurdle came when it was time to refuel. Aerial refueling was a delicate matter under ideal conditions, and in poor weather it bordered on impossible. Already tonight, an Intruder flight from USS *Kennedy* aborted its H-2 raid after a failed attempt with the tankers.

The *Saratoga* Intruders fared better, but it wasn't easy. Each pilot fought the turbulence, holding steady behind the big tanker while matching its speed and heading. A long hose snaked toward him in the darkness. At the end of the hose fluttered a cone-shaped basket, his target for a refueling probe extending from the rounded A-6 nose. A good connection was rewarded with a gush of jet fuel. Failure left the basket thumping against the canopy or possibly snapping off the probe. U.S. Air Force planes used a slightly different method. Instead of a probe they had a fuel receptacle, into which tanker operators would insert a boom. This method carried its own risks in bad weather.

With the unpleasant business of refueling finally over, the Intruders dropped to 500 feet. H-3 was a short distance past the border. To each pilot's right sat a bombardier/navigator, hunched forward as he studied his radar through a blackout boot. At fifteen miles out, the ground fire began to simmer. No one doubted the target area would be at full boil. They had the option of climbing above it, but that meant exposure to deadly missiles like the Soviet SA-6 and French-built Roland.

The abortive *Kennedy* Intruders had planned to bomb H-2 from medium altitude, around fifteen thousand feet. Their strike leader deemed the AAA batteries too thick for a low-level attack, and he planned instead to take his chances outwitting the SAMs. The dilemma went all the way back to sorties over North Vietnam, when pilots began searching for the ideal altitude, a sweet spot that minimized the risk from both guns and missiles. They never found it, and through bitter experience, most airmen came to accept SAMs as the lesser evil. Of course, missile technology was much improved since Vietnam.

Chuck Horner and Buster Glosson, during their prewar pep talks to air force squadrons, counseled a medium-altitude approach. They noted that 70 percent of the aircraft shot down over North Vietnam were AAA victims. Still, medium altitude was not a mandate, more like fatherly advice. Horner and Glosson believed that mission planning belonged with the men who risked their lives.

The *Saratoga* strike leader, Cdr. Mike Menth, viewed H-3's missile rings as the deadlier threat. He wanted to sneak in low and avoid them. Menth knew AAA would be a concern, but the air base was huge, giving the gun batteries an awful lot of black sky to cover. An intense barrage couldn't last long, he reasoned. The Iraqis would either run out of ammunition or melt their barrels. He split his four-ship flight in half, with the two pairs attacking along different vectors. Behind Menth, in a trailing A-6, were Lt. Bob Wetzel and Lt. Jeffrey Zaun.

The Iraqis were ready for them. Roving searchlights and wafting flares turned night into dusk, while ropes of antiaircraft fire twisted and crisscrossed over the target area. As Menth weaved through the thick streams of hot metal, his bombardier/navigator released a half-dozen Mark-83 unguided bombs. As soon as the last bomb came off, Menth cut sharply for the dark desert.

Wetzel and Zaun approached the target along the same axis, less than thirty seconds behind their leader. They watched in disbelief as a low-flying missile—probably intended for Menth—streaked past their nose. Then they spotted another missile, at the two o'clock position, tracking directly for them. Wetzel began a defensive turn, and the chaff dispenser spat out two bundles, but the missile was on them too quickly.

A blinding white glow lit the cockpit, and the plane bucked and reeled. An engine-fire warning light came on, and they heard the right engine scream as it disintegrated. Ejection was the only option. Zaun escaped injury, but the force knocked Wetzel unconscious. He awoke on the ground with both arms broken. Zaun gingerly tried to free him from his parachute harness.

Meanwhile, the second pair of Intruders were having similar trouble. The lead plane successfully dodged heavy fire, but a missile showered the trailing jet with shrapnel. Despite heavy damage the jet remained flyable, and after jettisoning their ordnance the crew coaxed it to a safe landing in Saudi Arabia.

In the desert near H-3, Wetzel and Zaun took stock of their situation. They could see aircraft hangars about a mile away. The Iraqis would soon come looking for them, but Wetzel's injuries made it difficult to move. A trek to Saudi Arabia, some forty miles distant, was out of the question. Soon headlights appeared. They managed to hide behind a hillock, but it only delayed their inevitable capture.

Back on *Saratoga*, Menth reflected on the disastrous mission. He'd thought his low-level plan was sound, but it cost him one plane and nearly a second. "We just can't do this anymore at low level. It's going to eat us alive," he told the others. "The gun barrels did not melt."[3]

CHAPTER 12

Basra Raid

ON THE WAR'S SECOND NIGHT, HALF A DOZEN F-15E STRIKE EAGLES—designated T-Bird flight—sped along the Iraq-Kuwait border at an altitude of 500 feet. They traveled in trail, each jet separated from the next by a distance of four miles. Their target, the Basra Oil Refinery, sat near a broad marshy plain, a fact that pleased the Strike Eagle crews because the Iraqis could place few defenses there. They planned to use the swampy wetland as the initial point (IP) for setting up their attack.

They were still some distance from the IP when a stream of red tracers sliced through the darkness. An Iraqi gunner had spotted them, likely with the aid of an infrared device, and was honing his fire on T-Bird Three.

"It was close," said the pilot, Capt. Merrick Krause. "It was maybe forty feet—less than a wingspan from us, leading us and getting closer. I rolled left and continued with a barrel roll right over the gun. It was a tight barrel roll, but sluggish in this pig of an airplane."[1] The F-15E was weighed down with two external fuel tanks, a dozen 500-pound bombs, navigation and targeting pods, and four Sidewinder missiles. "The gunner lost us, and after, we rolled upright," Krause said. "I was pretty tense and had to force myself not to hyperventilate, and to concentrate on keeping in formation."

The Strike Eagles would be lofting their bombs into the refinery. Loft bombing, or toss bombing, was like the underarm throw of a ball. A pilot pulled up sharply and released his bombs in climb, leaving the bombs to arc forward to the target. Lofting permitted pilots to avoid flying over a dangerous target, ideal for an oil refinery filled with exploding storage tanks and angry gunners. But the technique was not without peril, especially at night.

"You start at low altitude and pull the nose up to your loft angle for bomb release," explained one pilot. "After release, you over-bank and pull away from the target while starting your descent back to low altitude. At night, this is entirely an instrument procedure as you have no ground references to look at."[2]

The F-15E used a system called LANTIRN (Low-Altitude Navigation and Targeting Infrared for Night), which featured a terrain-following radar and a forward-looking infrared display. Although advanced for its time, LANTIRN did not yet interface with the plane's autopilot. A pilot needed to keep his eyes in the cockpit throughout the loft and recovery maneuver, watching his instruments and potentially missing outside threats.

As the Strike Eagles reached their IP, they observed an orange glow that illuminated the sky for miles. A navy strike package had already hit the refinery, and enormous flames from burning oil tanks were reflecting off the low overcast. Already the F-15Es were visible from the ground. Their flight lead came on the radio and instructed everyone to loft from maximum range, which in this case was about four miles.

Another surprise awaited them—an entire Republican Guard division was camped between the marsh and the refinery. Republican Guard units were the core of Saddam's power, and he lavished them with the finest equipment. This particular division happened to be straddling the T-bird ingress route, and it was on full alert after the navy's attack. Potent antiaircraft guns such as the four-barreled ZSU-23-4, which pilots called the Zeus, stood ready.

"As we turn from the IP, all hell breaks loose—AAA coming up from everywhere," said Capt. Ned Rudd, piloting T-Bird Two. "I was initially flying in at five hundred feet, but I stepped down to three hundred feet, then two hundred feet, then one hundred feet. I was down there. And at this time I've got like sixty hours [of experience] in the airplane, and I'm at one hundred feet with bullets coming from both sides over the top of me."[3]

"It was like nothing I could ever have imagined," said Capt. Chris Hill, who was in T-Bird Four. "Picture a football field with firemen along the sidelines. Each one has a high-pressure hose and out of those hoses comes red and orange Kool Aid. That's just what the tracers looked like. They only put tracers every seventh bullet, so for every one thousand tracers there are six times as many bullets."

The flight lead, T-Bird One, proceeded into this gauntlet, swerving smoothly around the deadly geysers. In the back seat, his weapon systems officer found the target and designated it. A diamond-shaped indicator, called the "carrot," appeared on the pilot's heads-up display. He steered toward it. The targeting system cued him to pull up at the correct distance for loft. He began his climb and pressed the pickle button, authorizing a bomb release. The computer calculated the exact instant for release. The bombs came away, and T-Bird One began his recovery.

Next it was T-Bird Two's turn. There were so many tracers that Ned Rudd felt like he was flying through a glowing tunnel. "I'm like shooting a curl in surfing," he said. "There is nowhere to go but straight ahead, and I don't want to go straight ahead." The young and inexperienced Rudd had been paired with a veteran weapon systems officer, Lt. Col. Keith Trumbull. The man they called T-Bull was considered one of the best backseaters in the air force. As Rudd twisted and turned the airplane, Trumbull calmly scanned his targeting map for their storage tank. He found the tank and designated it, placing a carrot on Rudd's display. The nervous pilot didn't notice.

"Take your steering," Trumbull said.

"What?"

"Take your steering," he repeated gently.

Rudd found the carrot and turned toward it. The loft distance began counting down. "We get in to about six miles, and I know I have to go straight now," Rudd said. "It would be silly to go through all this and miss the target because I jinked. I start easing the altitude down and I'm bending the throttles forward without going into afterburner, flying my steering and watching the countdown."

The cue to pull up finally appeared, and Rudd began his loft. An eternity passed before the bombs left their racks. "Now I'm pulling down from my loft recovery, and I'm watching out for the ground and I kind of level off, and I'm jinking trying to avoid bullets. Then I hear T-Bull in his calm voice saying, 'You are at two thousand feet and 280 knots.' What a mouthful that is. He is saying, 'Get down and speed up. Now!' But in his ice-cold voice, he just says two thousand feet and 280 knots, which told me everything I needed to know." They cleared out of the target area, making way for T-Bird Three.

Back in North Carolina, when the Strike Eagle pilots practiced single-file attack, they learned that if a pilot needed to abort his bombing run he could always loop back to the end of the line and queue up for another attempt. For the second time tonight, Merrick Krause in T-Bird Three watched an Iraqi gunner draw a bead on him. As the tracer stream veered closer, Krause broke left. He made a 180-degree turn and then took his place behind T-Bird Six.

The Four and Five ships made their lofts without incident, but by now the entire plant was a raging inferno. "The heat of the fires at the refinery had my HUD almost completely washed out," Krause said. "I had trouble reading the symbology. But I could see a black spot ahead of me. It was Six."

Piloting T-Bird Six was Maj. Tom Koritz, M.D., a flight surgeon who also flew fighter jets. While many flight surgeons served supporting roles in an aircrew, an advanced pilot-physician like Koritz was rare. He immersed himself fully in both professions, earning a special respect within the squadron. His weapon systems officer, Lt. Col. Donnie Holland, had spent fifteen years in F-4 Phantoms before transitioning to the F-15E. Koritz pulled up into his loft and tossed his bombs and then radioed that he was leaving the area.

Krause moved in, but once again the Iraqis seemed to have his number. He swerved and began his climb two seconds too soon, enough to spoil an accurate loft. T-Bird Three was soaring upward at thirty degrees, headed into the heart of the AAA fire, with a targeting computer that stubbornly refused to release his bombs. Krause decided to forget about lofting and switched from automatic delivery to manual. He rolled the plane over, pulled the nose down slightly, and did half an aileron roll. The maneuver gave him a commanding view of the entire oil complex.

"I picked a tank that we were supposed to be hitting, put my pipper on it, pickled, and started pulling up again to stay above secondary explosions and the frag," he said. "The last I saw of the target, the flames were several hundred to a thousand feet high, there were explosions, and big fireballs were coming off the refinery."

Krause turned sharply for the egress route and noticed an isolated fire burning outside the plant. "While doing the hard left turn, I reached down and jettisoned the gas tanks. And just then I looked out to the left, and said something to the effect that somebody's bombs fell short."

His weapon systems officer heard the comment and glanced down just in time to see the flaming debris. Neither man gave it much thought. Their aerobatics over the refinery had placed them well behind the others, and they were anxious to catch up. A few minutes later the flight lead called for a radio check. T-Bird Two checked in, and Krause checked in T-Bird Three. Four and Five also checked, but then the radio went silent. They called for Six to respond, but heard only static. Tom Koritz and Donnie Holland were not answering.

Krause remembered the burning debris and felt his stomach knot. He keyed the radio. "This is T-Bird Three. We're behind the package. We are the last ones out, and the last we heard is Six calling off target."

The flight lead replied, "If you are the last guys in the flight, look on the radar to see how many people you have out in front."

The scope showed only four airplanes. T-Bird Three brought the total to five. Tom Koritz and Donnie Holland in T-Bird Six never made it out of the target area. Both were dead; the burning debris had been their airplane. Either they were shot down at low level, or they crashed into the ground during the difficult loft-recovery maneuver.

CHAPTER 13

Pain and Suffering

IRAQ'S AIR FORCE ACCEPTED THE FUTILITY OF FIGHTING BACK. SADDAM chose to save his best aircraft for the next war. Meanwhile, coalition bombs continued falling on strategic targets across the country, from H-3 air base in the far west to the deep-water port of Umm Qasr in the southeast. Baghdad was enduring around-the-clock harassment, with Tomahawk strikes by day and F-117 raids at night.

Two major obstacles continued to slow the campaign. The weather, which turned foul shortly after the campaign's kickoff, showed no sign of improvement. Pilots recalled fondly the calm and cloudless skies of autumn. Winter brought to the Persian Gulf gusting winds and heavy cloud cover. During the next three weeks, nearly half of all attack sorties were altered by poor weather. Some sorties were diverted to an alternate target, but more frequently the mission was scrubbed and the planes sat idle on the tarmac. Delays to the air campaign would impact the start of the ground war, tentatively scheduled for mid-February.

The second obstacle was Iraq's air defense network, which was turning out to be more resilient than expected. The network's brain was a French-designed computer system called Kari ("Iraq" spelled backward in French). Kari was sophisticated yet simple. An illiterate soldier, sitting in one of nearly 500 observation posts and radar stations across the country, could tap a few buttons and let the system do the rest. Tracking information for the aircraft he detected automatically went to a mid-level operations center, where with the stroke of a stylus an officer alerted the appropriate squadrons and batteries. The tracking data also went to a sector operations center, which oversaw the country's air defense on a macro level.

Before the war, American intelligence agencies parsed Kari using satellite imagery and electronic emissions collected by surveillance aircraft. The French manufacturer, with some prodding, furnished critical design details. Soon a game plan emerged: Airstrikes would sever Kari's communications links, essentially dividing the monster into manageable segments. But so far the plan hadn't worked. Kari was surviving with the aid of backup landlines, extra microwave relay stations, and buried fiber-optic cables. Iraqi gunners continued to receive warning of inbound strike packages and were ready and waiting.

Coalition tactics aggravated the Kari problem. Low-level attacks were giving Iraqi gunners and missile operators too many targets. Chuck Horner and Buster Glosson urged pilots to stay above 10,000 feet, but Cold War habits died hard. Medium-level bombing, while safer, was far less accurate, particularly with the thick cloud cover now enshrouding Iraq. Some weapons, such as the British JP233 bomblet dispenser, only worked at low level. U.S. Air Force squadrons obeyed their generals and stayed at medium level, with disappointing bomb damage. Elsewhere, the low-level tactics remained in place.

On the night of January 18, the Royal Air Force suffered a fatal loss. Wing Commander Nigel Elsdon was leading a four-ship flight of Tornados on an airfield attack near Basra. Elsdon and his navigator, Flt. Lt. Max Collier, streaked along the runway with their JP233 dispensers popping and flashing in fearsome brilliance. Night raids were typically safer, except for those six seconds when the JP233 dispensers fired, making the jet a high-speed fireworks display. Elsdon and Collier finished their run and pulled away from the airfield. They felt two heavy thumps as the empty dispensers automatically jettisoned.

Nobody knows exactly what happened next. The trailing Tornado crews were occupied with their own attack runs; they lost sight of their flight lead, and they heard no radio call. The prevailing theory is that Elsdon and Collier suffered a catastrophic SAM hit and died instantly. Elsdon would be the highest-ranking coalition officer killed in the war.

Other allied nations also took losses. An A-4KU Skyhawk of the Free Kuwait Air Force went down south of Kuwait City. The pilot, Lt. Col. Muhammed Sultan Mubarak, was hit while bombing the same air base he had been forced to flee six months earlier. He ejected safely and was captured.

Italy's contribution to the air war was small, just eight Tornados stationed at Abu Dhabi. Their government had dithered about sending them at all, so the Italian aviators arrived on the eve of war, with no time to train or become acclimated to the theater. Their inexperience showed during their first mission, when the Italian Tornados rendezvoused with a U.S. Air Force KC-135 tanker. Bad weather was making aerial refueling difficult for everyone, and to the newcomers it seemed nearly impossible. All but one Tornado gave up and returned to Abu Dhabi still toting their weapons. The remaining aircrew, Maj. Gianmarco Bellini and Capt. Maurizio Cocciolone, felt honor-bound to proceed alone. They were shot down shortly after dropping their bombs and taken prisoner.

American crews flew 85 percent of all combat sorties, so they were taking the most losses. On the night of January 18, a flight of four A-6E Intruders took off from USS *Ranger* in the Persian Gulf. Their mission was to mine the waterway leading to Umm Qasr, home of Iraq's small navy. It was a tough but necessary assignment—speedy Iraqi missile boats posed a threat to capital ships like *Ranger*. The Intruders flew in trail at 500 feet with thirty seconds of separation. The weather was bleak, with low-hanging clouds that formed a solid background for Iraqi gunners defending the channel.

Spotters on a coastal island likely reported their ingress, because the AAA barrage was already well underway when the Intruders arrived. The jets weaved their way through pulsing tracer ribbons before transitioning to a low and steady flight path once they reached the waterway. In turn, they seeded the passage with Mark-36 naval mines, each plane peeling off in a different direction afterward. The low clouds flickered with the furor of 1,000 shells.

High over the Gulf, an orbiting E-2 Hawkeye waited for each Intruder to call "feet wet," meaning they had reached open water and were headed for the carrier. Since they flew below radar coverage, a radio call was necessary to report successful egress. The flight lead checked in with the Hawkeye, as did his third and fourth planes. The second Intruder in the flight, manned by Lt. William Costen and Lt. Charles Turner, never made the call or returned to *Ranger*.

During the overnight hours, rumors swirled of a radio call from a downed crewman in a salt marsh north of Bubiyan Island. At daybreak, a combat search-and-rescue helicopter pounded for the salt marsh as *Ranger* Intruders and F-14 Tomcats zoomed overhead. But heavy ground fire boiled up as soon as they neared the coastline, and the mission was aborted. After the war, the navy would recover the remains of Costen and Turner. They never ejected and almost certainly died instantly. The mysterious radio call was likely an Iraqi ploy to ambush rescue aircraft.

Southern Kuwait
January 18, 1991
0630 Local

At forty-six, Chief Warrant Officer (CWO) Guy Hunter was older than his commanding officer, Col. Cliff Acree, who now sat in front of him, piloting their OV-10A Bronco. They were Marine Corps forward air controllers, charged with meandering enemy territory in their forty-foot turboprop, finding ground targets for the fighter-bombers. The work was perilous, but Hunter always felt blessed with good luck. He served four tours in Vietnam without a scratch.

As the gray morning brightened, Acree scanned the desert with binoculars, seeking a cluster of mobile rocket launchers that threatened marine battalions on the other side of the border. For the past six months, Iraqi troops had been content to dig sand berms, string razor wire, and plant land mines. But with the air war underway, their intentions became less predictable. The Third Marine Air Wing was removing obvious threats like the rocket launchers. Acree and Hunter had searched in the same vicinity yesterday, finding the Iraqis below ignored their little plane.

The OV-10 Bronco was originally designed to ferret Vietcong guerillas from thick jungle, a nearly impossible task for supersonic jets. This twin-tailed little airplane could rumble down rough forward airstrips for three-hour patrols, sipping high-octane gas if aviation fuel was unavailable.

The Bronco carried four machine guns and a few small rockets, as well as flares and white-phosphorous target markers. It could be configured to haul more than a ton of cargo, or five paratroopers, or two litter patients. The December 1964 issue of *Popular Science* called it the "Flying Jeep."

The U.S. Marines, Navy, and Air Force acquired the Bronco from North American Aviation and eagerly deployed it to Vietnam. The plane proved versatile, but too slow and underpowered for combat. More than eighty Broncos went down in Southeast Asia, some by crashing into steep mountains because they could not climb quickly enough. After the war, the navy transferred its remaining stock to the marines, and the air force began hunting for a replacement. The Marine Corps stuck with its Broncos, going so far as to equip some with infrared vision for night use.

The plane's high-mounted wings and oversized canopy gave Acree and Hunter a sweeping view of the Iraqi fortifications. They saw long, oil-filled trenches, which apparently the Iraqis planned to set ablaze. Tanks hid like scorpions inside deep revetments, and tiny figures popped in and out of underground bunkers. The desert, it seemed, had been transformed into a giant, mine-laden obstacle course. The marine spotters persisted and eventually found their quarry, the rocket batteries.

"We located them and reported their position," Hunter said. "We were waiting for a flight of four A-10s, and once they arrived we would show them where the target was and mark it for them. Then they would roll in and drop their bombs on it."[1]

Acree moved the Bronco off the target to loiter in safety as they waited. Hunter kept his binoculars glued to the rocket launchers, so he never saw the missile streaking toward them. Acree would later say he caught a glimpse of it just before impact. The lightweight Bronco had no chance of surviving a close-proximity missile blast.

"It shattered the left engine and blew the canopy off," Hunter said. "Fortunately for me, I had my helmet on tightly and my visor down, because otherwise it probably would have taken the left side of my face off and my eye out. As it was, it did enough damage."

He blacked out.

"When I came to, a few seconds later, we were going downhill at a very rapid rate in the aircraft. There was a lot of loud noise because the canopy was gone. There was a lot of smoke and fire. I immediately grabbed the control stick to try to pull the aircraft back out of the dive, but the controls were stuck solid. My next inclination was to eject from the aircraft, and I leaned over to do it, and lost consciousness again."

Acree had suffered a serious gash to his neck but was able to pull the ejection handle. Soon they were both drifting, while the battered Bronco plummeted for the desert floor. Hunter awoke once more and foggily imagined himself steering the parachute all the way to the Persian Gulf. He was still daydreaming when the ground rose up to meet him. He collapsed in a heap on hard-packed sand.

"I rolled over and got out of my parachute, and immediately snatched out the survival radio," Hunter said. He had a concussion. Blood streamed from his forehead and the torn lid of his left eye. "I looked around a short distance and saw these two figures walking toward me, so I started walking the other way." He kept speaking into the survival radio as he fled, but there was no response. "Then Colonel Acree called out to me. It turned out he was the two guys. I was seeing double."

They staggered around together, dazed and bloodied, desperately trying to raise someone on their radios, until an Iraqi truck pulled up and rifle-toting soldiers piled out.

* * *

A total of ten coalition planes went down in the first forty-eight hours, and it could have been worse. Aircraft were coming back speckled with shrapnel, their crews describing flak so thick it blotted the sky like man-made hurricanes. A flight of French Jaguars limped home after a low-level raid on Al Jaber airfield—all with battle damage. One plane had an Iraqi bullet penetrate the canopy. It passed through the pilot's helmet, sliced open his scalp, and continued out the other side. Upon landing he climbed from the cockpit drenched in blood.

Prior to their mission, the French obtained satellite photos and other intelligence from a U.S. Air Force F-16 squadron. When handing over the data, the Americans recommended a medium-altitude approach, given the airfield's fierce defenses. But like many other NATO members, France emphasized low-level training designed to exploit the folds and wrinkles of European terrain. The Jaguar pilots felt most comfortable going in low, so they did, but the fury of Al Jaber changed their minds. From now on, French jets would stay above 10,000 feet.

The U.S. Navy was reaching the same conclusion. Vice Admiral Stanley Arthur, commander of the Seventh Fleet, was pleased with the air campaign's progress but concerned about the losses. Arthur knew plenty about risk—the old A-4 Skyhawk driver flew more than 500 missions in America's last war. Now he felt duty-bound to share some of that experience with the next generation.

"Gentlemen, far be it from me to dictate specific combat tactics," Arthur wrote, "but I must inject my early observations relative to the age-old argument of low altitude delivery versus high. With a quick look at what has happened to the multinational air forces to date, one cannot escape the fact that the current AAA environment makes low altitude delivery a non-starter."[2] Arthur noted that low-flying strikers needed the benefit of surprise, and right now they didn't have it. "We learned a hard lesson in Vietnam relative to AAA," he reminded his wing commanders. No more navy planes made low-level attacks.

The last holdouts were the RAF squadrons, who still believed in ultralow tactics. The Brits were determined to deny the Iraqis the use of their runways, which meant more JP233 attacks. The two lost RAF Tornados were chalked off as unfortunate costs of war, and the harrowing airfield raids continued.

CHAPTER 14

Package Q

AT DOHA INTERNATIONAL AIR BASE IN QATAR, SIXTEEN F-16S SAT with engines idling. The planes belonged to the 614th Tactical Fighter Squadron, also known as the Lucky Devils. Each pilot was strapped in, running through checklists. A modern fighter like the F-16 required extensive preparation before takeoff, especially during combat operations.

Major Emmett "ET" Tullia reached down and flicked a switch. A videotape recorder whirred to life. "Mission number 2365," he announced. "I'm going to be attacking an oil refinery in the southern part of Baghdad."[1] Tullia gave further details about his aircraft and mission, speaking in an aviator's measured tone, as if today's assignment were no different from the hundreds of training sorties he'd flown.

A crewman signaled to Tullia that it was time to pull the arming pins on the Mark-84 bombs slung beneath his wings. The pilot raised his arms in the air, proving his hands were clear of all controls. As the arming crew went about their work, Tullia—his hands still aloft—scanned the dials, displays, and switches around him. Everything looked ready for combat. His eyes stopped at the digital clock. Eight minutes until takeoff.

He and the other Doha-based F-16 pilots didn't know it at the moment, but they were about to become part of a grand experiment.

During the war's first two days, Black Hole planners treated Baghdad with extreme caution. The Iraqi capital was ringed by some of the fiercest antiaircraft defenses in the world—at least 60 SAM batteries and 1,800 guns. By comparison, American pilots raiding Hanoi at the height of the Vietnam War faced less. Stealthy F-117 Nighthawks visited Baghdad each night, followed by waves of Tomahawk cruise missiles during the day, but the city was off-limits to non-stealthy, manned aircraft. Prewar computer simulations predicted roughly half would be shot down. But after two solid days of attacks, the planners suspected—or at least hoped—that Baghdad's defenses might be weakening.

The prospect of a traditional raid tantalized them. Nighthawks and Tomahawks were extraordinary weapons, but stealth and precision came at a cost: less explosive punch. An F-117 carried just 4,000 pounds of bombs, and the Tomahawk's warhead was far less than that. The stalwart F-16, meanwhile, hauled more than 15,000 pounds under its wings and belly. Some of that load would be spent on external fuel tanks for the long flight to Baghdad, but a flight of F-16s could take out sprawling targets—like an oil refinery—which the precision bombers could barely scratch.

The F-16 was the combat workhorse of the U.S. Air Force, a multirole aircraft designed to shoot down enemy fighters in the air and fling bombs at targets on the ground. When it entered service in 1978, generals christened it the Fighting Falcon, but those who flew it called it the Viper. According to legend, the nickname came from the science-fiction show *Battlestar Galactica*, and indeed the sleek, single-engine jet looked like a starfighter. An innovative fly-by-wire control system—which replaced conventional pulleys, cranks, and tension cables with computer circuits— enhanced the F-16's futuristic image. It also made the plane lighter and more responsive. Viper pilots reported a special synergy with their aircraft. They didn't just fly it; they wore it like a glove.

Desert Storm was their opportunity to showcase the Viper's abilities. Yet a daylight raid on the Iraqi capital gave them pause. Before the war Capt. Mike Roberts, a Lucky Devil, glimpsed an advance copy of the Air Tasking Order and could scarcely believe his eyes. "I remember thinking, 'Wow, day three, downtown Baghdad in the daytime. They'll change that by the time we get there,'" Roberts said. "But sure enough, day three came and no changes. Everybody was pretty nervous about it."[2]

Friendly Airspace
Northern Saudi Arabia
January 19, 1991

Strike Package Q, as it was called in the Air Tasking Order, included seventy-two Vipers, four F-15C Eagles, a pair of EF-111 Ravens, and a flight of F-4G Wild Weasels. It would be the largest package of the war, and the biggest F-16 strike in history.

The plan called for everyone to rendezvous over Saudi Arabia and receive fuel from the tankers, then head north toward Baghdad. As usual, weather was a factor. Two morning missions to Baghdad were scrubbed due to dreadful weather, and now Package Q was threatened. "The clouds were so thick that it was difficult for us to refuel," Emmett Tullia recalled. "The tankers were diving and climbing, trying to find us some clear space to refuel."

Bomb-laden F-16s struggled to stay with their tankers and avoid a midair collision in the low visibility. The formation frayed, and then it unraveled entirely. Four planes trying to draw fuel from the last tanker straggled so far behind the group that they had no hope of catching up. The mission commander ordered them back to base. Briefly, he considered diverting the entire strike package to its backup target—a mass of dug-in tanks belonging to Iraq's elite Republican Guard—but when the clouds finally dispersed he chose to press on to Baghdad.

The huge formation lacked any benefit of stealth or surprise, and Iraq's early warning radars tracked them while they were still in Saudi airspace. Antiaircraft rounds greeted them soon after they crossed the border. Most of the flak remained well below the jets, but some 100mm shells climbed to their altitude, blossoming into menacing black clouds. More planes fell behind while ducking the bursts and were sent home.

As Package Q approached the city, two-thirds of the formation peeled off toward the primary target, a nuclear power plant and research facility ten miles southeast of town. The Lucky Devils, meanwhile, continued north toward their assigned targets: Republican Guard headquarters, Iraqi air force headquarters, and an oil refinery. They didn't realize it at the time, but all of the Wild Weasels and Ravens went with the group headed to the nuclear plant. The Lucky Devils would be going "downtown," as Roberts had put it, all alone.

The Baghdad Nuclear Research Facility was no stranger to air raids. Most nations considered it the centerpiece of Saddam's nuclear weapons program, and on two occasions, wary Middle East neighbors tried to put it out of business. The first attempt came in 1980, when Iranian jets bombed the newly built facility, inflicting only minor damage. Less than a year later, Israel's air force gave it a try. Flying sand-colored F-16s, which they had only recently acquired from the United States, the Israelis caused greater destruction but failed to shut down the site permanently.

Those early attacks taught Saddam to protect his investment. Now, a decade later, the American F-16s arrived to find the nuclear facility nestled behind a sand berm more than 150 feet high. Smoke generators surrounded the area, producing a thick white haze. Most pilots could not see their specific aim points, and—following standing orders intended to limit civilian casualties—simply pulled off without releasing any ordnance.

Pilots who pressed on faced a cauldron of antiaircraft fire. The Weasels and Ravens quickly became overwhelmed as dozens of radars swept the skies. Within three minutes, twenty-seven SAMs filled the air. Artillery bursts sparkled everywhere, their smoke congealing into a solid cloud layer. No bomb hit its target, although by this point nobody really cared. The attackers sought nothing more than escape. They jinked and rolled, releasing flares to distract heat-seeking missiles, and then they punched the afterburners for lifesaving speed and altitude.

Their survival was the result of skill and training, but also good fortune. One pilot would later write about the experience, calling it the "Mission from Hell."[3] The nuclear plant raid had been a terrifying experience and a sobering failure. But as bad as it was for them, none would have traded places with the Lucky Devils, who were just now setting up their attack downtown.

Hostile Airspace
Daura Oil Refinery, Baghdad

From 26,000 feet, Emmett Tullia peered through breaks in the low-hanging clouds, trying to find the refinery. On Tullia's right was his good friend, Jeff Tice, who was flying under the call sign Stroke One. Tullia was Stroke Three. They planned to roll in on the target together, but that changed once the SAM launches began.

A shrill warning announced the presence of an SA-2 Guideline surface-to-air missile. Nicknamed the "flying telephone pole," the SA-2 was a thirty-five-foot Vietnam-era relic that could usually be defeated by chaff. Still, its speed and sizable warhead posed a threat, and both pilots broke into defensive turns.

The missile pursued Tullia's plane.

"[This is] Stroke Three, defending [against an] SA-2," he radioed, informing the others of his status. The high-G turn pushed him deep into his seat, putting a strain in his voice. Still, he felt no panic. The situation was manageable.

"Stroke Three, you're on your own," Tice called out, confirming that they would now proceed to the target separately.

From Tullia's view, the missile below was a glowing orange dot that slowly grew larger as it closed. He jerked the control stick and watched with fascination as the orange dot altered its course to stay with him. He did it again, and once again the dot shifted to match him. But the reaction was not instantaneous. The SA-2's circuitry needed two or three seconds to recalculate its intercept path. Those few seconds were its weakness.

Fighter doctrine for defeating a SAM boiled down to a game of chicken. If chaff and evasive maneuvers failed, the pilot positioned the missile off his wingtip and waited. Once it drew close enough—usually four or five seconds from impact—the SAM would have no more time for course corrections. A hard break would, according to the textbooks, force an overshoot. But the brinksmanship required perfect timing: too early and the missile could adjust; too late and it might pepper the aircraft with shrapnel.

Tullia was ready. He executed the tactic flawlessly and the SA-2 sailed past, exploding at a safe distance. Next he needed to get his bearings and reacquire the target. The city was vanishing beneath a veil of smoke, clouds, and AAA explosions. He dipped the Viper's nose and scanned for landmarks. Incredibly, the oil refinery appeared directly before him, through a convenient hole in the gray blanket.

He pushed the plane into a dive and watched the refinery slide onto his heads-up display, then slewed the targeting pipper onto a distillation tower. He thumbed the weapon release button. Seconds passed as the targeting system waited for the precise instant to drop, factoring in wind and other variables. Tullia could hear the excited radio chatter of other pilots dodging missiles. At last a pair of tremors announced the Mark-84s coming off his wings.

Suddenly free of all the extra weight and drag, the aircraft felt once more like a jet fighter. He pulled from the dive and turned south, anxious to leave Baghdad. But almost instantly the piercing warning tone returned, followed by another, and another. Multiple SAMs were nearby.

"Stroke Three, check right," someone called to him. "Break right!"

It was Jeff Tice, who had already delivered his bombs and was egressing the target area. Tice could see the missiles streaking toward his friend.

Tullia obeyed, pulling into a hard right-hand turn. An SA-3 soared from behind and exploded off to his left, filling the cockpit with blinding white light but inflicting no damage.

"Wait, somebody got hit," a pilot called out in dismay.

The radio chatter trailed off for an instant while everyone absorbed that information, then resumed.

"Stroke Three [is] egressing southeast," Tullia announced. The measured calm of his voice was gone now, replaced with adrenaline-laced urgency.

Tangled knots of SAM contrails—visible remnants of high-speed pursuit—scrawled across the sky, and more missiles were on the way. New warning tones filled Tullia's ears as he yanked the plane left and right. He grunted through each high-G turn. The defensive maneuvers were working, but each one robbed him of speed and altitude. He was already down to 11,000 feet, nearly within reach of the AAA guns. So far he had managed to stay above the flak with quick bursts of afterburner, but the burner guzzled precious fuel, and he was deep inside enemy territory.

"Stroke Three, you still there?" Tice asked, no longer in visual contact.

"Stroke Three is still heading southeast," Tullia replied through clenched teeth as he twisted yet again.

Other pilots continued calling out SAM launches, and he swiveled his head to see if any were coming his way. The plane's warning receiver would alert him to radar-guided missiles, but it offered no help against the heat-seekers, which stalked in silence at low altitudes.

The warning receiver chirped again. Tullia looked off to his right to spot an SA-6 Gainful heading for him.

"Stroke Three defending six," he barked.

This missile seemed different. It was closing more rapidly than the others he had evaded, and when he jinked to shake it, the SA-6 responded almost instantly. It sped toward him without wavering. For the first time, Tullia felt certain he would be hit. Despite the sharpest turn he could muster, the missile still pointed straight at him. For a split second, he envisioned it spearing his airplane.

"Whoa!" he exclaimed, as the SA-6 passed so near he could hear the engine. It continued a short distance and detonated, once again bathing him in white light but inflicting no damage.

The SA-6 encounter had lasted less than twenty seconds, but it felt so much longer. He was drenched in sweat and breathing heavily into his oxygen mask. He needed to escape before his luck ran out, but the missiles wouldn't stop coming.

"There's another one! Stroke Three defending again!"

This time he decided to push the F-16's nose over, trading altitude for escape speed. The maneuver would put him within AAA range but he was outside the city now and the guns were fewer. In any case, he could not risk another near-miss. He passed through 10,000 feet, then 9,000, twisting wildly the entire time. After what seemed an eternity, the SAM lost its lock and drifted away. He slid the throttle forward and climbed to relative safety.

Six minutes of aerobatics left Tullia exhausted, low on fuel, and separated from his squadron. He switched the HUD to navigation mode and began the long flight back to Doha. His primary concern was reaching friendly airspace and finding a tanker. He had no idea how the other Lucky Devils fared, or if the mission was a success.

A surprise awaited him when he finally landed at Doha. As Tullia shut down the engine and descended the ladder, his crew chief began inspecting the F-16 for damage. A plane with so many close scrapes was sure to be a little dinged up, but the chief could find nothing wrong. Then he reached the chaff and flare dispensers near the tail. In a high-threat environment, pilots were known to keep tapping the countermeasures button long after all the chaff and flares were gone. But Tullia's dispensers were still fully loaded, the result of a malfunction. He had evaded six missiles on maneuvers alone.

* * *

Emmett Tullia was the luckiest of the Lucky Devils that day. Two others had been less fortunate, suffering missile impacts over Baghdad. The first was Mike Roberts, the captain who had wondered privately about the wisdom of going "downtown." Roberts dodged one SAM only to catch shrapnel from another. At first, he thought the damage was minor.

"I remember trying to light the burner on the airplane to get some airspeed back, and instead of feeling that kick in the pants from the burner lighting, I felt the motor just dying underneath me," he said. "We have what we call 'Bitching Betty' in the airplane—a voice warning system that starts talking to you when things are going bad—and Betty's bitching, and lights are lighting up everywhere, and the motor had quit running. The flight controls weren't responding."[4]

Roberts accepted reality and ejected, but in the chaos nobody saw his parachute. The squadron presumed him killed until a few days later, when he turned up on Iraqi television as a POW.

The second stricken aircraft belonged to Jeff Tice. After releasing his bombs, Tice loitered over Baghdad to spot missiles for Tullia, an act of professionalism and friendship. But it had cost him. Once Tullia became separated from the group, Tice turned for home. He was near the outskirts of Baghdad when an SA-3 tagged him. (See the prologue for details.) As with Mike Roberts, the Lucky Devils wouldn't learn his fate until they saw him on an Iraqi broadcast of allied POWs.

Package Q was a failed experiment. Daura Oil Refinery burned furiously—and would continue to rage for the next six weeks—but all other targets escaped damage. The Iraqis had put up a vigorous defense. Two aircraft were destroyed, their pilots captured, and other planes suffered damage or came within moments of running out of fuel. One bone-dry F-16 surely would have crashed if not for a plucky KC-135 tanker crew from the Kansas National Guard, who ventured into Iraqi airspace to meet it.

The mission was a wake-up call for the Black Hole planners. Baghdad's air defenses were still a potent threat. From now on, Nighthawks and Tomahawks would have exclusive domain over the city. Nobody wanted another Package Q.

CHAPTER 15

Eagles Go Hunting

SADDAM'S NEW AIR STRATEGY WAS ONE OF HARASSMENT. OUTRIGHT victory was impossible, he realized, given the size and sophistication of the coalition air armada, so most Iraqi aircraft remained on the ground trying to ride out the storm. There would be no large-scale dogfights in this war, just short, violent encounters between small groups of adversaries.

During the first twenty-four hours, the Iraqi air force scrambled roughly a hundred planes, by far its most active day. When nine of those aircraft failed to return, Saddam's generals took pause. Day two of the war was quiet, with few Iraqi sorties and no losses, despite waves of allied warplanes crisscrossing the country. By day three, the Iraqi generals apparently were game for another try. AWACS operators noted increased bandit activity, particularly in western Iraq, around the air bases of H-2 and H-3. Flights of F-15C Eagles descended on the area.

Among those flights was Capt. Richard Tollini's four-ship, which had just come off a tanker when AWACS called out multiple bogeys. Tollini led his Eagles north to confront two separate formations of Iraqi fighters, both of which appeared to be angling toward a coalition strike package. A flight of MiG-29 Fulcrums was speeding in from the northwest, while farther away and due north, a flight of MiG-25 Foxbats approached. The Fulcrums were the more potent and immediate threat. But when Tollini's group tried to engage the MiG-29s, they turned and fled, perhaps hoping to draw the Americans into a trap.

Instead, the Eagles turned to meet the two Foxbats, which were closing quickly. With just twenty-five miles of distance between them, the opposing formations would merge in seconds. Tollini and his wingman,

Capt. Larry Pitts, both obtained a radar lock. Immediately, the Foxbats broke into a hard right turn, released large amounts of chaff, and dove for the desert floor. It was an effective maneuver that broke the American radar locks, as the tracked planes became lost in ground clutter.

Clearly, these two Iraqi pilots were well trained and experienced. They had just used a classic Soviet evasion tactic, and they showed no sign of panic or confusion. Their Soviet-built jets, although admittedly aging, possessed superior speed and were still formidable fighters, particularly when in skilled hands.

Back in 1970, when the MiG-25 first entered service, it shocked Western air forces by setting world records for speed and climb, which hinted at unprecedented combat ability. The F-15 was still under development at the time, and Pentagon officials worried the Eagle would be no match for the vaunted Foxbat. They pushed McDonnell Douglas to make the F-15 a better fighter.

In 1976, a Soviet pilot defected to the United States via Japan. Western analysts got their first hands-on inspection of a Foxbat and realized it wasn't quite the world-beater they assumed. Despite Mach 3 speed, the plane's combat performance was pedestrian at best, with a heavy airframe that limited maneuverability. Meanwhile, the F-15 Eagle had been transformed into a truly extraordinary fighter based on the exaggerated threat, a happy mistake.

The two Iraqi Foxbats now sped unseen along the desert floor. All four F-15C pilots scanned furiously, trying to pick up the MiGs before they moved into firing position. Wingman Larry Pitts was the first to reestablish contact—he spotted one of the bandits streaking low across his nose. He called it out, and Tollini gave him the green light to pursue.

"I roll inverted and do a split-S maneuver from ten thousand feet," Pitts said.[1] Upon reaching the bottom of this high-G maneuver, he found himself directly behind the Foxbat and about two miles distant. The Iraqi pilot realized he was vulnerable and countered with a hard right turn. At supersonic speed, it was a mistake. "His turn radius is the size of Texas," Pitts explained. "I'm very quickly inside his turn. Before he completes the one hundred and eighty degrees of turn, I'm already within weapons parameters."

The MiG's long afterburner plume glowed white, and Pitts toggled his weapon selector for a heat-seeking AIM-9 Sidewinder. The missile locked instantly and he punched the pickle button, sending the Sidewinder on its way. It tracked for a few seconds until the MiG began pumping out flares. The missile became confused by the decoys and went astray.

Pitts decided to try a radar-guided missile. He toggled to an AIM-7 Sparrow and fired. This missile tracked directly to the target but failed to explode—a dud. He launched another Sidewinder, but it too fell victim to the MiG's steady stream of flares.

"This guy is fighting hard," Pitts said. "I'm thinking to myself, 'If the missiles aren't going to work, I'm going to have to go gun this guy,' which is not an easy solution when he's at three hundred feet, doing five hundred knots, and not in a turn." He toggled back to his last radar-guided AIM-7. This one, he hoped, was not a dud. "I fired the missile from six thousand feet behind him, and it looks to me like it goes right up his tailpipes and blows up the back end of his airplane."

Pitts pulled up to avoid the brown debris cloud and then put the kill out of his mind. There would be time to process it later. Right now he needed to regain some situational awareness. Another MiG-25 was still out there. He looked up and caught sight of Richard Tollini, engaged high on the left.

The flight lead was going nose-to-nose with a rapidly approaching aircraft, which logically would be the other MiG-25. Yet Tollini wasn't certain. From a distance, the twin-tailed Foxbat resembled an Eagle. Before firing, he had to be certain the oncoming plane wasn't a member of his own flight. Tollini squinted and saw a long white plume broiling out the back of the jet.

"Is anybody in afterburner?" he called out. The other Eagle pilots answered negative, and now Tollini was certain. He unleashed a Sidewinder. The MiG spat out a torrent of flares and defeated the heat-seeker.

The Iraqi pilot had seen enough. His wingman was gone. He was outnumbered four to one and had just survived a close call with an American missile. He chose to flee. The decision was prudent, but his execution was not. Disengaging from a dogfight requires just as much poise and skill as any other element, but the Iraqi simply turned away. He never considered the hazard of going "belly up"—displaying his plane's broadest outline—to the onrushing Eagles.

"Now we're seeing the underside of his belly, which is not a great place for the MiG to be," Pitts explained. "Rick selects an AIM-7 Sparrow radar-guided missile and fires it. That airplane just turns into a ball of dust."

The F-15Cs expended most of their fuel tangling with the Foxbats, so they headed south for a tanker and then home. The Iraqi air force, meanwhile, remained undeterred in its quest to control the western desert. Fighters continued to launch from H-2 and H-3.

Soon after Tollini's flight departed the area, a coalition strike package passed through, making its way back to Saudi Arabia. The strikers were wary of being stalked from behind, so they requested additional fighter escort to cover their six o'clock. But AWACS had nobody to send, except perhaps the four F-15Cs flying HAVCAP (High Asset Value Combat Air Patrol). These Eagles protected the tankers and other support aircraft orbiting high above Saudi Arabia, including the AWACS planes.

An AWACS commander got on the radio and discussed the request with HAVCAP flight lead Capt. Cesar Rodriguez. So far in the war, no Iraqi fighters showed any interest in coming south to Saudi Arabia and going on the offensive. But that could change at any time. HAVCAP could not leave the support aircraft unprotected, so Rodriguez proposed splitting his flight in half. He and his wingman, Capt. Craig Underhill, would head into Iraq to cover the strike package, while the other two Eagles remained on station. The AWACS commander approved the plan, and Rodriguez and Underhill sped north. Within moments they picked up a pair of bogeys near H-2. AWACS confirmed them hostile, but as soon as the Eagles approached, the Iraqi jets turned and ran.

Almost immediately afterward, a new contact appeared from the west, only thirteen miles distant. Events began to unfold rapidly. Rodriguez and Underhill turned toward the new bogey, who was approaching at supersonic speeds. AWACS called it hostile. Underhill got a lock on the bandit. He fired a missile.

At nearly the same instant, the bandit locked up Rodriguez, who released chaff and dove for the desert floor. He wanted to hide in the ground clutter, just as the MiG-25 Foxbats had done during the earlier engagement. Rodriguez heard Underhill call "Fox One!" and knew a radar-guided missile was in the air.

"I turn left in my cockpit, and I actually pick up the motor of his AIM-7," Rodriguez said.[2] The Sparrow shot past him, barely 200 feet away. With the Iraqi plane less than four miles distant, Rodriguez expected to come under fire at any second. He desperately hoped the Sparrow tracked true. "I'm really caught right now at the mercy of what that missile is going to do," he said. "Sure enough, the minute I picked up the [bandit's] silhouette, it couldn't have been more than two or three seconds later, and boom!"

The jet disintegrated into a greasy smudge.

"Splash one," Rodriguez called, as he began climbing from the defensive maneuver. He was eager to regain some altitude and get back into a position to mutually support his wingman. They had done what they needed to do—the strike package was safely away—and picked up a kill in the process. "To be honest my thought process was, 'Let's get the hell out of here,'" Rodriguez said. They turned south for Saudi Arabia and a tanker track.

A few minutes later, AWACS picked up a new bogey. This jet was ten miles distant at their six o'clock. Rodriguez didn't know if the plane was pursuing them or had different intentions entirely. Rather than waiting to find out, he decided to confront it. The Eagles snapped around, a maneuver that placed Underhill out in front. He quickly acquired a radar lock.

Their sudden move startled the bogey, who broke into a sharp left turn. Again, this "belly up" maneuver was a mistake, since it exposed his plane's full length and width to the opposing radar, making him an easy target. Underhill assumed he was about to get his second kill. He selected a radar-guided Sparrow and was just about to punch the button, when something totally unexpected happened.

"He lights up as a diamond on my scope," Underhill said. "It goes from a solid radar contact to a diamond, which tells me he's a friendly."

An avalanche rushed through Underhill's mind. Maybe it was a malfunction, he thought. Then he considered the possibility that this guy really was a friendly. Maybe AWACS screwed up. He thought about the jet he destroyed just a few minutes ago. If this guy was a friendly, then maybe that one was, too. "I tell you, that was just a terrible feeling," Underhill said. "Fratricide was something the Eagle community took very seriously."

They were approaching the merge. His questions would be answered once they had visual identification. The bogey suddenly became aggressive, turning and rolling, trying to slice its way behind the two Eagles. Underhill climbed and maintained his radar lock, while Rodriguez stayed low with the bogey, trying to identify it. "I could see the Iraqi colors on his tailfin, the flag, and the MiG-29 silhouette," Rodriguez said. "I called that it was a MiG-29."

Small and lightweight, the MiG-29 Fulcrum excelled at close-quarter dogfighting. It was easily the finest aircraft in the Iraqi air force, and the best fighter a Soviet client state could buy. Mikoyan designers endowed the Fulcrum with tremendous agility, but they skimped on avionics. The plane was newer than both the F-15 and F-16, yet it lacked the Eagle's sophisticated radar and the Viper's fly-by-wire control system. Western analysts believed the best chance for defeating a Fulcrum was from a distance, before its dexterity became a factor. Unfortunately for Rodriguez, that opportunity had passed. He was already inside the tiger's cage.

"I start a left-hand turn, and he starts a left-hand turn," he said. They began a downward spiral, as Rodriguez and the Iraqi raced to get behind each other for a shot. By 8,000 feet, the Fulcrum was leading the way down the corkscrew. Rodriguez strained against heavy G-forces as he tried to keep pace. They passed through 7,000, and then 6,000 feet. The MiG couldn't shake him, yet it remained outside his weapons parameters. On his heads-up display, Rodriguez saw the 5,000 mark go by.

"The desert floor starts to become a definite factor," he said.

Cockpit layout was another element the Mikoyan engineers had ignored. Fulcrum pilots used controls that were virtually unchanged from earlier generations of MiGs. Modern innovations such as HOTAS (Hands-On Throttle and Stick) placed important buttons and switches directly on the flight controls, enabling fighter pilots to work key systems as they flew the airplane. An intuitive and ergonomic design like HOTAS kept the pilot's eyes outside the cockpit, improving his situational awareness.

The Iraqi lacked any ergonomic benefit. His hands moved furiously about the cockpit as he tried to stay one step ahead of his pursuer. He was pulling heavy Gs. The blue sky outside his canopy was vanishing, being replaced with gray desert. He needed to break from the spiral immediately, and he did. He rolled the Fulcrum over and pulled into a split-S. His intent was to come out of the maneuver in a vertical position and rocket skyward. He never had the chance.

"Before he actually hits perpendicular, he hit the desert floor," said Rodriguez, "causing a fireball that just tumbles and tumbles for what seemed like an eternity to me." Rodriguez had outmaneuvered a Fulcrum at close quarters, earning a kill. He and Underhill flew back to Saudi Arabia.

Elsewhere, the Eagles continued hunting. A pair of F-15Cs flying out of Incirlik, Turkey, encountered two F-1 Mirages in northern Iraq and destroyed them with Sparrow missiles. The heavy losses of January 19 convinced the Iraqi air force to seek another strategy, since challenging the Eagles clearly was a waste of pilots and machines.

For the F-15C pilots and other coalition aviators, their strategy was changing as well. They had achieved air superiority in just three days. Now they would pursue a more permanent goal, one aimed at fostering peace and stability in the region—the wholesale destruction of the Iraqi air force.

CHAPTER 16

Great Scud Hunt

IN FAR WESTERN IRAQ, NOT FAR FROM THE JORDANIAN BORDER, AN eight-wheeled Scud missile launcher rumbled through the darkness toward a presurveyed desert location. Upon arriving, the crew hopped out and immediately began running through their launch sequence.

Soviet technicians, who trained the first Iraqi Scud crews nearly a decade ago, claimed a proper launch sequence took about ninety minutes. But in the intervening years, the Iraqis became launch experts. They drilled for speed and efficiency, trimming away nonessential steps and abbreviating the essential ones. A good Iraqi crew could fire a missile in under thirty minutes and be gone before enemy aircraft arrived. The crews knew their "shoot-and-scoot" tactics were vital in this war, since American planes were scouring the western desert.

Within minutes, the forty-foot missile was upright and locked into firing position. The Scud was a primitive weapon, a direct descendant of the German V-2 rockets that terrorized London. But simplicity was part of the Scud's appeal. It could be launched from a fixed site or a mobile TEL (transporter/erector/launcher) vehicle, which was roughly the size and shape of a big rig. Once fired, a Scud sped to the fringes of the atmosphere at Mach 8 until its fuel was gone, and then fell to the target unguided. When the Soviets designed the missile in the 1950s, they had tactical nuclear warheads in mind, so pinpoint accuracy was not critical.

Accuracy was also not a concern of Saddam Hussein, who—like Hitler with the V-2—wished to terrorize enemy cities. Saddam first began lobbing Scuds at Iranian population centers in 1982. The Iranians obtained their own missiles and retaliated, leading to the so-called "war of the cities," another brutal chapter in the Iran-Iraq conflict.

Saddam desperately wanted a long-range missile that could reach Tehran, but the Soviets refused, so he built his own. The Al-Hussein Scud traded any semblance of accuracy for greater distance and was prone to breaking into pieces during descent. As long as the warhead remained intact, Saddam did not care. During a three-month period in 1988, nearly 200 Scuds rained down on the Iranian capital, triggering a panicked exodus from the city. He had achieved his goal.

In 1991, against the coalition, Saddam planned a similar Scud strategy. Missiles would threaten not only the cities of any Arab nation who dared oppose him, but also Israel. Experience told him that any attack on Israeli soil would draw a swift counterattack, thus making the Jewish state a de facto member of the coalition. Arab nations suddenly would find themselves allied with a sworn enemy in a war against fellow Arabs. The coalition would disintegrate.

In Washington, the Bush administration anticipated Saddam's Israeli gambit and fretted over it. But in Riyadh, the top military commander could not help viewing Scuds through a soldier's eyes. Norman Schwarzkopf saw only a crude and ineffective weapon. The rickety missiles should be ignored, he felt, since they were more likely to dig random holes in the desert than hit any targets of value. Schwarzkopf agreed to opening-night strikes on Scud launch pads, but only because Washington insisted. As soon as the Apaches of Task Force Normandy opened up the radar-free corridor, F-15E Strike Eagles sped toward concrete launch pads in the western desert, pounding them with laser-guided bombs.

Saddam expected the attacks on his vulnerable Scud launch pads, so he let them sit idle. The mobile TELs would carry out his missile strategy. American intelligence agencies knew he had mobile launchers, and their prewar estimates ranged from eighteen to forty-eight TELs. The actual number, they would soon discover, was closer to 225. Saddam's missile crews would lie low by day, hiding their vehicles in a culvert or under a highway overpass. They stayed off the air to avoid being tracked by radio transmission. And they planted in the desert full-size TEL decoys, a product of the former East Germany, which looked remarkably real from the air.

The first two Scuds of the war were fired at Israel. They missed, landing instead in the Mediterranean Sea, sending up huge offshore geysers. A few hours later one struck a Tel Aviv neighborhood, its half-ton warhead causing property damage but no casualties. The next Scud was launched at Saudi Arabia and began its descent on the city of Dhahran. In the first combat use of an antimissile missile, a U.S. Army Patriot rose up at Mach 3 and intercepted it. Altogether, seven Scuds went into the air on the second night of the war, but none caused serious damage.

Tel Aviv's emergency workers were still sifting through the rubble when Defense Minister Moshe Arens called Washington. The Israeli government previously turned down an offer of Patriot batteries. Now the missiles were welcome, Arens said, and the sooner the better. He also asked for the coalition's IFF (Identify Friend or Foe) codes, which would enable the Israelis to distinguish between Iraqi and allied fighters. Seventeen hours later, thirty-two Patriot missiles were on the ground in Israel.

The IFF issue was more problematic. Israeli fighters needed those codes to operate over Iraq, so furnishing them meant condoning an Israeli counterattack. Saddam would be getting precisely what he wanted. After a White House meeting, Cheney called Arens and declined the IFF request. Instead, Cheney assured him that coalition aircraft would be stepping up their efforts to find and destroy Iraqi TELs.

The Great Scud Hunt was on.

Riyadh, Saudi Arabia
January 18, 1991
0650 Local

The Tactical Air Control Center suddenly resembled the floor of the New York Stock Exchange at the height of a sell-off. Aircraft needed to be yanked from assigned missions and sent out into western Iraq. Planners thumbed through the mammoth Air Tasking Order, the campaign's daily game plan, looking for available planes. Liaison officers worked the telephones, frantically calling squadrons around the theater with new orders.

Lieutenant Darren Hansen and another A-10 pilot were among those tapped for Scud hunting. "Just before we walked out the door we got a priority call from Riyadh, and they stopped us. They said we were going to Al Jouf. I had never even heard of it," Hansen recalled.[1] "Now we are sitting in our jets, holding, waiting for more information, and they come running out with a map. They unfolded it and said, 'Right here it is, see?' I'm saying, 'That's five hundred miles to the west—what are we going to do way out there?'"

The A-10 drivers journeyed west across Saudi Arabia, making a quick refueling stop along the way. When they finally landed at Al Jouf, which barely qualified as an airstrip, they looked around and realized it was a Special Forces forward operating base. An army ground crew refilled their tanks while a colonel briefed them over the radio.

"Basically, he said, 'Here are some coordinates where you might find Scuds. Good luck and Godspeed,'" Hansen remembered. "We could see that we were going at least seventy miles into Iraq, without a map, without knowing exactly what a Scud or Scud launcher looks like, and we were doing that in an A-10."

The A-10 Thunderbolt II was built strictly for close air support. Manufacturer Fairchild Republic never envisioned the plane straying more than a few miles from the battlefront. The A-10's imagined purpose was shredding Soviet tanks and armored personnel carriers as they pushed across Western Europe. The rugged little jet was meant to pop up from behind a mountain, pour fire on an advancing column, and then retreat to a forward airstrip for more fuel and weapons. Forays deep into enemy territory went beyond its design specifications.

The A-10's problem was speed, or rather, a distinct lack of it. Two turbofan engines operated quietly and efficiently but topped out at about five hundred miles per hour, roughly a third of the F-16's speed. Viper pilots made jokes—an A-10 cockpit had no clock, just a calendar; the A-10 was at serious risk of bird strikes, from behind. Yet this plodding, snub-nosed airplane, known universally as the Warthog or simply the Hog, held several Scud-hunting advantages over its supersonic colleagues. The most important was loiter ability, or time over target (TOT).

"Scuds started popping up all over the place and the question was: Who are we going to send after them?" said an A-10 pilot working at the TACC as a liaison. "There were already packages of F-16s airborne. Instantly they could divert some of them out to western Iraq where the Scuds were being launched. But the generals vetoed that. They didn't want F-16s; they wanted A-10s out there. The F-16s would get out there and have a two-minute TOT, and they still wouldn't know where the Scuds were. They knew that the A-10s could get out there with at least a one-hour TOT—more with tanker support—and could do a lot of searching."[2]

The first few Scud sorties turned up nothing, hinting at the enormous challenge they faced. Western Iraq was a barren expanse, and Scud crews were adept at hiding. Ten Warthogs took up residence at Al Jouf, flying in pairs during the daylight hours. The pilots quickly became bored and frustrated, like desert highway patrolmen who worked an entire shift without seeing a single vehicle. Squadron commanders eventually showed mercy, setting up a five-day rotation schedule for Scud duty. None of the Hog drivers looked forward to their stint at Al Jouf.

Al Kharj Air Base, Saudi Arabia
January 20, 1991
1400 Local

A-10s were daytime hunters, so nocturnal Scud missions fell to the LANTIRN-equipped F-15E Strike Eagles. Infrared equipment enabled them to scour desert roadways from an altitude of 15,000 feet, and any missile launchers they found could be hit with laser-guided bombs. But like the Warthogs, they were finding little.

On the afternoon of the war's fourth day, a major tasking revision came in from Riyadh. Intelligence officers had identified a major facility, north of H-2 air base at Al Qaim, where the Iraqis assembled and stored their Scuds. The new orders scratched a meticulously planned ammo-dump raid. Instead, two twelve-ship flights of Strike Eagles were going to Al Qaim, a place so heavily ringed by surface-to-air missiles that the pilots called it Sam's Town.

Now the F-15E crews scrambled to throw together a mission plan in just a few hours. They needed ingress and egress routes, attack profiles, and support from Wild Weasels and Ravens. Ground crews hurriedly swapped out each plane's ordnance for the new target. Late in the afternoon, Riyadh called to change the attack time, and then called to change it yet again. This mission was critical, the caller explained. The Israelis had endured another night of missile attacks and were preparing their own massive counterstrike. Washington wanted to prove that the coalition could handle the Scud problem on its own.

The Strike Eagle crews resented the shove in the back. Political considerations were trampling professional military preparation, a classic Vietnam-era mistake. Afternoon quickly gave way to evening, and soon they were suiting up to fly. Colonel David Eberly, an experienced pilot and the 4th Tactical Fighter Wing's director of operations, tried to hide his concerns from the others as they walked across the flight line toward their jets. The mission commander, a lieutenant colonel, strode beside Eberly and quietly voiced his own misgivings. "This thing is a goat rope," he murmured. "It's the kind of mission that gets people killed."[3]

A rough aerial refueling in heavy weather set the mission's tone—nothing was going to be easy on this one. The Wild Weasels, who were supposed to lead the way into Sam's Town and soften up the defenses with HARM missiles, were late. They had missed the second time change made by Riyadh.

The Strike Eagles circled patiently, but after half an hour they could wait no longer. Scrubbing the mission did not seem a viable option. Before the war, Buster Glosson visited the squadrons and told them there was nothing in Iraq worth dying for, meaning they should always err on the side of caution. But the Strike Eagle crews sensed this mission was an exception to that rule, so they proceeded into Iraq without Wild Weasel escort. They would rely solely on jamming aircraft to distract the Sam's Town radar operators.

Two EF-111 Ravens arrived southeast of Al Qaim, on schedule, and prepared to clutter the radar scopes with a blizzard of electrons. But then another complication arose, this time in the form of a MiG-25. An Iraqi pilot found the orbiting pair of EF-111s and pursued them. After dodging three air-to-air missiles, the unarmed Ravens fled south. Word never reached the Strike Eagles that they were going in alone.

Sam's Town greeted David Eberly and his colleagues with a chorus of warning tones. "Approaching the target area at twenty-one thousand feet and 580 knots, we became aware that surface-to-air radars were locked onto our aircraft," Eberly said. "For a split second I thought of the gunfight scene at the O.K. Corral."[4]

The nightmare at the Basra Oil Refinery had convinced the Strike Eagles to stay above AAA range, but higher altitudes meant exposure to radar-guided missiles. As the piercing tones grew more insistent, glowing orange dots appeared on the ground below. Each dot was an SA-2 or SA-3 missile launch.

Eberly and his backseater, Maj. Thomas Griffith, were third in line to drop their bombs. Griffith marked the target and they began their run. At nine miles out, Eberly glanced outside and spotted a reddish plume hurtling toward him. The missile did not drift or deviate but seemed frozen in place—tracking straight for him. "As it came closer I pulled the aircraft right to force the missile to overshoot, and then rolled back left to get the target symbol onto the heads-up display," he said.

They put the SAM out of their minds as soon as it sailed past. The slight detour had disrupted their bombing run, leaving just a few seconds to get back on target. They worked quickly, desperately hoping to get their bombs off and avoid the need for another pass. Neither Eberly nor Griffith saw the second missile that was tracking them. They saw only a blinding white flash. Eberly opened his eyes in a daze.

"Something was different in the cockpit," he said. "My eyes were drawn to the fire lights on the left side of the instrument panel. I struggled to focus." Years of aircraft emergency training sliced through his foggy thoughts, forcing a well-rehearsed response. "Instinctively, my hands were reaching to grip the ejection levers to the sides of my seat. There had been no fumbling around. I could feel the friction of the metal on metal as I raised and squeezed the levers."

CHAPTER 17

Search and Rescue

An orange glow shimmered in the distance. David Eberly watched it, transfixed, as his mind tried to catch up with reality. The thoughts came slowly. He was dreaming. No, this was real—he was on his knees with hard ground beneath him.

Perhaps he was outside his tent in Saudi Arabia. Maybe he had been sleepwalking to the latrine and stumbled. It was winter. The war had started. Had he been flying? He looked around and spotted an inflated life raft, then his parachute. He was holding a survival kit. This was Iraq. The distant orange glow was Al Qaim.

Eberly stood and walked to the parachute, which he didn't remember unbuckling. Its flowing nylon would stave off the cold. He knelt in the raft and swaddled himself, then peered up at the stars, feeling infinitely alone. A faint whir broke his reverie. As the sound grew louder, he recognized it as an engine, but not an aircraft engine. Headlights appeared, and he felt panic. A large structure loomed nearby—a power-line support tower. He hid behind its concrete base.

A truck stopped fifty yards away, and the driver got out and lit a cigarette. Eberly watched, afraid to breathe, certain his pounding heart would give him away. But after a few minutes, the man climbed into the truck and drove off in the same direction he had come. Eberly resolved to get as far from Al Qaim as his legs would take him, walking beneath the power lines for guidance.

As he listened to his boots scuffle the gravel and scrub brush, he debated calling for help on the survival radio. Any transmission would be picked up by the Iraqis, who could use it to triangulate his location. He thought of three older pilots he knew, and their dreadful POW experiences in Vietnam. Eberly felt he owed it to those guys to at least try. He took out the PRC-90 survival radio.

"Mayday, mayday, this is Corvette Three on Guard," he called, indicating the emergency frequency. "This is Corvette Three in the blind. How do you read?"[1]

No reply. He called a few more times, but still there was nothing. He kept walking and eventually stumbled across an ejection seat. It was empty, which he hoped meant Griffith was still alive. He called again, and this time got an answer. A familiar voice said: "Three Alpha, this is Bravo." It was Griffith. After a few more transmissions, they found each other. There were no celebrations—the situation was grave and both men knew it. They walked along in silence, the power lines stretching overhead, until the first hints of morning light. Then they crawled beneath some bushes, wrapped themselves in the parachute, and went to sleep.

Combat search and rescue (CSAR) evolved into an art during the Vietnam War, with rescue forces emerging as the most highly decorated group of airmen in that conflict. Air force and navy rescue aircrews plucked 778 downed fliers from hostile situations and whisked them away to safety. The rescue commitment was a point of pride and a moral imperative, but also a morale booster for combat pilots, who flew into dangerous missions knowing that someone would come looking for them, no matter the risk. And often, the risk was great. More than 100 rescue aircraft were shot down during the war, with 76 crewmen killed or captured.[2]

Occasionally the unwavering SAR commitment became a morass, with the rescuers needing to be rescued. An incident in April 1972 lasted eleven days and occurred in the midst of a major North Vietnamese offensive. Lieutenant Colonel Iceal Hambleton was the lone survivor from an EB-66 electronic warfare plane shot down while escorting a flight of B-52s. Hambleton, using call sign Bat 21, parachuted into a region overrun by North Vietnamese units. He evaded capture as a string of rescue attempts met with disaster. Ultimately, Hambleton was extracted by commandos, but not before five rescue aircraft were shot down, resulting in the deaths of eleven airmen and the capture of two more.

The Bat 21 incident triggered a painful examination of existing search-and-rescue protocol. CSAR crews accepted risk as part of the job, but sending them into hopelessly lethal situations seemed irresponsible. After Vietnam, the Pentagon concluded that a rescue mission needed at least a modest chance of success.

Additional changes took place during the 1970s and 1980s. CSAR training and equipment languished amid budget cuts and administrative reshufflings. By Desert Storm, the once razor-sharp attention to CSAR had dulled. David Eberly's antiquated PRC-90 survival radio transmitted on just two frequencies, giving any competent enemy a chance to home in on it, or draw rescuers into a trap with false signals. The vastly superior PRC-112 radio had yet to be purchased for all air force squadrons. Navy aviators, who received the PRC-112 on the eve of combat, found it didn't fit in their survival vest pockets.

Rescuing Eberly and Griffith would be a challenge. The other crews of Corvette flight did not see them go down, didn't know if they were alive, and could provide only a vague notion of where to look. At the Joint Rescue Coordination Center in Riyadh, staffers marked off a sprawling twenty-mile search area. Al Qaim was a hornet's nest. Slow-moving rescue helicopters would be easy prey, even during a pinpoint extraction. A plodding search was impossible.

Back at the F-15E squadrons, expectations were high. This generation of fighter pilots grew up hearing stories of miraculous rescues in Southeast Asia, and they anticipated the same for their war. Word arrived that an RC-135 Rivet Joint intelligence-gathering aircraft had intercepted Iraqi radio traffic about a manhunt near Al Qaim. The F-15E crews imagined their friends hiding out there, somewhere in the frigid desert, and hoped the CSAR guys would bring them home soon.

In daylight, Thomas Griffith could see a nasty cut on the back of Eberly's neck, so he tore a strip from the parachute as a bandage. Griffith then went through his pockets and realized he still had some mission-planning documents. He scratched a shallow hole and buried them, in case of capture. An empty road ran in the distance, and a hillock stood about a quarter of a mile away, which seemed safe and inviting. Its crest would offer a decent view of the surrounding area and, they hoped, better range on the survival radio. The sky was clear and the daytime temperature felt around forty degrees. They were hungry but a more pressing concern was water, since they only had about two pints.

"We stayed on that hill all day," Griffith remembered. "We watched trucks going down the road, but they all appeared to be commercial. After we were on the hill, we decided to sit tight, thinking that we would get rescued that night. We didn't think rescue assets would come looking for us during the day."[3]

Of the seven CSAR bases set up before the war, none were remotely close to the Corvette Three search area in west-central Iraq. The big MH-53 Pave Low helicopters—descendants of the Vietnam-era Jolly Green Giant—would need a C-130 tanker escort. Their safest route was through Syria, since Eberly and Griffith were thought to be within twenty miles of the Syrian border. Syria was a coalition partner, but the Americans would still need overflight permission. There was also talk of sending a ground team across the border to snatch the airmen.

Meanwhile, in Amman, Jordan, an Iraqi Bedouin walked into the U.S. Embassy claiming to know the whereabouts of downed American pilots. He offered his assistance in retrieving the aviators in exchange for a new Toyota pickup truck. Hours passed before the man was revealed as a fraud.

That afternoon, a flight of F-16s was skirting Sam's Town when the flight commander picked up a stray transmission: "This is Corvette Three. Does anybody read?" The commander was unaware of any other flights in the area. He had heard the Iraqis were making fake radio calls, exploiting the old PRC-90 survival radios. Earlier that day, someone in western Iraq was claiming to be Crest 45A, a bogus call sign. Regardless, he called AWACS.

"Hey, who is Corvette Three?"[4]

"Why? Did you hear something?" replied the AWACS operator.

He described the call, and the operator thanked him but furnished no answers.

Back at base, the F-16 commander went into the intelligence shop. "Who the [heck] is Corvette Three?" he demanded. They told him it was a downed Strike Eagle crew. He shipped his mission tape over to the F-15E squadron, and they immediately confirmed the voice as Eberly's.

Night fell, and with it the temperature. Eberly and Griffith sat bundled in the parachute, straining to hear approaching aircraft. They were famished now, and thirsty, but preserved their last precious drops of water. Suddenly, the Al Qaim defenses came alive, suggesting another attack was underway. Griffith pressed the transmit button.

"Allied aircraft in the wadi area, this is Corvette Zero-Three," he called.

An F-15E from their squadron was in the middle of a bomb run when the transmission came through. "It's Griff! It's Griff!" the pilot and weapons officer yelled. They finished dropping their ordnance and then switched over to the emergency frequency. "Corvette Zero-Three, this is Chevy Zero-Six," they replied. "Hang tight. We'll get somebody looking for you."

Despite the contact, the night slipped away without a rescue attempt. Syrian officials were still mulling the overflight request. At Al Kharj Air Base, frustration boiled upward from the F-15E crews all the way to the wing commander, who called Riyadh repeatedly demanding an attempt. Tired of excuses, he finally shouted into the telephone, "Is this incompetence or is it just sheer cowardice?"[5]

Eberly and Griffith began their second day on the hilltop with renewed hope. The PRC-90 radio was buzzing with chatter—several obviously American voices, all trying to coordinate a rescue. At last the CSAR guys were coming. Eberly kept calling, trying to get their attention, but they didn't answer. The voices just kept talking to one another. Minutes passed. Eberly kept on the radio, while Griffith scanned the horizon. The Pave Low helicopter had a big profile; you could see it coming from miles away.

Slowly, the truth dawned. A rescue mission was indeed underway, but it wasn't for them. It was for someone else.

* * *

U.S. Navy lieutenants Devon Jones and Larry Slade had been flying escort on a predawn airfield raid when their F-14 Tomcat was struck by an SA-2. The plane careened out of control and was in a flat spin when they ejected at 10,000 feet. They briefly saw each other's parachute before becoming separated in the clouds and darkness. The F-14's impact created a fireball, which both men steered away from, knowing it was the first place the Iraqis would look. They landed far apart and were unable to establish radio contact.

Pilot Devon Jones looked at the thick smoke plume climbing from the crash site. He wanted to head due west, away from the airfield. Jones remembered the winds had been blowing west, so he walked in the direction the smoke plume was drifting. Half an hour later the sun rose directly in front of him and he realized the winds had shifted. He was walking east, directly toward the airfield. He immediately began to backtrack.

Larry Slade, the radar intercept officer, had injured his back upon landing but he too started walking. The featureless desert offered no place to hide, and soon a pair of armed Bedouins came along in a battered white Datsun pickup. They ordered Slade into the truck and drove him to their tent, where they fed him a leisurely meal and then loaded him back into the pickup and asked where he wanted to go. Slade said Saudi Arabia, but after four hours they pulled up at an army camp outside Baghdad. Saddam's regime offered a handsome reward for captured fliers, and the Bedouins had planned on turning him in all along.

Devon Jones came to realize he shouldn't be traipsing around in broad daylight, but like Slade he couldn't find a hiding place. Finally, he dropped to his knees and started digging with his helmet, eventually excavating a hole about three feet deep. He collected some scrub brush for camouflage and settled into his makeshift bunker to wait out the day. Shortly before noon, he heard a vehicle and peeked over the lip to see two Iraqis a few hundred yards away. They appeared to be farmers drawing water from a cistern. Jones had mixed feelings about this latest development. The big blue water tank meant frequent visitors, but at least he knew he wouldn't die of thirst.

Once the farmers left he decided to try the radio again. He didn't expect any rescue contacts until nightfall, but he still had hope of raising Slade. After a few calls, a faint voice replied: "Slate Four-Six, how do you read?" Jones's heart raced. The voice wasn't Slade's but it was definitely American, and the speaker knew his call sign. Maybe they were coming for him in the daytime. Jones tried to relax and think clearly; he needed to go one step at a time.

The voice belonged to Capt. Paul Johnson, an A-10 pilot. Johnson and his wingman, Capt. Randy Goff, were flying search-and-rescue alert, keeping up the proud tradition of A-1 Skyraiders and A-7 Corsairs over Vietnam. Like those predecessors, A-10s flying CSAR duty used the classic "Sandy" call sign.

"Slate, this is Sandy Five-Seven," Johnson called. "How do you read?"[6]

"Sandy, this is Slate," Jones replied calmly. "Loud and clear."

Johnson needed to verify that he was speaking with the actual navy pilot and not some Iraqi impersonator. Authentication was standard procedure, but also Johnson had his doubts about this guy. He sounded too relaxed for someone who had just jumped from a burning airplane into enemy territory. AWACS passed along some personal questions that only Devon Jones could answer, and after a few correct responses Johnson felt satisfied he had the real Slate Four-Six. The next step was pinning down his location.

The Warthogs were equipped with radio direction finders, but Jones's signal was too weak for a fix. They tried flying farther west but the signal did not improve, nor did it strengthen when they went east. Then they turned north and the needle began moving. The search coordinates were off by sixty miles—Jones was nearly on the same latitude as Baghdad, in a wasteland far west of the city.

As Johnson drew closer, he began dropping flares. Jones spotted one and talked the Warthogs to his position. But almost as soon as the planes arrived, they had to turn around and depart. They had not expected to roam so far north.

"The last thing I wanted to do to a survivor was leave him, but I had to leave for fuel," Johnson explained. "If I had been Devon, I would have taken out my pistol and shot at me. But Devon said, 'Fine. Talk to you when you get back.' I thought he was a very calm fellow all day long. I don't know that he had much choice. He may have said some choice words after he left the radio."

With a solid fix now established, the CSAR operation went to full throttle. Two Pave Low helicopters thundered across the border at an altitude of fifteen feet. A pair of F-15C Eagles roared north to patrol the rescue area. Meanwhile, Paul Johnson and Randy Goff were running critically low on fuel and unlikely to reach the nearest tanker track over Saudi Arabia. A KC-10 Extender turned north to meet the Warthogs thirty miles inside Iraqi airspace. Johnson and Goff filled their tanks and raced to rendezvous with the Pave Lows. They flew a racetrack pattern over the helicopters for cover.

Obstacles lay in their path, such as the busy Baghdad-Amman Highway, which the formation crossed without incident. A known Roland SAM site also stood in the way, so AWACS vectored them around it. Whenever possible the helicopters flew low along dry creek beds, known as wadis. They established radio contact with Jones and then hovered in the distance while the Warthogs moved to clear the area.

"As the planes came in, everything seemed to be heading to a big crescendo," Jones recalled. "About half a mile down the south road, I spotted a truck, an army truck, with the canvas covers—a grunt truck. I think we all saw it at the same time because the A-10 called, 'We've got a fast mover on the dirt road.'"[7]

Johnson called, "Slate, confirm the truck is headed in your general direction."

"The truck is headed straight for me!" Jones replied.

Johnson had a decision to make. From the air, he couldn't be sure the truck was a threat—perhaps it was civilian. But it also might have been an Iraqi army vehicle, using direction-finding equipment to home in on Jones's signal.

"When Randy and I rolled in, I had little confidence that it was a military truck," Johnson later said. "Randy still believes it was not a military truck. He thought it was what we called a water truck, going out to supply animals, or farms, or homes. He thought it was some farmer who was lost. Devon is convinced beyond a shadow of a doubt that it was an Iraqi military truck."[8]

Despite their reservations, both Warthog pilots knew they needed to treat the vehicle as hostile. "Unfortunately, the truck was in the wrong place at the wrong time," Goff said. "We couldn't afford to have him be there."[9] They strafed the truck and it exploded. "To this day, I don't know if I killed one poor Iraqi farmer or fifteen grunts sitting in the back seat," Johnson acknowledged.

With the area clear, a Pave Low moved in. "That truck was down there burning," said Johnson, "orange flames and black smoke pouring out of it, and the helo comes in and lands. Then, just a hundred yards away from the burning truck, [Devon] jumps up out of his hole and runs to the helo."[10]

"One of the Special Forces guys jumped out and waved me on," Jones said. "I jumped in and off we went."

CHAPTER 18

Desperation

DAVID EBERLY AND THOMAS GRIFFITH REMAINED ON THEIR LONESOME hilltop, trying to figure out what to do. They had picked up transmissions from the Slate Forty-Six rescue and tried repeatedly to break into the conversation, but were too far away. Nobody heard them calling on their outdated PRC-90 radios.

Now they had a decision to make. It was cold and they had not eaten in two days. Syria beckoned to the west. Their choices were simple—either stay put and continue to await rescue, or try walking out of Iraq. They stared across the desolate, windswept landscape and discussed it.

"If we left right then, we were pretty strong, we had a little drinking water, and were fairly well hydrated," Griffith explained. "We figured that it was about five miles to the Syrian border, and another couple of miles to a town that was on our map. We figured we could make it in our present condition. However, we were fairly secure where we were, and if the helicopters came we would be in an easy place to find. The risk was that if we stayed on the hill and the helicopters didn't come in a day or two, we would be too weak to do anything."[1]

The mind-numbing waiting game held little appeal. So far it had yielded nothing but frustration. Walking offered some control over the situation, and at least it would keep them warm. They decided to go at nightfall. The afternoon was spent cutting the parachute into crude Bedouin robes for disguise. They stuffed the remnants into their flight suits for additional warmth. Then the low winter sun finally set, and they climbed down the hill and began walking.

Back at Al Kharj, the Strike Eagle crews were going crazy. They called Riyadh constantly for updates, and they offered to fly up to Sam's Town and pinpoint Eberly and Griffith's location. They were told to stay put, as F-15Cs were already flying combat air patrols in the area, trying to establish contact with Corvette Three. The Syrian government still had not responded to the overflight request. Some of Griffith's friends had not slept in thirty-six hours, and now they talked about getting into a Humvee and driving up there.

As Eberly and Griffith trudged through the darkness, they picked up the odor of farm animals and then spotted a small cluster of Bedouin tents. A pack of mangy dogs charged from the camp, snarling and circling, nipping at their legs. The airmen were sure someone would hear the racket and come to investigate, but no one did, and after a few minutes the dogs lost interest and wandered away.

Later in the evening their radio crackled to life. An F-15C, call sign Mobil Four-One, was trying to raise them.

"Go ahead," Griffith said hopefully.

"We are just trying to get hold of you to see if you're still around," said Mobil Four-One. "What is your physical condition?"[2]

"Physical condition is good. Alpha and Bravo are together. We are approximately ten miles northwest of [garbled]."

"Corvette Zero Three, we read you. We will be flying closer to get better radio contact."

"Do you understand our position?"

Suddenly an unidentified voice broke in, shouting: "SAR in effect! Get off of this frequency!" This third party was never identified, and the contact with Mobil Four-One was lost.

"At that point we didn't know what was going on, but we were ready to get the hell out of there," Griffith said. "We were tired and thirsty, and then this guy gets our hopes up. We took a break and as we were sitting there, we could see what looked like an abandoned building. We talked about it, and since we were getting desperate for water now, we start thinking that maybe somewhere close there would be a well where we could get some water."[3]

In survival school, the instructors always stressed the importance of avoiding buildings, even buildings that appeared empty. Both men eyed the run-down shack and knew to stay away, but they were hungry, thirsty, sleep-deprived, and shivering in the biting wind. They needed a break, and, hopefully, the shack was it. They crept ahead, alert for any sound or movement. Just as they were sure the building was vacant, it came to life. Automatic weapons fire sailed over their heads and kicked up sand at their feet. Ten men emerged pointing AK-47s and yelling commands in Arabic. The shack, it turned out, was an Iraqi border post.

The next morning and afternoon, patrolling aircraft reported no joy in raising Corvette Three. Pressure to launch a rescue mission now became unbearable, and the CSAR commanders reluctantly gave the green light for an attempt. Two Pave Lows and a C-130 tanker lifted off from Batman, Turkey. They lacked overflight clearance from Syria, but as they approached Syrian airspace, permission finally was granted. Their receivers warned that a Syrian SA-6 missile site was tracking them, but they ignored it.

The Pave Lows waited inside Syria, just one mile from the Iraqi border. Their plan was to enter Iraq while a coalition airstrike pounded Al Qaim. Theoretically, the strike would stir up enough chaos that nobody would notice a couple of low-level helicopters. The choppers flew figure-eights behind a slight rise in the earth, pacing like caged animals. The bombardment began, and with it the pulsing AAA barrage of Sam's Town.

The lead helicopter ascended 500 feet and began calling Corvette Three. Nobody answered, but immediately they saw a direct link between their transmissions and the antiaircraft fire. "I got on the radio and started trying all the different frequencies to contact him," the Pave Low co-pilot said. "Somewhere at that point, we realized that the SAR net was nothing more than a radio-controlled AAA, pilot-controlled AAA. We would key the mike and they would start firing."[4]

"We started to notice that the Iraqi AAA started to get real intense once we had talked on the radio," agreed the pilot of the second Pave Low. "Then the fighters joined in, trying to get them up on the radios. Corvette Zero-Three only had PRC-90s, and we knew as long as we were there and talking on the radio, the odds of the mission being compromised were greater. Bottom line is that we stayed down there for almost thirty minutes orbiting and calling on the radio. Never heard a word from Corvette Zero-Three. Then, reluctantly, without radio contact, we were done. We flew back to Turkey."

The chopper crews could not have known the futility of their search. By this time, Eberly and Griffith were already on their way to Baghdad prison cells. The missed opportunities to retrieve them disillusioned the aircrews who still grappled with Iraq's air defense network. "Before the war, the Special Operations guys came down to talk to us," a Strike Eagle pilot remembered. "'No sweat,' they said, 'we'll come and get you anywhere you are.' That, from my perspective, was a big lie. Nobody was going to come and get you."[5]

A few days later, the Pentagon received an urgent message from the air force director of operations in Riyadh. It was a request for hundreds of the modern PRC-112 survival radios.

* * *

The Third Marine Aircraft Wing continued to focus on targets in Kuwait and southeast Iraq. Two divisions of marines would be pushing into Kuwait once the ground war started, so the wing sought to soften Iraqi resistance with strikes by A-6E Intruders, AV-8B Harrier IIs, and F/A-18 Hornets.

Of these aircraft, only the AV-8B could claim a uniquely marine pedigree. The Intruder and Hornet were navy planes adapted for Marine Corps use, but no navy pilot flew the Harrier. A direct descendant of Britain's Hawker Siddeley Harrier jump jet, the AV-8B was a vertical/short takeoff and landing (V/STOL) aircraft. A collection of underside engine nozzles gave it the ability to take off and land in spaces normally reserved for helicopters, yet still reach a maximum speed approaching Mach 1.

Marine Corps interest in V/STOL dated all the way back to the 1960s, when a number of manufacturers experimented with jump jets. When considering airpower, marines naturally thought first of close air support. At the time the army was banking on helicopters for that job, but Marine Corps leaders wanted more. V/STOL promised an aircraft that could operate from crude forward bases like a helicopter, yet still bring significant speed and firepower into battle.

The original AV-8A, which made its marine debut in 1971, was a disappointment. It had a smaller payload and shorter range than the old A-4 Skyhawk, a holdover from the 1950s. Yet the corps refused to abandon its V/STOL dream. The plane underwent years of redesign and testing, resulting in the second-generation AV-8B, which finally arrived in 1985. The new Harrier had improved range and payload but still lagged behind conventional jets in both categories. The marines didn't care, for at last they had a serviceable V/STOL aircraft. Desert Storm offered a chance to prove its combat effectiveness, and eighty-six Harriers were deployed to the Gulf.

On January 28, Capt. Michael C. Berryman led a two-ship Harrier element into southern Kuwait. They were searching for some rocket launchers that had been harassing a marine outpost at the Saudi border town of Khafji. Mobile launchers were difficult to find, and Berryman and his wingman came up empty, but they did stumble across an Iraqi vehicle convoy moving along the coastal highway south of Kuwait City. They rolled in and attacked.

"Coming off target, I got hit with a surface-to-air missile," Berryman said. "The airplane started spinning end-over-end, and finally ended up upside down at about ten thousand feet. It started spinning down towards the ground."[6]

The Harrier fought all attempts at recovery, and Berryman realized an ejection might be in his immediate future. His thoughts turned to the Persian Gulf, shimmering about three miles away. If he could push the jet out over the water, he'd have a better chance of rescue. He struggled with the controls, trying to bring the Harrier out of its downward spiral. "At that time, I didn't know that the tail had been blown completely off the airplane," he said. "I started seeing the ground rushing up at me and I thought, 'Well, it's probably time to think about getting out.'"

Weeks earlier, he had told himself to forget about ejecting if he was hit. The prewar intel briefings featured grisly images of Kuwaiti resistance fighters who had been captured by the Iraqis. Some men had their ears cut off, or their noses, or had messages carved into their chests. Berryman looked at those photos and decided that instant death was preferable to slow torture. Just ride it in, he had told himself. But now, with the reality of death just seconds away, he felt differently: "I finally decided that I've got to give myself a chance to live through this, rather than dying with the airplane."

He pulled the ejection handle, but nothing happened. "I looked down to make sure I had, in fact, armed the seat. It was armed. About that time, the canopy exploded in place and I felt the cold air rush in. I watched my maps and stuff get sucked out, and I watched the rocket motor fire between my legs. The next thing I felt was this big jerk as the parachute opened above me."

The ejection's force disoriented him, but Berryman soon became aware of Iraqi soldiers shooting up at him as he drifted. Upon reaching the ground, he lay there, dazed, until the staccato of automatic weapons spurred him to action. He ran from the gunfire toward a sand dune, only to find an armored personnel carrier waiting on the other side. A dozen soldiers surrounded him.

"They started beating on me, and kicking me, and pulling off my flight gear," he said. "In my G-suit pockets I had kept three days of rations just in case something went wrong. When they found those survival rations, they just kind of backed away from me and started passing out the food amongst themselves."

Despite the beating he had just received, Berryman pitied the Iraqi soldiers. "These guys, they were starving, and you could tell they were a ragtag bunch," he said. "Of course, as soon as they got through eating all my food they jumped right back on me, and started kicking and beating me again, and I didn't feel sorry for them anymore."

He was taken to a bunker that appeared to be a company headquarters, where a medic bandaged cuts on his neck and face from the ejection. Berryman then began the lengthy process of being passed up through the Iraqi chain of command. He went to what he suspected was a battalion headquarters, followed by that of a regiment and then division, each time encountering officers of successively higher rank. By this point his questioners were more skilled and fluent, but he continued to resist.

"The interrogator started asking me some questions, and I was just giving him name, rank, and serial number, per the code of conduct," Berryman remembered. "He finally jumped up and said, 'Okay, Michael, you've just made a big mistake.' And he stormed out of the room. I was concerned then."

Two men entered the room and gave him a fierce beating, and then they took him outside, where a long row of soldiers waited. They pushed him through the gauntlet, letting soldiers strike and spit on him, and then tossed him into the back of a vehicle. They turned him over to the Republican Guard at Basra, where he endured worse interrogations and beatings. A guard shattered his left knee with a lead pipe. As he writhed on the ground, an interrogator said, "Michael, if you don't want them to break your other leg, you will start answering my questions."

He became more cooperative, furnishing information of little tactical value. Many of their questions were elementary, almost childlike. When they asked pertinent questions—such as his squadron's location—Berryman fabricated lies, and he was relieved to discover his interrogators rarely compared notes to find flaws in his story. They had great skill at inflicting physical pain, which they did frequently, but their mental tricks were less effective. They often put a pistol to his head, promising to pull the trigger if he didn't answer truthfully, but Berryman learned to recognize the threat as empty.

"Almost invariably, right before he put the pistol to your head, you'd hear a click, and you'd know that the click was the clip coming out of that pistol," he said. "The only thing you had to worry about was if he had been smart enough to take the round out of the chamber."

The interrogations became routine, an unwelcome but familiar part of POW life. Berryman eventually came to think of them as a game. He would answer some questions, refuse to answer others, endure a beating, and then offer up some lies before being dragged back to his cell. As an active player in the game, he felt he held some small bit of control. The knowledge that he wasn't totally helpless made him feel better. In his filthy cell, he passed the time with sleep or by thinking of food. He liked to plan elaborate meals he might someday enjoy.

The days blurred. At some point he was moved to a large city, probably Baghdad. He knew only hunger, pain, and boredom. One day a pair of guards opened his cell door and led him to the interrogation room for another round of the game. He played deftly, dealing out answers, lies, and silence like cards on a blackjack table. Then something unexpected happened. The guards removed his handcuffs. Each man grabbed an arm and splayed his hands on the table.

"The interrogator took out a knife, and he stuck this knife in the table, right between my fingers," Berryman remembered. "He said, 'Okay, Michael, I'm going to ask you five questions. For every question you don't answer, you're going to lose a finger.'"

A bolt of panic surged through him. He suddenly felt helpless. His tormentors were changing the rules of the game. Bruises would heal, bones would mend, but severed fingers were gone forever.

"I knew that no matter what I told him—whether it was true or not—he was going to start chopping off my fingers, just to prove that he had ultimate and complete control over me," Berryman said.

The panic tightened into a knot of sheer terror, gripping him so tightly he could not think. His mind went blank, leaving him unable to utter a single word, not even his own name. He sat there, frozen, unable to take his eyes from the blade.

"I just kept waiting for him to start cutting off one of my fingers," he said. "Finally, I think it dawned on him that I was so scared that I was of no use to him anymore."

The interrogator put the knife away and ordered the guards to return Berryman to his cell. But, he warned Berryman, they were not finished. In a few days the knife would return, and next time there would be no mercy.

CHAPTER 19

Bag of Tricks

SADDAM HUSSEIN HAD ASSUMED THE BOMBING CAMPAIGN WOULD BE brief. He anticipated three or four days of air attacks, mostly against his front-line conscripts, followed by the start of ground combat. He did not believe the coalition was capable of a sustained bombing operation that lasted weeks or even months, and he certainly didn't anticipate a precision campaign aimed at his communications and supply lines.

Saddam needed the ground war to begin soon so his troops could inflict large-scale casualties, which he felt certain would shatter the coalition's resolve. Americans and Europeans were unfamiliar with the grisly realities of ground war. As mangled bodies mounted, the populations of those countries would demand a negotiated peace. Saddam knew of America's antiwar movement during Vietnam—the massive demonstrations, the moral outrage, the civil disobedience—and counted on a similar reaction to this war.

Yet the coalition's ground troops remained completely inaccessible, ensconced in desert camps and ships at sea. Scud missile attacks were generating tremendous media attention but had yet to draw Israel into the conflict. Saddam needed the coalition to start feeling some discomfort.

The first set of POW "interviews" aired on Iraqi television on January 22, the sixth day of the war. Each battered and dazed airman sat before a stark white background as the video camera rolled. An off-camera interviewer asked pointed questions, leading the prisoner to condemn himself and his nation for perpetrating unwarranted attacks against "the peaceful people of Iraq." Also off camera, an armed guard stood ready to shoot. But Saddam's tactic backfired. The forced confessions from bruised and dirty faces only drew worldwide condemnation of Iraq and strengthened coalition resolve.

On the same day, Iraqi soldiers began dynamiting Kuwaiti oil wells. Most of the wells caught fire and spewed blazing columns 200 feet into the air, while others gushed noxious, obsidian lakes. Saddam's scorched-earth policy appeared to have military as well as political motive. His generals might have believed the greasy smoke plumes, some of which rose as high as 22,000 feet, would interfere with coalition air operations. The black clouds became a complication but never really hindered the campaign.

Weather was a different matter, and the daily pounding of Iraq would have been far worse if not for poor weather. Winter cloud cover in the Gulf was usually predictable, with two-day storm fronts followed by four or five days of clear skies. But this time the storms refused to depart, and the campaign's first week was a vexing hash of fog, wind, and low ceilings. Aircraft sat idle or returned with ordnance still beneath their wings, as thousands of sorties were scrubbed or aborted. During one two-day period, A-10 Warthog squadrons that had been scheduled for more than 400 sorties flew a grand total of 75.

On day eight of the campaign, the weather finally cleared, enabling coalition air bases and carriers to launch a full slate of strikes. The blue skies also permitted Saddam to reach into his bag of tricks.

Al-Kut Airfield
Southeast of Baghdad
January 24, 1991

Four F-1 Mirages departed the airfield and took a southeasterly heading toward Kuwait. After a week of heavy losses, the Iraqi air force had cut back on patrols significantly but still made a token effort. Many more sorties tried to avoid the enemy; they were a survival tactic to disperse planes across the country. The Mirage flight had another purpose altogether. These jets were going on the offensive, their handpicked pilots hoping to attain a small measure of revenge, and possibly trigger the start of the ground war.

Iraq's air force kept a small aerial refueling capability, and now two tankers came up to meet the Mirages near Tallil. The six aircraft flew in formation for a while and then began a leisurely turn toward Baghdad, suggesting to radar observers that their exercise was complete. The formation kept a careful distance from a U.S. Navy strike package, which had already dropped its bombs and was now egressing toward the Gulf.

Once the strike package was past, two Mirages abruptly broke from the formation and followed. But it was not a pursuit. The pair remained well behind and 10,000 feet below the navy jets.

During the past week, Iraqi analysts had studied American tactics and learned quite a bit. They knew that U.S. fighter-bombers used specific exit points when leaving Iraq, which permitted coalition radar operators to more readily monitor the heavy volume of traffic. Any plane not using one of the predefined egress points would receive extremely close scrutiny. Aircraft that followed the preapproved flight paths were not automatically presumed friendly, but neither would they stand out as hostile. The Mirages were trying to look like stragglers from the strike package, hoping to slip through the fighter screen unnoticed.

A radar operator aboard a U.S. Navy E-2C Hawkeye was the first to suspect trouble. He observed two jets at low altitude over Bubiyan Island, trailing a formation of carrier-bound jets. He could account for all the planes in the navy formation, but not the stragglers. He decided to check with the air force and see if anyone knew who these guys were.

Before the war, a digital link-up had been established between air force AWACS and navy Hawkeye planes, enabling them to share tracking data. On this particular day, however, the computer link was down, leaving the two services to hash out the issue with voice-only communications. Meanwhile, cruisers of the navy's defensive screen in the Persian Gulf also noticed the unidentified jets. Like the surveillance aircraft, they were concerned but not alarmed. With so many coalition planes in the air, an occasional snafu was to be expected.

Suddenly, the two jets snapped south and accelerated. Now the alarms sounded. Iraqi fighters were known to carry French-built Exocet antiship missiles, which they used deftly during the war with Iran, and in the USS

Stark incident of 1987. These two fighters were already well within Exocet range of several navy vessels. Those ships went to general quarters.

The Hawkeye summoned a flight of F/A-18 Hornets on patrol over Bubiyan Island. Minutes earlier the Hornets would have had an easy intercept, but now the Iraqis were far away, streaking south along the Saudi coastline with unknown intentions. Soon it became evident that the Hornets would not catch them. The Hawkeye crew asked their AWACS colleagues for assistance, but all available air force fighters were too far inland. The Mirages were speeding along a seam in the air force and navy zones of responsibility, like a line drive hit directly between two outfielders.

The coalition's daily Air Tasking Order always left the Saudis responsible for patrolling their own territory, including the coastline. American attitudes toward the Royal Saudi Air Force were mixed. Many Saudi pilots flew advanced U.S. aircraft. They received extensive training in the United States, and they performed well in joint exercises. But the Americans knew that royal politics permeated every element of Saudi society, including the military. Wealth and family connections mattered just as much as professional ability, which meant that some Saudi fighter pilots were merely playboy dilettantes. Right now, nobody else was in range.

AWACS vectored two pairs of Saudi F-15C Eagles toward the Mirages. The Eagles were coming from the west, while the Iraqis raced south—a difficult right-angle intercept. The first pair of Eagles missed the merge, and by the time they realized their error the Mirages were gone. The second pair also missed, but not as badly, and curled around in time to give pursuit. Captain Ayedh al-Shamrani and his wingman throttled forward and began reeling in the Iraqis. Fuel quickly became an issue, especially for the wingman, and after a few more minutes Al-Shamrani ordered him back to base. Before departing, the wingman took a potshot with an AIM-7 Sparrow, which fell harmlessly into the water.

The Iraqi pilots, now aware they were being pursued, punched off their fuel tanks and began jinking. Al-Shamrani stayed with them. He drew within the fringes of AIM-7 range and fired a Sparrow, but it too missed. His fuel state was critical but he continued the chase. This engagement was not about liberating Kuwait or cementing regional stability. His country was under attack and fate had placed him here, as the only pilot able to prevent it.

Al-Shamrani's last two missiles were AIM-9 Sidewinders. The heat-seekers had a shorter range than the radar-guided Sparrow. He waited, got a solid lock, and fired. The Sidewinder sped away and tracked for twelve seconds before reaching its target.

"Target destroyed!" he shouted into his headset. "The first target destroyed!"

He immediately locked up the second Mirage and fired again. Another white plume. Another explosion. "Splash! Target destroyed," he bellowed.

Al-Shamrani checked his position. The Iraqis had led him so far south he was near Dhahran. By now his F-15C was running on vapors so he made an emergency landing there.

At the time, intelligence analysts could only speculate about the purpose of Saddam's Mirage gambit, but during the ground war American troops would uncover mission documents at Tallil Air Base. The goal had been to strike vital Saudi oil complexes near Dhahran. Captain Al-Shamrani became a national hero. Embarrassed U.S. officials, meanwhile, tried to save face by implying that American fighters had been held back, permitting the Saudis some glory. In reality, a clever foe had nearly pulled off a cunning plan.

As for the Mirage pilots, they must have known it was a one-way mission. Even if successful, they had no fuel for a return leg.

❧

Taif Air Base, Saudi Arabia
January 26, 1991
1700 Local

Five F-111F Aardvark tactical bombers waited nearly twenty-four hours for the order to go. Their mission was urgent. The Aardvarks were tasked with halting Iraq's latest ploy: ecological warfare. Saddam was turning the Persian Gulf into a gigantic oil slick.

The tactic became apparent on the morning of January 25, when reconnaissance aircraft spotted a menacing black oval off the Kuwaiti port of Al Ahmadi. At first it appeared the Iraqis had emptied some tankers, which was bad enough, but then the true breadth of the problem emerged. The Kuwait Oil Company used a floating platform eight miles offshore for loading deep-draft supertankers. Underwater pipelines ran from the massive storage facilities at Al Ahmadi all the way out to the loading platform. Iraqi troops had opened these pipelines and turned on the pumping stations.

Two years earlier, in March 1989, the tanker *Exxon Valdez* spilled 260,000 barrels of crude in Alaska's Prince William Sound, an environmental disaster. Yet it paled in comparison to the nightmare now unfolding in the Gulf. The open pipelines were creating an *Exxon Valdez* spill every few hours. Saddam had political and military motives. Seventeen thousand U.S. Marines waited offshore, ready to make an amphibious landing. He hoped the thick sludge, combined with vast naval minefields, might be enough to deter the invasion. The oil spill might also create a water crisis by clogging Saudi desalinization plants, and at the very least it would be one more bargaining chip in any peace negotiations.

In Riyadh, exiled Kuwaiti engineers furnished blueprints of the Al Ahmadi facilities. Two pumping stations, nestled among sprawling tank farms, pushed oil out to the loading platform. Without those pumps the flow would slow to a trickle. Buster Glosson and his Black Hole team sketched a plan to destroy the pump houses with laser-guided bombs. Heavy coastal defenses meant the bombers would use "buddy lasing" to guide their weapons on target. As one Aardvark negotiated the ground fire to get close enough for bomb release, a second plane stayed safely away and steered the bomb to the pump house. The plan called for four ships; they would take a fifth as a spare.

By late evening on January 25, the F-111 crews were ready to roll, but a last-minute hold came from Riyadh. Kuwaiti government officials were worried about collateral damage. Al Ahmadi was the heart of the petroleum industry, with key infrastructure and thousands of workers. Precious hours lapsed while the Kuwaitis were reassured, and then low clouds settled over Al Ahmadi, forcing another delay. Meanwhile, the oil flowed.

The jets finally departed at nightfall on January 26 and headed northeast for the Gulf. One Aardvark had a warning light, forcing a return to

Taif, and the spare took its place. The F-111 was an old warbird, originating under the Kennedy administration. This would be her final conflict, but in the coming weeks she would prove invaluable.

In 1961, Kennedy recruited Robert S. McNamara, a studious auto industry executive with slicked hair and wire-rimmed glasses, as his defense secretary. The young president thought the Pentagon could benefit from McNamara's statistical methods and devotion to efficiency. Many McNamara initiatives made sense. The intelligence-gathering efforts of the army, navy, and air force frequently overlapped, so he merged them into a single agency, saving time and money. He pushed the air force to adopt the navy's brand-new fighter, the F-4 Phantom, which became a Vietnam workhorse. Other ideas, such as convincing all the branches to wear the same uniform, failed miserably.

His F-111 project, also known as McNamara's Folly, began when the air force was seeking an all-weather tactical striker and the navy needed a Mach 2 fleet defender. McNamara wanted a plane they both could use, but their design requirements were far too dissimilar. After years of compromise and bickering, the navy managed to extricate itself from the project and instead pursued the F-14 Tomcat, a plane that would borrow several F-111 innovations, including variable-geometry "swing" wings.

The air force Aardvarks now hurtling toward Kuwait bore hints of their navy parentage. Pilot and weapons officer sat side by side, sharing some controls and displays, like in the navy's A-6 Intruder. They did not have ejection seats, as the air force would have preferred. Instead, the entire cockpit was a self-contained escape capsule, which rocketed away from the rest of the aircraft and parachuted to safety. The capsule offered protection in heavy seas, but it made for some bone-jarring ground landings. The air force overlooked these quirks in light of the Aardvark's excellent performance, and it became one of the earliest platforms for laser-guided munitions.

The skies over Al Ahmadi were clear now, offering unlimited visibility as they set up their attack. The Three and Four ships darted for the beach, while One and Two paralleled the coastline. As planned, Three released its bomb at 15,000 feet and then peeled away to avoid the thickening AAA. The weapons officer of One began guiding the falling GBU-15, but after a few seconds it stopped obeying his commands. This bomb had gone "stupid," so they'd need to make another attempt.

"I've got it! I've got it!" a voice suddenly called over the radio. Captain Bradley Seipel, the weapons officer of the other "buddy" Aardvark, had established a data link with the GBU-15 and could see the grainy, black-and-white video from its nose camera.

"I think I've got the pump house," Seipel announced, nudging his joystick to center the squat little building in his screen. His data link was tenuous, making the video skip and jump. "It's intermittent, but I've got it," he said. As the pump house grew larger on the screen, he struggled to keep it centered. "Okay, I've got the target. A little to the right. Come on!"[1]

The GBU-15 smashed through the roof and detonated, obliterating the little building. Next Seipel turned his attention to the bomb coming off Four. The remaining pump house was three miles distant, hiding among storage tanks and service buildings.

"I've got the general target area," he reported. "I've got the tank farm." The data link for this bomb was strong, with crisp video and rapid response to his joystick commands. "Is that the building? Yep, I've got the target." He placed the pump house in his crosshairs, making slight adjustments while it slowly filled his screen. "Looking good," he said as the bomb reached its terminal phase. "Looking sweet. Come on, baby!"

His screen went white as the second pump house disintegrated.

Crude oil would continue to dribble into the Gulf, but an environmental disaster had been averted. After the war, the Aardvark crews learned they had some help on the ground from resourceful Kuwaiti workers. During the chaos of the attack, the Kuwaitis scurried about the tank farm, shutting off valves to individual tanks. The Iraqis never noticed.

CHAPTER 20

Taking Shelter

IRAQ HAD NEARLY 600 HARDENED AIRCRAFT SHELTERS AT BASES AND airfields across the country. The steel-and-reinforced-concrete hangars varied in age and design, but most offered ample protection for two to six fighters. After a disastrous first week, the Iraqi air force decided to stay on the ground, tucking its jets into the hardened shelters and sliding the blast doors closed. The coalition needed to penetrate these vaults and destroy the treasure they held.

Prewar experiments in the New Mexico desert suggested a near-miss might be more effective than a direct hit. The near-miss concussion would buckle the shelter's floor, potentially damaging aircraft from below. Chuck Horner and Buster Glosson dismissed the idea as inadequate. They wanted to give Saddam's fighters a knockout punch, not a glancing blow, which meant cracking open the shelters. But with forty-ton armored doors and a three-foot concrete shell, each trapezoidal bunker seemed impervious. The coalition's first few shelter-busting missions left only blackened pockmarks.

Subsequent attempts revealed that a 2,000-pound bomb outfitted with a delay fuse usually penetrated the shell, but only if it struck at a right angle. The blast chiseled a neat little hole, through which a follow-up bomb could be tossed to destroy the shelter's contents. This technique required laser-guided precision, meaning F-111 Aardvarks and F-117 Nighthawks. Later, a few F-15E Strike Eagles and Royal Air Force planes joined the effort.

Bomb damage assessment was tricky. The structure's thick shell typically held the blast, giving few hints of the destruction inside. A few pilots observed their shelter burst apart at the seams, or saw its gigantic steel doors fly off, but usually they had to rely on subtler clues. Pilots learned to watch the original impact hole for a fiery geyser, which they called "smoodge." A shelter bellowing smoodge almost certainly had been converted into a blast furnace.

When squadron intelligence officers viewed a mission tape and saw smoodge, they counted the shelter as destroyed, and so did the TACC staff in Riyadh. But Washington's intelligence agencies had no access to mission tapes, only satellite reconnaissance photos, which were usually taken hours or days after the attack. Intelligence analysts studied the satellite photos and saw an intact structure with a tiny hole in the roof. They considered the shelter operational and urged Riyadh to hit it again.

The agencies would not be swayed by claims of smoodge or any other explanations. During Vietnam, grossly inflated progress reports had misled government decision-makers and the American public. There would be no exaggerated results in this war, they vowed. Without solid proof of a kill, it didn't happen.

For Aardvark crews in Taif and Nighthawk pilots in Khamis Mushait, frustration mounted as previously struck shelters kept showing up on the Air Tasking Order. They had always accepted combat's risks as part of the job, but now they were being asked to take those risks to re-bomb dead targets. It was discouraging and wasteful, and soon, quietly, they developed a work-around.

"We'd call [Taif] up and both of us would go carefully over the same map of the airfields," said one F-117 pilot. "We would put an X on the bunkers they'd already hit, and they'd put an X on the ones we'd taken out. So, when the [Air Tasking Order] came down and they wanted us to hit a shelter or bunker that had already been marked, we would change the target and go after one we knew was still intact."[1]

The Iraqis soon realized that their decades-long investment in hardened shelters wasn't paying off. Cramming fighters inside them merely aided the coalition, since two laser-guided bombs were enough to destroy up to half a dozen jets. If the Iraqi air force was going to survive this conflict, only one option remained—fleeing the war zone.

On the morning of January 26, the first Iraqi warplanes departed for Iran. Before the war, Saddam had arranged for Iran to give his aircraft safe harbor. In exchange he returned all remaining POWs and territory captured during their eight-year war. By the end of the day, twenty-seven Iraqi planes were in Iranian territory.

The exodus caught Riyadh by surprise. Nobody had anticipated Iraqi MiGs and Mirages dashing east for Iran. The Iranian government pledged that all incoming aircraft would be detained until hostilities ended, but the coalition was wary. If Iran permitted Iraqi pilots to launch strikes from within its borders, warships in the Persian Gulf would have ninety seconds to respond. Chuck Horner and Buster Glosson decided the best approach was to knock down any planes seeking escape, and they established special combat air patrols—MiGCAPs—for that purpose.

~•~

Saudi Arabian Airspace
Near the Jordanian Border
January 26, 1991

The four F-15C Eagles of Chevron flight were in the air for ninety minutes and just back from their first refueling when AWACS spotted a flight of bandits leaving H-2 air base. The Eagles were guarding the lumbering E-3 Sentry, but by this point in the war it was only a formality, so when Chevron flight asked permission to pursue, the AWACS commander gave his blessing. Flight lead captain Rhory Draeger led them into Iraq at Mach 1.

Draeger's wingman, Capt. Tony Schiavi, thought they were chasing a long shot. The bandits were more than 100 miles away, probably heading for a base closer to Iran, where they could stage a sprint across the border. Chevron flight would hit bingo fuel long before catching them. Still, the young wingman admired Draeger's aggressive attitude. They roared northeast in pursuit.

"We close it to about eighty miles, and we're probably just about at the point where we need to turn back," Schiavi said. "Getting too far up there, into an area where they have ground threats. So right at this point, just as we're saying, 'We're not going to be able to get these guys,' four more take off right behind them from H-2."[2]

The arrival of four more bandits on the scene gave them pause. Chevron flight wondered if the new jets were coming up to engage them, or if the Iraqis might be running some sort of a trap. Schiavi imagined the first group of Iraqis snapping back around, trying to box the Eagles between two hostile elements. But those concerns faded as the first group continued northeast until they fell off the radar. Now their focus shifted entirely to the second group, which followed the same heading. An RC-135 Rivet Joint electronic intelligence aircraft reported that the four Iraqi planes speeding along the desert floor appeared to be MiG-23 Floggers.

One MiG suddenly doubled back and landed at H-2, apparently with technical issues. The three remaining Floggers slid into a standard V formation and continued their journey, oblivious to the Americans racing up from the south.

"We're coming in about thirty miles from the merge," Schiavi explained. "We punch our wing tanks off, but keep the centerline tank on. Okay, so we have better maneuverability now if we get in an engagement in this thing. If our missiles don't work or whatever, we'll be able to turn more tightly without those tanks."

Draeger handed out the target assignments. He would take the lead MiG, while Schiavi would fire on the northernmost plane, and Chevron Three and Four both targeted the southern one. Draeger cautioned everyone against making a preliminary missile lock. This was shaping up as a textbook beyond-visual-range engagement, and they didn't want to alert the Iraqis. The Eagles were within twenty miles, descending rapidly. A low cloud deck obscured the ground. Once their missiles vanished into those clouds, they'd be unable to see the results. Draeger watched as everyone moved into firing position.

"Okay, heads up, Four. Watch out so you don't shoot through me," he warned.

"Fifteen miles," Schiavi called. They were close enough for AIM-7 Sparrows.

"Fox! Fox from One," called Draeger, as his Sparrow left the rail.

"Fox from Two," Schiavi announced a few seconds later.

Chevron Three and Four also fired. Schiavi had doubts about his first missile so he launched another. Three did the same. A hole opened in the clouds, and for the first time they could see their targets. The MiGs wore a desert-camouflage paint scheme. They still flew in V formation at less than 1,000 feet above a highway. The Iraqi pilots were trying to stay below radar, and likely using the road for navigation.

"Captain Draeger's missile hits his man," Schiavi remembered. "Hits him right in the back—the old Flogger running across the ground there—and he's flying so low you can see the dust kick up around it. He calls 'Splash,' but then he looks again. The airplane flies right through the fireball and comes out the other side. It hit him but didn't just knock him out of the sky. He's burning but not down. Captain Draeger goes to a heater [AIM-9 Sidewinder] to put some heat on this big fire. But before he can do this, the fire reaches the wing root and it suddenly explodes in a huge fireball."

The trailing MiGs broke hard right, but it was too late. They exploded in quick succession. Three black clouds hung over the highway.

* * *

In the coming weeks, F-15C Eagles would pick up more kills, mostly while flying MiGCAP along the Iran-Iraq border. But guarding the entire 900-mile boundary proved impossible, and for the rest of the war small flights of fast-moving aircraft slipped past. Saddam had at last found a way to shelter his warplanes from coalition attacks, with an estimated 130 planes escaping to Iran.

Ultimately, the ploy backfired. Iranian anger still simmered from the eight-year conflict with Iraq, a war which Saddam had started and then prosecuted with singular cruelty. Iran would keep his aircraft as war reparations, folding them into its own air force.

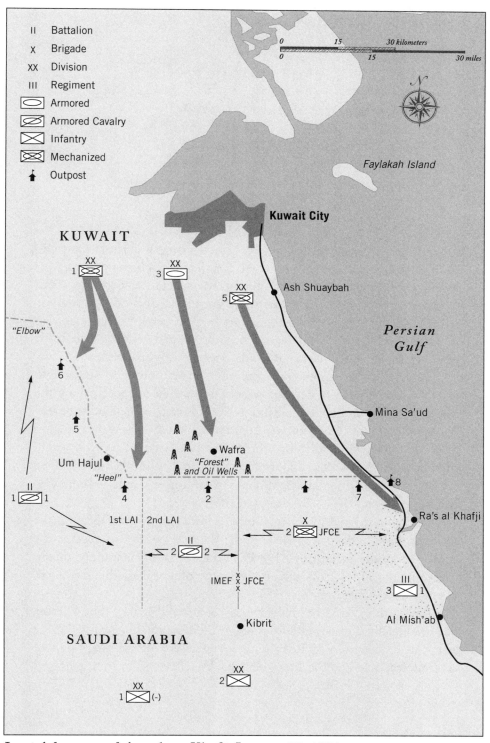

Legend:

- II — Battalion
- X — Brigade
- XX — Division
- III — Regiment
- Armored
- Armored Cavalry
- Infantry
- Mechanized
- Outpost

KUWAIT

Kuwait City

Ash Shuaybah

Faylakah Island

Persian Gulf

Mina Sa'ud

"Elbow"

6

5

Um Hajul

"Heel"

"Forest"
and Oil Wells

Wafra

7

8

Ra's al Khafji

1 [II] 1

4

2

1st LAI | 2nd LAI

2 [II] 2

2 [X] JFCE

3 [III] 1

IMEF x JFCE

Al Mish'ab

Kibrit

SAUDI ARABIA

1 [XX] (-)

2 [XX]

Iraqi Advance and Attack on Khafji, January 29, 1991

CHAPTER 21

Khafji

ON THE EARLY MORNING OF JANUARY 27, A LINE OF VEHICLES SNAKED from Baghdad and drove south for Basra. Saddam Hussein was traveling to a meeting with his corps commanders. Iraqi strategy was about to change, induced to a new course by ten brutal days of coalition airstrikes and the threat of more to come. Iraq's starving legions could no longer wait behind their defenses as airpower sapped their strength. If the ground war didn't begin soon, it would not be much of a contest.

Saddam's field commanders proposed a multipronged attack into coastal Saudi Arabia. A mechanized division would roll south along the coastal highway and seize the Saudi town of Khafji, while a wave of seaborne commandos came ashore south of town and disrupted the coalition response. Meanwhile, thirty-five miles west, an armored division would rumble across the border, supported and screened by another mechanized division. After stirring sufficient chaos, these forces would withdraw to Kuwait and await the coalition counterattack.

Saddam approved the plan and then climbed into his vehicle for the six-hour drive back to Baghdad. Along the way two F-16s spotted the convoy and rolled in, destroying several vehicles. Saddam's was not among them, and the Viper pilots remained unaware of how close they'd come to eliminating the dictator.

The death of Saddam Hussein was not a stated goal of the coalition, but unofficially it was highly desired. American intelligence-gathering assets, including RC-135 Rivet Joint aircraft, were intercepting far more communications than the Iraqis realized. Whenever solid leads emerged of his whereabouts, planes hit the location. But years of paranoia made Saddam a constantly moving target, and he always departed before the bombs arrived. Riyadh stayed vigilant. In the unlikely event Saddam took to the air, F-15Cs would be issued the coded command "Horner's Buster," which meant they needed to shoot down the target at all costs, even if it meant running out of fuel and bailing.

Marine Observation Post Four
January 29, 1991
1926 Local

Coalition ground forces were camped well south of the Kuwait border, safely beyond the reach of Iraqi artillery. Khafji's 15,000 residents had been evacuated for the same reason, leaving the border town to marine reconnaissance teams. More marines occupied a string of decrepit border outposts once used by Saudi police to deter smugglers. The recon teams were an early warning network, a trip wire in case of attack.

The sand-crusted marines had observed a surge in Iraqi activity during the past forty-eight hours. Just the previous night, they glimpsed distant columns of Iraqi tanks and armored personnel carriers near the border. They called in artillery and airstrikes, and cheered the orange splashes of flame from exploding vehicles. The marines didn't know they had caught the vanguard of an invasion force as it crept into position.

Other warning signs existed, including a report of more than a dozen large amphibious vessels staging in a Kuwait City port. At the time, the clues of impending battle were lost in a sea of intelligence data. Iraqi units were always on the move, shuffling positions to strengthen their defenses and confuse the spy satellites. The landing craft seemed like just another deception, when in fact they were being loaded with commandos.

Marine Observation Post Four (OP-4) sat at a sharp angle in the Saudi-Kuwait border, where the boundary ceased its meandering and instead made a beeline for the coast. Now, in the green hue of night vision, the OP-4 marines spotted an armored vehicle coming straight toward them. Then they saw another. Soon the green horizon was filled with boxy shapes. A young lieutenant leapt to his radio and called it in, but nobody heard—the Iraqis were jamming the frequencies.

The other outposts were also under siege, and one managed to get a message to the rear. Marine vehicles and aircraft scrambled to respond, but the size of the Iraqi offensive was alarming. At least fifty armored vehicles advanced on OP-4 alone. The recon team managed to hit a T-55 tank that had drawn within 300 yards, but clearly OP-4 would not last much longer. A flight of Harriers streaked overhead, releasing Rockeye antitank cluster bombs. The team had just enough cover to reach their Humvees and slip away.

Marine light armored vehicles arrived with TOW (Tube-launched, Optically tracked, Wire-guided) missiles, bringing the battle to full pitch. In the frantic whirl of shadows and flame, a marine gunner mistook one of his own vehicles for an Iraqi T-55, firing a TOW that shredded its target and instantly killed four men. Fratricide was frighteningly difficult to avoid in a nighttime tank engagement, and from overhead the battlefield looked even more jumbled. A flight of hastily diverted A-10s was about to take on the challenge.

Ruggedly simple Warthogs lacked night vision, but during the Desert Shield buildup some A-10 squadrons trained specifically for night sorties. They climbed into dark Saudi skies, releasing flares to strafe targets by the flickering light. Hog drivers also made creative use of the infrared AGM-65 Maverick missile, which had a four-inch targeting monitor. This grainy little video feed had a narrow field of vision—pilots compared it to viewing the world through a soda straw. But the Night Hogs, as they had begun calling themselves, mastered the technique of finding targets through it and flew successful night missions against front-line Iraqi armor and artillery.

When the A-10s arrived over OP-4, they saw shadowy knots of vehicles intermingled with glowing tracer streams. Distinguishing friend from foe was impossible. The marines helped, pointing out high-priority targets with concentrated machine-gun fire, and twice the Night Hogs identified an Iraqi tank bathed in tracers and sparks. They rolled in and disabled them, then popped off some flares and asked the marine air controllers to identify more targets.

The controllers sent one of the jets after a maneuvering T-55, which the pilot quickly located on his little green targeting screen, just like in training. On infrared, the tank's hot engine glowed white, giving the Maverick a solid lock. Everything was working precisely as intended. He punched the pickle button and the Maverick leapt away on a course for the Iraqi tank engine.

Milliseconds later, the missile went "stupid." An electronic malfunction caused the onboard tracking system to lose its target lock. The Maverick plunged for the ground, until its infrared seeker acquired a new heat source—a marine vehicle. It crashed through the roof, killing seven and injuring two.

The death toll now stood at eleven, all victims of friendly fire.

* * *

The fighting that raged around the desert outposts stood in stark contrast to the invasion's eastern thrust, where Iraqi tanks and armored personnel carriers rolled down the coastal highway virtually unopposed. Not long after midnight on January 30, they rumbled to a halt at their objective, the Saudi town of Khafji.

The Iraqis surveyed the empty streets and assumed they were alone, unaware that two six-man marine reconnaissance teams crouched on rooftop perches. The recon teams had passed up an opportunity to withdraw to safety, staying behind to direct coalition air and artillery. Now, as Iraqi soldiers conducted a house-to-house search, the marines hoped they would overlook the rooftops, which they did.

At sea, fifteen boatloads of Iraqi commandos ran into trouble almost as soon as they left port. The commandos had planned to come ashore south of Khafji and disrupt any counterattack, but British warships spotted them and sent Lynx helicopters to investigate. The helicopters attacked with missiles, rockets, and machine guns, sinking more than half of the landing craft and forcing the rest back to shore.

In Riyadh, Buster Glosson was working the night shift. He and Chuck Horner always covered for each other, overseeing the air campaign while the other slept. Glosson was in his office, meeting with a Saudi air commander, when news of the incursion reached him. He rushed downstairs to the TACC, where the staff seemed paralyzed by confusion. They had grown accustomed to the campaign's clockwork efficiency but now, for the first time, the coalition was on the defensive. Glosson woke Horner and together they rallied the staff and organized a response, rerouting aircraft from across the theater.

A key to halting the invasion would be J-STARS. The E-8 Joint Surveillance Target Attack Radar System was brand-new technology, rushed to Saudi Arabia just in time for the war. Only two J-STARS prototypes existed, and Operation Desert Storm permitted the modified Boeing 707s to skip further testing and go straight into a combat environment. As the name suggested, J-STARS was a joint project of the air force and army. Its purpose was to give ground commanders a sweeping view of the battlefield, as AWACS did for air generals. The plane's belly bulged with an enormous side-looking radar, capable of finding moving and stationary targets as small as an individual vehicle. The J-STARS software was so new and sophisticated that manufacturer Grumman sent a team of civilian experts into the war zone to maintain it.

Until now, J-STARS spent most of its time searching western Iraq for Scud launchers. As the big plane swung east and scanned the Khafji area, a vivid map of the invasion appeared. Iraqi columns flowed south along a forty-mile front. Horner recognized it as precisely the scenario he had fretted about back in August, when Schwarzkopf left him in charge of Saudi Arabia's defense. He realized the Iraqi offensive was not a crisis, but an extraordinary opportunity. Hundreds of armored vehicles had crawled from their revetments and were on the move. Without air cover, they were fully exposed to attack.

Soon so many planes were stacked up over Khafji that pilots worried about a midair collision. Harriers and Night Hogs were joined by F-16s, F/A-18s, and A-6 Intruders. J-STARS furnished targeting details, while AWACS and EC-130E Airborne Battlefield Command and Control Center (ABCCC) aircraft orchestrated the attacks. Air controllers on the ground and in two-seat marine F/A-18Ds guided the jets to individual targets.

Marine AH-1W Cobra helicopter gunships skimmed the desert, popping up to unleash a TOW missile or burst of 20mm cannon fire, before vanishing behind the dunes. High above, waves of B-52s swept toward Iraqi staging areas in southern Kuwait. Within the first twenty-four hours, Saddam's forces lost approximately sixty vehicles. Before the three-day battle ended, the number would approach 300.

Saudi Coastal Airspace
January 31, 1991
0530 Local

Ground troops cherished low-flying mudfighters like the Cobra heli-copter and A-10 Warthog, but one aircraft held their highest esteem. When in contact with enemy forces, nothing sounded better than the deep propeller-drone of an AC-130 Spectre gunship. The Spectre's precision firepower instantly solved most problems on the ground. Horner told Special Operations Command to get some AC-130s to Khafji.

Spectres were a highly modified version of the C-130 Hercules transport, perhaps the most versatile aircraft in military history. Since the 1950s more than thirty C-130 variants entered service. Aside from its primary mission of tactical airlift, the four-turboprop C-130 filled such diverse roles as airborne assault, search and rescue, and scientific research.

The idea of arming a cargo plane for combat dated back to the AC-47 Spooky, which prowled the skies of Southeast Asia, hosing down enemy positions with machine-gun fire. Spooky's success led to the rapid development of a weaponized C-130, which offered longer loiter time and more firepower. During the war's final years, Spectre gunships protected firebases and ravaged convoys along the Ho Chi Minh Trail. As ground commanders became aware of the gunship's precision, they called for ever-closer fire support, occasionally summoning a steel blizzard within their own perimeter.

An extreme vulnerability to ground fire limited the AC-130 to night duty. Escort aircraft tried to compensate by suppressing nearby AAA and SAM batteries, but the big, sluggish plane still proved susceptible. In 1972 alone, four Spectres were lost to ground fire. The gunship was a powerful weapon, but, clearly, it needed to be used judiciously. During the first two weeks of Desert Storm, Air Force Special Operations Command worried that Riyadh was overextending the Spectres, sending them into high-threat environments in southern Iraq. On one mission, an AC-130 pilot trying to evade a SAM executed a turn so sharply it damaged the airframe.

When the call came for AC-130 support at Khafji, Special Operations Command set up a three-ship rotation over the battle zone, maintaining constant coverage during the nighttime hours. Spectres joined the swirling vortex of planes and helicopters hammering away at southbound Iraqi columns. They kept a safe distance, operating over coastal waters, where the threat of return fire was minimal.

As dawn approached on January 31, the final Spectre of the night, call sign Spirit Zero-Three, neared the end of its shift. On the plane's port side, an array of heavy machine guns and 105mm cannon blazed as the crew of five officers and nine enlisted men responded to requests for air support.

By now it was becoming obvious to both sides that the Iraqi incursion had failed. American airpower pounced on reinforcements, leaving long trails of charred wreckage. The previous night the commander of Iraq's III Corps, Major General Mahmoud, radioed Baghdad for permission to withdraw. His request was denied. Mahmoud was reminded that he was fighting the "Mother of All Battles." During the overnight hours he twice repeated his request, and twice received the same reply. "The mother is killing her children!" he finally exclaimed, but his orders did not change.

By 0600, the night sky was turning cobalt with hints of the new day, and Special Operations Command inquired about the status of its last engaged Spectre. At 0619, an AWACS operator instructed Spirit Zero-Three to depart the area and head for home. But the plane lingered. Marines north of Khafji wanted an Iraqi rocket launcher destroyed, and the crew wished to honor this last request before calling it a night.

At 0623, the AWACS operator repeated his instructions to return to base. Daybreak loomed.

"Roger, roger," replied the copilot.

Two weeks of stellar success had a psychological impact on some aircrews. Combat was becoming familiar, its inherent danger less obvious.

Spirit Zero-Three should have departed the area immediately when ordered. A touch of overconfidence, and an intense desire to assist the marines, kept the plane in harm's way as the sky brightened.

Somewhere on the beach north of Khafji, an Iraqi soldier stood with a shoulder-fired missile, most likely a heat-seeking SA-7 Grail. In the morning twilight he glimpsed a ghostly silhouette over the water, about a mile offshore. Man-portable air-defense systems (MANPADS) like the SA-7 had limited range, making them useful only against helicopters and other low-flying targets. The large aircraft he spied was well within reach. He lifted the thirty-five-pound weapon to his shoulder.

Less than a minute after hearing the copilot's last reply, the AWACS operator picked up another transmission. "Mayday, mayday," a faint voice cried.

The missile's impact sheared off the port wing, sending the AC-130 into a death spiral. The stricken plane burrowed into the muddy shallows, instantly killing all fourteen aboard. It was the worst single loss of the air war.[1]

Khafji would fall later in the day, bringing an end to Saddam's grand offensive.

CHAPTER 22

Preparing the Battlefield

RIYADH ONCE AGAIN CONTROLLED THE PACE OF THE WAR. THERE WOULD be no more ground fighting until coalition airpower had sufficiently "prepared the battlefield," which Norman Schwarzkopf defined as a 50 percent reduction in Iraqi forces. The strategic air campaign entered a new phase, with special emphasis on troops in the field and their supply routes.

The U.S. military had come a long way since Vietnam, when the services missed precious opportunities to work together for better results. Yet it was hardly the smoothly integrated "joint" force that Congress wished to create with the Goldwater-Nichols Department of Defense Reorganization Act of 1986. Interservice rivalry and distrust always simmered near the surface, and the war's latest phase triggered an eruption.

Ground commanders complained that the promises of battlefield preparation were going unfulfilled. Saddam's front-line defenses, which stretched across southern Kuwait and continued west into Iraq, remained virtually untouched. Air planners replied that more than 600 sorties per day were hitting the Iraqi army. They explained that many strikes were far from view, in the reserve areas where Saddam held his elite Republican Guard divisions. The commanders remained unimpressed. When the ground war kicked off, they would be facing front-line troops, not reserves.

To resolve the controversy Schwarzkopf placed his deputy, U.S. Army lieutenant general Calvin Waller, in charge of a target-selection committee. Top ground commanders nominated the front-line Iraqi targets they wished to see destroyed, and then Waller worked with Buster Glosson to make it happen. The committee annoyed Glosson, who thought it a shortsighted distraction from the campaign's broader objectives, but he dutifully added nominated targets to the daily Air Tasking Order.

Glosson had a bigger worry these days. Airstrikes were having a minimal impact on Iraqi armor, especially the dug-in tanks of the Republican Guard. Many Guard tanks were buried in sand up to their turrets. If Glosson didn't find a way to ferret them out, Schwarzkopf's goal of 50 percent attrition would never be met.

During the last week of January, he began thinking about the seven Warthog squadrons stationed at Dhahran. The idea of all those rugged tank-killers tantalized him. Beneath the snub nose of every A-10 was a seven-barreled Gatling-type autocannon, which fired armor-piercing rounds the size of beer bottles. He wanted to rain down all that heavy metal on the Republican Guard. The trouble was distance. A-10s were not deep-strike aircraft, and the nearest Republican Guard unit, the Tawakalna Division, was seventy miles inside heavily defended territory. Conventional wisdom held that subsonic aircraft like the A-10 would be too vulnerable.

Glosson was ready to challenge conventional wisdom. The A-10 had performed so well during its inaugural ten days of combat that even its sharpest critics—including Chuck Horner—took notice. Warthogs were active throughout the border area, knocking out radar sites and artillery emplacements, and making life miserable for front-line Iraqi troops. Perhaps, the critics admitted, there was still room on the modern battlefield for a slow-mover. "I take back all the bad things I have ever said about the A-10," Horner announced during one of his morning pep talks to the TACC. "I love them! They're saving our asses!"[1]

Glosson placed a call to Dhahran and told the A-10 squadrons to start mapping out large-scale raids against the Tawakalna Division. Hog drivers welcomed the newfound respect for their aircraft, but they had concerns about venturing so far behind the front lines. They'd need to be careful and clever.

Red-bereted Republican Guards were better trained, disciplined, and paid than ordinary Iraqi soldiers. They had the best weapons Saddam's money could buy. The Tawakalna Division possessed more than 200 Soviet T-72 main battle tanks, nearly 300 armored fighting vehicles, and a multitude of mobile air defense systems. The division built a lengthy combat record during the Iran-Iraq War. It had romped through Kuwait in August 1990, before pulling into a reserve position in southern Iraq.

The first A-10 raid began on the morning of January 29, as four Warthogs rolled in with Maverick missiles, Rockeye cluster bombs, and a full load of 30mm ammunition. The flight lead took out an SA-6 radar with a Maverick, while the other planes hit a radio transmitter and an SA-9 launcher. With the Tawakalna air defenses now fully occupied, a second four-ship element swept in, destroying long-range artillery pieces and other high-value targets. Within ten minutes, all eight planes had expended their ordnance and were heading south.

The Iraqis barely had time to catch their breath before a second wave arrived. This flight split into four two-ship elements, fanning out over the division to target ammo dumps and dug-in armor. Soon stockpiled ammunition was cooking off, resulting in huge secondary explosions, and burning vehicles sent thick plumes into the sky. Wave two pulled off, making way for wave three.

"When we went in, we could see the target area from sixty miles away because of the black smoke from the strikes ahead of us," said the lieutenant colonel leading wave three. "As we came off our strike I remember looking back, and black smoke was coming off where we had hit, and you could see bright flashes of things still exploding. When we came back on the turn, it was still smoking so bad we had trouble finding targets."[2]

The Tawakalna defenders were on their heels but still fighting back, creating some tense moments. The closest call of the day belonged to Capt. Rick Turner, who spotted an SA-9 launcher and plunged into an attack dive. Turner locked up the four-wheeled vehicle and was just about to thumb the pickle button when he saw two heat-seeking missiles streak from their launch tubes. He immediately broke from the dive, pulling a tight defensive turn while pumping out flares, and managed to defeat the missiles.

Raids continued long into the afternoon, and by sunset more than 150 Warthogs had visited the Tawakalna Division. The squadrons refined their tactics for additional raids on January 30 and 31. Glosson called each night asking for an update, but the results were hard to quantify. The pilots knew they were causing destruction, but with all the smoke and chaos it was hard to say how many tanks and armored personnel carriers were destroyed, particularly given the Iraqi fondness for decoys.

Satellite and aerial reconnaissance photos were also inconclusive, so to get the answers Glosson needed, a pair of four-ship Warthog flights headed north on February 1 to perform armed reconnaissance. They would go in low, binoculars in hand, and count the burned-out hulks. The pilots were free to defend themselves and attack any obvious targets of opportunity, but their primary goal was damage assessment.

"We dived down from high altitude, built up all the speed that we could, and flew over them," said the first flight lead. "What we found was that they had a lot of targets down there, but they also had old, beat-up pickup trucks and other junk in some of the revetments, and they had camouflaged a lot of stuff. From higher altitudes, you would think they had a lot of stuff in there. We did one pass, caught a little bit of AAA, and then went back and did another pass and that's when we started getting a lot of it."[3]

The second flight found similar results: armored vehicles interspersed with plywood decoys, derelict pickups, and even a few farm tractors. They counted the actual kills while dodging flak and occasional SAM launches, and then they fired their Mavericks into some camouflaged bunkers and headed home.

Back at Dhahran, the eight pilots marked up a large-scale map with their observations. Certainly the Tawakalna Division still had plenty of functional armored vehicles, but it had also suffered some pretty heavy losses during the past three days. The wing commander went around the room, asking each pilot for a frank assessment of the division's strength. The most conservative estimate was 50 percent, so he reported that number to Glosson.

Naval Support Facility Diego Garcia
February 2, 1991
1200 Local

A round-trip flight between this Indian Ocean atoll and central Iraq lasted about sixteen hours. The three B-52G crews who now embarked on the 6,400-mile odyssey would spend ninety seconds dropping their bombs, and the rest of the time monitoring various systems. On a time-worn aircraft like the Stratofortress, warning lights were common.

The B-52 was the terrifying brute of American airpower, and it had been for more than three decades. The heavy bomber stood at the opposite end of the spectrum from the stealthy, surgical F-117 Nighthawk. There was no subtlety or laser-precision with a B-52G. The behemoth screamed in at just a few hundred feet, leaving a wake of utter destruction, or flew so high that its victims never heard it coming.

Schwarzkopf had insisted on a strong B-52 presence, as much for the psychological effect as the raw destructive power, and the BUFFs (Big Ugly Fat F[ellows]) were delivering. A far-flung fleet pounded the Iraqi army daily. Altogether, the B-52s numbered about seventy, with some in Saudi Arabia but most coming from as far as England or Diego Garcia. Their best day so far was January 30, when they hit the Republican Guard with 470 tons of high explosives. Ultimately, BUFFs would account for about a third of the war's total bomb tonnage.

One of the B-52Gs now departing Diego Garcia was typical of the variant. Tail number 59-2593 entered service nearly thirty-two years earlier, making it older than most of the current crew. The bomber, which today flew under the call sign Hulk Forty-Six, had received normal maintenance and equipment upgrades during its lifetime. Four crew members, including pilot and copilot, occupied the main deck, while on the lower deck two bombing and navigation officers sat before a daunting wall of electronics. Nobody reported any problems during the long flight to Iraq.

The bombing run also proved uneventful. Weather conditions were good, with a low-hanging cloud deck that offered the planes an extra measure of protection. A typical three-ship flight carried more than a hundred and fifty 750-pound bombs. They released in unison, saturating a swath of desert that stretched a mile wide, and a mile and a half long. As far as they could tell, the Iraqis were not shooting back. The bombers finished the run and turned for the return leg of their journey.

On the way home, Hulk Forty-Six began experiencing some minor problems. The crew observed a fuel gauge problem, followed by a cranky electrical generator, but they were accustomed to dealing with the old plane's petty ailments. "Gauge malfunction, the electrics, these are things you saw on normal flying missions," said Capt. Kevin Kent, the pilot.[4]

Another warning light came on, this time indicating a problem with the Number Five engine. A different engine then flamed out entirely but the copilot, Capt. Jeffrey Love, managed to get it restarted. Engine problems were more troubling, but nothing the crew couldn't handle. Their mission was nearly finished—the bright lights of Diego Garcia waiting just over the horizon, a comforting beacon in the dark ocean.

They were preparing for approach when, without warning, the nagging glitches mushroomed into a full-blown emergency.

"Everything went black," Kent remembered. He was flying without electrical power, unable even to lower the flaps for a landing.

Love grabbed a flashlight and reached for the emergency procedures. He began reading instructions from a checklist, then stopped. Something else was wrong. He swung the flashlight's beam to the engine gauges and felt a chill. All eight turbofans were winding down.

He and Kent jammed the throttles forward, which caused a reassuring surge. But it didn't last, and soon the RPMs resumed a steady retreat. They had flown nearly four minutes without electrical power. Diego Garcia was still fifteen miles away. Their altitude had slipped to just 2,000 feet.

"Pilot, we need to leave the airplane," Love said.

"No, wait," Kent replied. There had to be a solution. He tried to think.

The entire crew was in peril, but none more than the two people in the lower deck. During an ejection, the bombing and navigation officers rocketed downward, out the plane's belly. They needed more altitude than the others.

"Let's just get the hell out," Capt. Jon Jeffrey Olson radioed from below.

"Pilot, we need to get out of the plane now," Love reiterated.

"Hulk Forty-Six is abandoning the aircraft at this time," Kent called to Diego Garcia. "No airspeed. We are losing everything."

Love yanked his ejection handle. The hatch above him popped off, flooding the cockpit with wind and moonlight. His seat thundered through the hatch and he was gone.

In earlier B-52 models, a tail gunner was forced to jettison his quad-mounted machine guns and then climb out, but the G-model placed the gunner directly behind the pilots, where he operated the tail turret remotely. Sergeant Steven Ellard heard his pilot give the bail-out command. He pulled the ejection handle and found himself arcing through the night sky, watching the plane continue on without him.

The electronic warfare officer, Lt. Eric Hedeen, punched out seconds later.

Kent continued yelling "bail out" into the intercom. Rushing air told him that at least some crew members had ejected, but he could not be sure about the two in the lower deck. Kent saw the altimeter reach 600 feet and pulled his handle. The parachute barely opened before he hit the water.

Love came to the surface near a chunk of flaming wreckage. He spotted his life raft, swam to it, and lit a flare, realizing belatedly that he was floating in a fuel slick. Love held the flare high overhead until it fizzled, and soon afterward he heard the distant beat of helicopter blades. The rescue chopper retrieved him, as well as Ellard and Kent.

Eric Hedeen suffered fatal injuries during the ejection. Rescuers found his body afloat in his life raft. The bodies of Jon Jeffrey Olsen and his lower-deck colleague, Lt. Jorge Arteaga, were never recovered. A cause for the massive electrical failure that triggered the crash was either never established, or never made public.

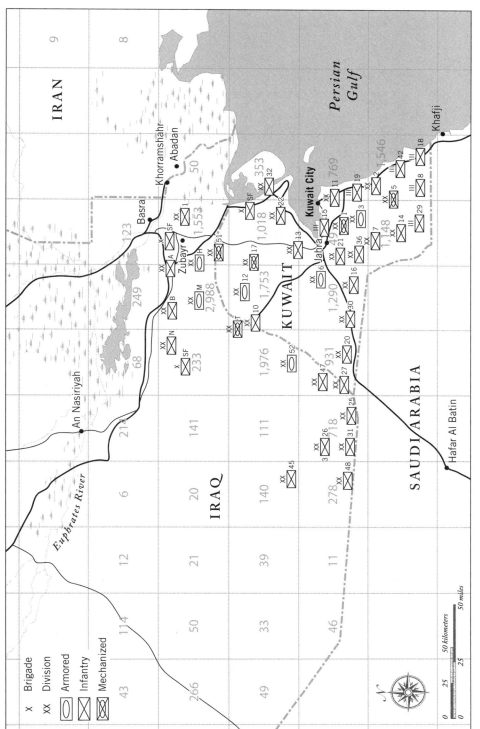

Strikes Targeted by Kill Box, January 17–February 28, 1991

CHAPTER 23

Kill Box

An armada of aircraft roamed Kuwait and southern Iraq, searching for armored vehicles and artillery. The region had been divided into thirty-five free-fire zones, dubbed kill boxes, where the hunters could operate independently and without fear of running into other aircraft.

Each thirty-by-thirty-mile kill box was a large area to scour, particularly for jets with only twenty or thirty minutes of expendable fuel. Satellite and aerial reconnaissance photos were supposed to provide leads, but typically those pictures were at least twenty-four hours old, and the Iraqis liked to move around. Glosson told his Black Hole planners to come up with ideas for making the kill boxes more effective.

The problem was not new. Vietnam-era pilots also had difficulty rooting out ground targets, and they relied heavily on airborne forward air controllers (FACs) to orchestrate the attack. FACs loitered over the target area in propeller-driven aircraft, marking enemy positions with white phosphorus rounds, and then talking the strikers on target. As the war progressed and North Vietnamese air defenses became more sophisticated, "Fast FACs" used old jets like the F9F Panther and F-100 Super Sabre, and finally the versatile F-4 Phantom. Still, the job remained a risky one, and Fast FACs often returned in shot-up aircraft, or not at all. After the war, Air Force FAC training virtually disappeared.

The Black Hole team thought it was time to resurrect the Fast FACs, using F-16s to patrol the kill boxes and guide strikers to targets. They first contacted the handful of pilots in the theater with actual FAC experience, and then recruited trainees who had good communication skills and an open mind.

A FAC obviously needed to be a team player, since he did the hard work of finding a target and then stepped aside while someone else blew it up. Glosson and company wished to convey that their FACs were not merely ushers, but key players in the tank-killing effort, so they came up with the name Killer Scouts. A Killer Scout would enter the kill box with enough ordnance for a strike of his own, and spend the rest of his time showing others the way.

Soon the Killer Scout program was up and running, with a pilot routinely assigned to the same kill box so he could learn its terrain and the rhythms of Iraqi activity. Productivity increased immediately, although some boxes were more fruitful than others.

"It depended on the abilities and experience of the Killer Scout himself," Glosson explained. "Some were more adept, especially the dozen or so who'd been FACs earlier. Those guys were really good at it. The others were starting from scratch, and had never been trained, so it took them a while to pick up all the techniques of how to talk the eyes of the pilot onto the target so he could drop his bombs. But compared to the first few weeks, these Killer Scouts were phenomenally successful."[1]

<hr />

Over the Medina Division
Southeast Iraq
February 5, 1991
2100 Local

A pair of F-111 Aardvarks, call sign Charger Zero-Seven and Zero-Eight, cruised a clear night sky at 18,000 feet. Republican Guard troops below heard them and sent up a desultory AAA reply, but the scattered neon streams were easily avoided. So far the Aardvarks had no indication of a guided-missile launch, which was the real worry.

They were here, deep in Iraqi territory, to test another Black Hole theory. Like the Killer Scouts, it was another scheme for reaching Schwarzkopf's 50 percent attrition goal. But this particular concept held tremendous promise, and it was so potentially game-changing that the

F-111 wing commander, Col. Thomas J. Lennon, decided to lead the test mission himself, piloting Charger Zero-Seven.

Back in December 1990, during the run-up to Desert Storm, American warplanes conducted an exercise called Operation Night Camel, in which they made simulated cluster-bomb attacks on the U.S. Army. Night Camel aviators using LANTIRN and Pave Tack infrared targeting systems made an interesting discovery: After sundown, armored vehicles glowed hot on their infrared display, despite having cold engines. They realized the tanks were radiating solar heat absorbed during the day, which contrasted sharply with the cool night air.

The Night Camel discovery had significant implications. Theoretically, any infrared-equipped aircraft could find idle tanks in the desert, even on the darkest night, and without any help from satellite photos or J-STARS.

There was only one drawback—the technique required a fair amount of altitude, in the range of 15,000 to 18,000 feet, and any airplane meandering at that level would be vulnerable to radar-guided SAMs. Missiles were the very reason non-stealthy, deep-strike aircraft like the F-111 used low-level attack. But after nearly three weeks of around-the-clock dismantling, the Kari integrated air defense system surely had lost its vigor, the Black Hole team reasoned.

Tom Lennon disagreed. When Glosson called to explain the idea, Lennon responded with profane disbelief. (Glosson termed the reaction as "visceral.") Neither man believed in tempering his opinions, which was why they always got along so well, going back to their days flying F-4s in Southeast Asia. Glosson knew Lennon as fiercely competitive and driven to succeed. If the infrared-tank-hunting test failed, it would not be for a lack of trying. Lennon, meanwhile, knew that Glosson wouldn't risk lives on a whim. He had vetted this idea and believed it would work.

The Aardvark commander gradually warmed to the prospect of his F-111s terrorizing the Republican Guard. Then Glosson mentioned using CBU-87 cluster bombs, which triggered a fresh round of outrage, as Lennon thundered that the cluster bombs are "not worth a shit because we can't hit anything with them."[2] They talked it over and settled on the GBU-12, a 500-pound, laser-guided bomb. When the two jets of Charger flight departed Taif on their test run, they each carried four GBU-12s.

Now, as Lennon settled into a mid-level orbit over the Medina Division, his weapon systems officer studied the Pave Tack monitor. The green murk held little promise, until suddenly a couple of ghostly white cubes slid onto the screen.

"Oh, yeah, I can really see them!" he told Lennon. "Come on, turn! Turn! Hurry up!"

Both F-111s found an abundance of warm armor hulls glowing on their infrared screens and began laser-designating targets. During the next thirty minutes, a succession of orange flashes interrupted the darkness as tanks and armored personnel carriers exploded. Iraqi gunners hosed the sky, hoping for a lucky hit that never came.

Back at Taif, Lennon reviewed the tapes for both planes, then picked up the phone and called Glosson. "Seven for eight," he reported gleefully. Without missing a beat, Glosson drawled, "Why didn't you get eight for eight?" Two nights later, forty-four Aardvarks went out and replicated the success. F-15E Strike Eagles and A-6 Intruders soon joined the party, since they too carried infrared and laser-targeting pods.

The new technique was not perfect—lasers couldn't penetrate cloud cover—but on a clear night the aircrews were totaling 100 kills or more. They dubbed the mission "tank plinking," a term that career army officer Schwarzkopf reportedly found distasteful. Yet he couldn't complain about the results. His goal of 50 percent attrition now seemed within reach. The infrared tapes showed Iraqi crews climbing from their tanks and running for cover at the sound of jet engines. They began sleeping in the open desert, far from their vehicles.

* * *

Iraqi armor and artillery units endured nonstop harassment, with Killer Scouts directing F-16s and F/A-18s by day, and high-tech tank plinkers hunting them at night. Still, Glosson wanted more. Previously, the Warthogs had worked over the Tawakalna Division to his satisfaction, and now he envisioned a larger role. He wanted to send the A-10s even deeper into Iraq, this time against the Medina Division.

The A-10 was proving invaluable in this war, an irony not lost on Hog drivers, who always felt like second-class citizens in the fighter community. In the early 1980s, air force generals discussed retiring the A-10 even before its production run had ended. The airplane with the gawky lines, armored cockpit, and gruntlike mission offended their supersonic sensibilities. Multirole jets could provide close air support just as well, the generals believed. To prove their point, they outfitted a squadron of F-16s with a four-barreled gun pod and deployed it to the Gulf. The experiment was a disaster, with the gun pods vibrating so violently they couldn't be aimed.

Glosson didn't care what an airplane looked like so long as it got him results. Sending the Warthogs into Medina territory would be a huge gamble, but Schwarzkopf's 50 percent goal consumed him. Glosson had developed a solid working relationship with the commander in chief, and he didn't want to let him down. He went to discuss it with Chuck Horner, who grimaced when he heard Glosson's plan for the A-10s.

"Buster, I'm not sure they can survive that far up over the Republican Guard."[3]

"We've beat the enemy down to the point that I believe they can," Glosson replied. "I feel obliged to try it because they've been so successful down in the first echelon. I'm going to do it unless you tell me I can't."

Horner had chosen Glosson to run the air campaign because he was aggressive and got things done. Difficult goals often required heavy risk, and so far Glosson's judgment had been spot on. "It's your decision," he said at last. "But I'm doubtful it's the right thing to do."

Over the Medina Division
Southeast Iraq
February 15, 1991
1500 Local

Lieutenant Robert J. Sweet was only twenty-four years old and just two years removed from learning to fly jets in the T-38 Talon. After A-10 training, he was assigned to the 353rd Tactical Fighter Squadron in

Myrtle Beach, South Carolina. Six months later he was in Saudi Arabia, preparing for war.

Captain Stephen "Syph" Phillis was thirty, and one of the finest pilots in the 353rd. When Sweet was graduating from the Academy, Phillis was finishing up at the elite Fighter Weapons School. Experienced flight leads like Phillis typically had green wingmen in tow, and on this day—the opening day of Warthog raids against the Medina Division—he was leading Sweet.

They were not the first to go, for the raids began early and continued all day. As Phillis and Sweet sat in their cockpits preparing to depart, two recently returned pilots climbed the ladders and gave them a scouting report. "We told them we hadn't seen any AAA fire all day," one remembered. "We briefed them that it was lucrative up there and that we took absolutely no fire."[4]

The veteran and the rookie took off from Dhahran and headed northwest, meeting up with a tanker before crossing into Kuwait. Soon they were through the emirate and into Iraq, not far from Basra. As they drew near the Medina Division, they could hear other A-10 pilots talking on the radio, describing abundant targets but also fearsome fire.

The radio chatter was unnerving, like sitting in a dentist's waiting room and listening to the drill. Sweet thought about all those Mavericks and cluster bomb units (CBUs) slung beneath his wings, weighing down his already sluggish airplane. He followed Phillis as they descended on their kill box. A paved road ran through the area, with trucks and armored vehicles parked along its shoulders.

"Syph rolled in and dropped his CBUs, and started taking pretty heavy AAA from north of his target," Sweet said. "So we decided to go south of the road, where there were a lot of targets but no shooting going on."[5]

A truck barreling down the road led them directly to a supply depot, and Phillis told his wingman to hit it with cluster bombs. Sweet rolled in and thumbed the pickle button. The CBU canister came off his wing and spilled open. Bomblets fanned out over the depot. "One detonated right in the center of the trucks, and I had another two that covered about half the encampment," he said. "I was happy that I got some of them."

They pulled off the depot and moved about five miles away, trying to remain unpredictable. Phillis didn't want someone on the ground zeroing in on them. They stumbled upon a tank formation and toggled to their Mavericks, but with daylight now fading, the electro-optical missiles would not lock, so they switched to the A-10's most basic weapon. Beneath each pilot, nestled in a cocoon of armor plating, sat a five-foot drum with 1,174 rounds of 30mm ammunition. They took turns strafing the tanks, firing in quick, destructive bursts.

Sweet was coming around for another pass when a flash of movement caught his eye. "I looked and saw a SAM coming at me from two o'clock low," he said. "It was guiding on me. I jammed on the flares and pulled a little bit, and it missed me, barely."

The missile left a smoke trail that pointed to its place of origin—a cluster of vehicles in the distance. Phillis attacked the group first, shredding a tank, and then cleared his young wingman for a pass. The plan was to let Sweet destroy the rocket launcher that had targeted him and call it a day.

"I was just about ready to roll in," Sweet said. "I was northeast of the target and the sun was low, which means that I'm easy to see. I was just about ready to roll in when there was a boom behind the airplane, and at that time I heard Syph call out two SAMs. But they had already hit me."

He twisted around, looking for damage, and felt a surge of panic. "The whole trailing edge of the right wing was gone and there was a fire. There were little tubes and wires sticking up with flames on the end of them. I didn't bother looking back any farther. I didn't even check the engines. I unconsciously firewalled the throttles and headed south. I was thinking that it was a long way to the border."

The plane still responded to his commands, which helped calm him. He radioed Phillis that he was in trouble and egressing immediately, and then he began a more thorough damage assessment. His caution panel was an unsettling mosaic of lights, none more disturbing than the hydraulics warning.

Without hydraulics, he'd need to fly in a backup mode called manual reversion. As the name suggested, manual reversion required a pilot to manipulate the control surfaces mechanically, using brute force, as a last-ditch method for getting a wounded Warthog home. The backup system was a credit to Fairchild Republic's engineers, who endowed the plane with multiple layers of survivability, but it wasn't easy to operate. The thought of landing a damaged A-10 in manual reversion would worry any Hog driver.

Sweet looked to his engine instruments, which indicated the two big General Electric turbofans were functioning normally. He was just beginning to think he might make it home when abruptly the right wing dipped and he began to roll. He yanked the stick full left, but the plane persisted in its right-hand roll, so he tried the rudder. Nothing. Reluctantly, he switched to manual reversion. Still nothing. His altitude dropped below 9,000, then 8,000 feet.

"The steep spiral had me forward in the seat, so I had to force myself back," he said.

Phillis was on the radio, trying to talk him through it, but nothing worked. The controls were useless. He spiraled through 6,500 feet.

"I'm out," he called. "I'm out."

He ejected north of the tank formation they had been strafing, but a strong southerly wind carried him directly toward the tanks. "I landed about thirty yards away from a T-72. There were about sixty guys there—guys that we had been shooting at. They were in their holes until I got real close to the ground, then they rushed out after me. I landed hard, tore a tendon in my leg, and then they all ran up and started beating the shit out of me with rifle butts to the head and all over."

Phillis circled overhead, calling for help. A nearby flight of A-10s from his squadron answered.

"My wingman is bag," Phillis told them, using the day's code word for "battle damaged." He began talking them toward his location. A rescue attempt seemed unlikely, but they weren't going to leave Sweet behind until they had to.

The nearby flight was almost there when they heard a chilling radio call.

"This is Enfield Three-Seven. I'm bag at this time also," Phillis announced matter-of-factly.

It was the last they heard from him, and upon arriving they found no trace of him.

The fate of Stephen Phillis would remain a mystery until after the war, when an American unit found his body among the wreckage.

The first day of Medina attacks took a heavy toll, with two ships down and a number of close calls. The A-10 wing commander, Col. Dave Sawyer, flew home with a tail full of shrapnel from an SA-13. As Sawyer nursed his plane to Saudi airspace, he passed a flight of F-16s working a target just fifteen miles from the border. Fast-moving Vipers—which counted deep-strike among their many roles—were getting front-line targets, while close-air-support Warthogs were being pushed ever deeper into Iraq. That night, Sawyer sat down and expressed his concerns in a letter to Chuck Horner.

Before the letter even reached Riyadh, Horner pulled the plug on Glosson's A-10 experiment. From now on, the Warthogs would remain within thirty miles of the border, where they belonged.

Remains of F-16C #87-0257 from the 614th Tactical Fighter Squadron, flown by Maj. Jeff Tice during the first daylight raid on Baghdad. U.S. forces discovered the wreckage during the ground war. The plane's canopy, which was not found until the 2003 invasion of Iraq, became part of a display at the Pima Air & Space Museum in Tucson, Arizona. CW2 KEVIN BELANGER

A Kuwaiti McDonnell Douglas A-4KU Skyhawk on the runway in Saudi Arabia. Advanced Skyhawk models such as the A-4KU featured a hump on the fuselage spine to house extra avionics. SGT. JEFF WRIGHT

Crew members prepare to bring military trucks down the nose ramp of a C-5A Galaxy in support of Operation Desert Shield. U.S. AIR FORCE

Horner during a visit to the 354th Tactical Fighter Wing at King Fahd International Airport. 354TH TACTICAL FIGHTER WING OFFICE OF HISTORY

Buster Glosson joined the U.S. Air Force in 1965 after earning an electrical engineering degree from North Carolina State University. He became an F-4 Phantom pilot, flying combat missions out of Thailand 1972–1973. U.S. AIR FORCE

A 37th Tactical Fighter Wing F-117 stealth fighter draws fuel from a KC-10 Extender while en route to Saudi Arabia. U.S. AIR FORCE

The MH-53J Pave Low III was the most technologically advanced transport helicopter in U.S. Air Force inventory, with enhanced navigation and integrated avionics for pinpoint accuracy during night and adverse-weather missions.
U.S. AIR FORCE

A BGM-109 Tomahawk Land Attack Missile (TLAM) launches toward a target in Iraq from the nuclear-powered guided missile cruiser USS *Mississippi.* SENIOR CHIEF MACHINIST'S MATE HENDERLITE

Three F-111F Aardvarks and an EF-111 Raven fly in formation during Desert Shield. Note the Raven's tail-mounted antenna pod, known as the "football."
U.S. AIR FORCE

The Air Combat Fighter Competition of 1974 ultimately produced two winners. The U.S. Air Force chose the YF-16, and the following year the U.S. Navy selected an upgraded version of the YF-17 to become the F/A-18 Hornet. U.S. AIR FORCE/R. L. HOUSE

Lieutenant Commander Michael Scott Speicher, whose fate remained unknown until 2009. In the intervening years he was promoted to the rank of captain. U.S. NAVY

An A-6E Intruder, armed with twelve 500-pound Mark-82 bombs, en route to target. U.S. NAVY NATIONAL MUSEUM OF NAVAL AVIATION

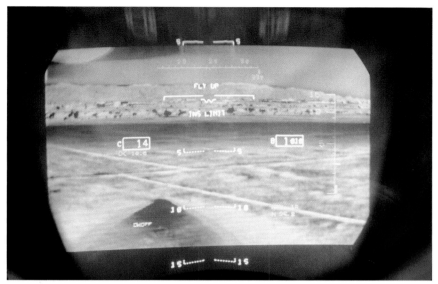

Using the Low-Altitude Navigation and Targeting Infrared for Night (LANTIRN) system, an infrared image is projected onto the heads-up display (HUD) of an F-15E Strike Eagle. SENIOR AIRMAN BRAD FALLIN

A Marine Corps OV-10D+ Bronco observation aircraft, not yet outfitted with its sand-camouflage paint scheme. The Bronco was phased out of Marine Corps service after Desert Storm but found new life flying for civil government agencies and some foreign air forces. USS *SARATOGA* PHOTO LAB

A ground crew member signals to a 614th Tactical Fighter Squadron F-16C pilot preparing for takeoff. STAFF SGT. LEE F. CORKRAN

Heavily armed F-16s draw fuel from KC-135 Stratotankers. Large strike packages were common in the first week but grew smaller as the campaign progressed. U.S. AIR FORCE

This F-15C Eagle is armed with four AIM-7 Sparrow missiles on the fuselage, an AIM-9 Sidewinder on the left wing, and an AIM-120 advanced medium-range air-to-air missile (AMRAAM) on the right wing. U.S. AIR FORCE

Military personnel examine a Scud missile believed to have been shot down by an MIM-104 Patriot tactical air defense missile. U.S. DEPARTMENT OF DEFENSE

This grainy photo, taken over the shoulder of an MH-53J door gunner, shows the first successful CSAR mission behind enemy lines since Vietnam. The rescue helicopter picked up U.S. Navy lieutenant Devon Jones 130 miles inside Iraq. AIR FORCE SPECIAL OPERATIONS COMMAND

Marine Corps AV-8B Harrier II attack jets from VMA-513 fly in formation during Desert Shield. U.S. AIR FORCE/ STAFF SGT. SCOTT STEWART

Iraqi F-1 Mirage pilots confer prior to a mission in the Iran-Iraq War. IQAF

Two reinforced concrete aircraft hangars at Al Jaber Airfield show the results of a coalition precision-bombing strike. The photo was taken by an F-14 Tomcat carrying the Tactical Air Reconnaissance Pod System (TARPS). U.S. NAVY

An AC-130 Spectre gunship conducts twilight target practice near Hurlburt Field, Florida. TECH. SGT. LEE SCHADING

An A-10 Thunderbolt II adorned with classic nose art. The rush to defend Saudi Arabia meant A-10s had to deploy in their standard gray-green "charcoal lizard" camouflage, rather than a paint scheme more suitable for desert operations. TECH. SGT. LEE SCHADING

A B-52G Stratofortress of the 1708th Bomb Wing takes off from Jeddah, Saudi Arabia, on a Desert Storm mission. U.S. AIR FORCE

An Iraqi T-54A or Type 59 tank destroyed by a precision "tank plinking" attack. SPEC. ELLIOTT, U.S. ARMY

Airmen prepare to load Mark-84 2,000-pound bombs onto F-16s of the 401st Tactical Fighter Wing. U.S. AIR FORCE

In addition to a 30mm chain gun, the Apache has four hardpoints mounted on stub-wing pylons, which typically carry a mix of AGM-114 Hellfire missiles and Hydra 70 rocket pods. U.S. DEPARTMENT OF DEFENSE

An A-10 pilot pauses between sorties for munitions specialists to reload the GAU-8/A Avenger cannon with 30mm ammunition. U.S. AIR FORCE

Civilian and Iraqi military vehicles litter a section of the "Highway of Death," where coalition aircraft attacked fleeing Iraqi convoys during the waning hours of Desert Storm. CAPT. R. J. WORSLEY

U.S. Army flight surgeon Maj. Rhonda Cornum speaks with Col. Richard Williams shortly after her release from captivity. Coalition POWs included forty-five military personnel and four civilians from CBS News. U.S. DEPARTMENT OF DEFENSE

F-15s and F-16s of the 4th Fighter Wing fly over Kuwaiti oil fires set by the retreating Iraqi army. The final blaze was extinguished eight months after the war ended. U.S. AIR FORCE

CHAPTER 24

Missteps

LIFE AT KHAMIS MUSHAIT HAD SETTLED INTO A COMFORTING RHYTHM. By day the heavily guarded air base in Saudi Arabia's extreme south appeared dormant, but in reality a legion of mechanics and technicians were at work inside hardened aircraft shelters, maintaining two squadrons of F-117 Nighthawks.

When darkness neared, the first wave of pilots suited up and prepared to depart. The air base could no longer mask its activity as dozens of black jets emerged, milling around the aprons and taxiways. A typical night saw three waves of stealth planes depart at various intervals, with the final wave returning shortly after daybreak and vanishing into their shelters.

The Bandits knew nothing but success. They had not lost an aircraft, despite penetrating deep into Iraq every night of the campaign. In the beginning they struck command-and-control targets like radar installations and communications towers, as well as Scud production facilities and fortified bunkers believed to house Saddam's chemical and biological weapons. More recently, they hammered targets vital to the Iraqi army, such as bridges and ammunition dumps. Frequently, a call from Riyadh added a target not listed on the Air Tasking Order. The mission-planning cells detested these last-minute changes, which upset meticulously planned routes designed to further minimize the F-117 radar profile. Grudgingly, they worked these new targets into the missions.

In Riyadh, the Black Hole maintained a master target list that had begun with Checkmate's "centers of gravity." Five months had passed since John Warden gave his Instant Thunder presentation, and since then the master list had grown exponentially. F-117s continued to visit Baghdad, even after most high-priority targets in the capital city had been serviced. The Black Hole didn't want Baghdad residents to think the war was over, or forget that Saddam Hussein had brought it to their doorstep.

Coalition ground commanders complained that aircraft were still being sent to Baghdad on the eve of the ground war. Those bombs should fall on Iraqi troops, they argued, rather than "making Baghdad's rubble bounce." The criticism had little impact, as the air force still hoped Saddam might be persuaded to leave Kuwait on the basis of airpower alone, or that his weakened regime might be overthrown.

Amariyah, Iraq
February 13, 1991
0430 Local

Fully unknown to the residents of this Baghdad suburb, a pair of Nighthawks had just arrived. The F-117s traveled separately to the target area, as was their practice, via entirely different routes. Yet they arrived at the same time and would attack the same target, which they knew as the Al Firdos command-and-control bunker. The people of Amariyah knew it by another name. They called it Shelter Number 25.

From the pilots' perspective, the mission went precisely as planned. The first plane's bomb bay doors opened, briefly raising its radar profile, and the pilot hit the pickle button. A 2,000-pound bomb sailed through the darkness, laser-guided toward the bunker's thick roof. It burrowed into reinforced concrete and detonated, carving an entry hole for the second plane's bomb, which was already on the way. The same technique worked perfectly on Iraq's hardened aircraft shelters, and it worked well here, too. Before departing, the pilots observed the billowing black plume they called smoodge, indicating the bunker's innards were melting.

The Al Firdos bunker was not crammed with military computers and communications gear, as the Bandits had been told. Rather, it mostly held civilians. An accurate body count was never established, but most estimates placed between two and three hundred people inside the shelter, including about a hundred children.

Many occupants perished instantly, either vaporized or torn to pieces in the blast, or burned alive in the subsequent inferno. By morning, images of charred, twisted bodies being pulled from rubble were broadcast around the world. Washington publicly insisted that Al Firdos had been a military bunker, even hinting that Saddam's regime might have planted civilians there intentionally. Behind the scenes, a scramble was underway to figure out exactly what happened.

Records revealed that American intelligence agencies first identified Al Firdos as a possible target in December, weeks before the campaign began. Analysts knew the two-level building was originally constructed as an air-raid shelter during the Iran-Iraq War. But they also knew that foreign contractors later upgraded and significantly strengthened the shelter, an unusual move for a regime that showed little regard for its citizens.

Once the air war started, Al Firdos became a hive of suspicious activity, beginning with workers trying to camouflage the roof, an odd choice for a civilian shelter. American electronic surveillance picked up communications traffic from the building, and reconnaissance photos showed a steady flow of sedans near the entrance, suggesting the presence of government officials. The CIA concluded that the Iraqi Intelligence Service, which operated a satellite office just a few blocks away, had transformed the shelter into a fortified command post.

Pentagon analysts fretted about the possibility of civilians, but, as the circumstantial evidence mounted, they came to accept the CIA assessment. Al Firdos was declared a legitimate target on February 10. Black Hole planners added the bunker to their master target list, and they incorporated it into the Air Tasking Order for February 13. When the F-117 mission-planning cell in Khamis Mushait examined the intelligence folder for Al Firdos, they saw nothing out of the ordinary. It looked like any other Baghdad command-and-control bunker, of which Saddam had many.

The CIA assessment had been partially correct. The Iraqi Intelligence Service had indeed appropriated the shelter, but not as a command post. Al Firdos was a place where privileged agency officials could stash their families, which explained the procession of sedans. The electronic traffic came from communications equipment on the lower level, where officials worked while staying with their families. In recent days, the agency had opened the shelter to neighborhood residents, a rare act of kindness that swelled the number of civilians who slept there each night.

For the Bush administration, Al Firdos was a public relations nightmare. No air campaign in history had taken such care to avoid noncombatants, and now an honest error had killed hundreds. The international criticism was not as loud or sharp as anticipated, and at home the reaction was muted. Many Americans assumed Saddam had made good on his "human shields" threat, this time sacrificing his own people to gain sympathy. No evidence ever emerged that he had done so.

Following Al Firdos, F-117 raids on Baghdad trailed off dramatically. Colin Powell sent word to Riyadh that any attack on the city first needed his personal approval. Glosson and his Black Hole team saw it as a rebuke, and they grumbled about a return to the Vietnam-era practice of letting Washington pick targets. In reality, Powell was thinking globally. A second civilian tragedy would surely tarnish all of the coalition's good work to date. Powell tended to agree with the ground commanders who were tired of seeing Baghdad's rubble bounce, and he ordered an end to the Tomahawk missile attacks as well.

A week after Al Firdos, a request crossed Powell's desk for an F-117 strike in downtown Baghdad: The Black Hole wanted to hit the Iraqi Intelligence Service headquarters. The agency handled Saddam's internal security, maintaining order through terror, so removing it would further weaken his regime and improve the odds of a coup. Powell granted permission.

The agency's menacing, three-story building was a place of imprisonment, torture, and murder. City residents called it the White Ship. Saddam's political enemies—either real or imagined—were taken there and often never seen again. Recently, the White Ship assumed a second function. Unknown to anyone outside the regime, this was also the place where Iraq held its prisoners of war.

* * *

They didn't know where they were, or even that they were all together, but everyone who had been shot down and captured was present. The group included Jeff Tice and Mike Roberts, the F-16 pilots who fell prey to Baghdad's air defenses during the ill-conceived Package Q strike. It included David Eberly and Thomas Griffith, the F-15E Strike Eagle crewmen who wandered the western desert, futilely awaiting rescue. There were navy and marine aviators, British and Italian fliers, and even a four-man CBS News crew who had bumbled across the border early in the war. All had solitary cells on the second floor of the Intelligence Service headquarters building, which they knew only as the Baghdad Biltmore.

The nickname was a grim nod to the Hanoi Hilton. Survival school instructors had recounted the POW horror stories from Vietnam, and so had the older guys in the squadrons. The stories ensured this new generation of airmen understood the brutal reality of life in captivity. Lessons had been learned: You can fight depression by keeping your mind occupied. Accept that nobody resists pain forever. Think of interrogation as a chess game—study your opponent's moves and develop countermoves. Divulge small truths, but slowly, and diluted with lies.

Every day at the Baghdad Biltmore was the same, with each prisoner sitting alone on a damp cement floor, huddled beneath a filthy blanket. Anyone making the slightest noise risked a beating, so the corridor was silent, except for a murmuring radio at the end of the hall. Meals came through a slot in the cell's steel door and typically consisted of cloudy broth with a slice of bread and cup of water. Fit, clean-shaven aviators grew gaunt and scraggly, shuffling around their little cells in baggy yellow uniforms. Some guards took pleasure in their suffering, but most were indifferent, and occasionally someone took pity and provided an extra cup of water or ladle of broth. Once there was even a handful of dates.

The prisoners remembered their survival training, and each fought the fear, boredom, and hopelessness in his own way. David Eberly developed an exercise regimen, doing push-ups and counting paces around his cell. A deeply religious man, he occupied his mind by compiling an alphabetical list of hymns. Michael Berryman, the marine Harrier pilot who had been threatened with having his fingers cut off, thought of food. Berryman had lost twenty-five pounds off his burly frame, almost a pound a day. He planned exquisite meals to celebrate his freedom, constantly revising the details of his appetizers, entrées, and dessert. For all the prisoners, sleep was a heavenly escape. They passed as many hours as possible in slumber.

The most dreaded sound in the Biltmore was that of footsteps in the corridor, which usually meant someone would be going to the interrogation room. Each prisoner listened, hoping for the footsteps to continue past his door. By now, they all knew the experience of being the unlucky one—the heavy bolt sliding back and the door creaking open, the guards issuing gruff commands.

The Intelligence Service interrogators were craftsmen, with skills honed by years of practice. As the guards delivered a beating, the interrogator studied his subject, watching for a wince or a yelp that indicated a particularly sensitive spot. For Jeff Tice, it was his left knee, the site of an old soccer injury. Afterward, whenever the interrogator wished to get his attention or punish him for an evasive reply, it was always with a blow to the left knee.

Tice and several other prisoners found that the guards were experts at perforating eardrums. Their technique required no tools. A hard, open-handed punch caused such a violent change in air pressure that the eardrum actually ruptured. They liked to deliver the blow as a prisoner entered the interrogation room, setting the session's mood.

The Intelligence Service men were secret police, experienced only in matters of internal security. They could keep a civilian population obedient by ferreting out any whiff of dissent, but military issues were beyond their purview. Tice realized this fact when they grilled him for basic details about the F-16, such as its weight, which could be found in aviation books and magazines. Pertinent questions, like the F-16's bomb-delivery profiles, eluded them.

The thorniest issue was the making of propaganda videos. North Vietnam had used pilot "confessions" as a propaganda tool a quarter-century earlier, and Saddam wished to replicate the success. Tice had no problem giving up innocuous details about his aircraft, but he drew the line at making a video. He would not be "news at eleven," as he put it. But the more he said no, the angrier they became, doling out fierce beatings and threatening him with death.

His injury list grew: busted knee, burst eardrum, and now a dislocated jaw. When the pistol butt knocked his jaw out of alignment, leaving him unable to speak, they tossed him from the interrogation room and began working on someone else. Tice lay there in the dank hallway, handcuffed, wondering just how much longer he could hold out. The physical pain was excruciating, but their mental games were just as bad. They explained that a video would show the world he was alive, making Iraq responsible for his safety. They said he could include a personal message to his wife and children. That idea tempted him immensely.

Tice pulled himself to his knees and sidled over to the wall. He pressed his face against the cool brick and pushed until his jaw popped back into position. The throbbing abated. It was a small victory, but he reveled in it. He felt strong enough to resist a little longer.

Twenty minutes later the guards returned and yanked him to his feet. They jostled him into the interrogation room and pushed him once more onto the little stool before the interrogator's desk. He heard the same promises and demands about making a videotape, and again he refused.

"Finally, one of the guys hauls off and hits me again in the jaw, and dislocates my jaw a second time," Tice said.[1] "Now I'm really hurting, and I thought, 'Oh, this is really going to get bad,' and he asked me if I wanted to make the tape now. I'm very much slumped over now. I've lost my composure to the point where I can't hold my head up very well any more. And I said, 'Well, what do you want me to say again?' And that was probably the wrong thing, because he knew that I knew what he wanted me to say. And he got pissed."

The interrogator barked a command in Arabic, and the guards began attaching a device to Tice's head. They slipped a metal wire on his right ear, ran it beneath his chin, and coiled it around his left ear.

Nearly every pilot owned a Sony Walkman to break the monotony of long, tedious flights. The loops of wire now connected to his ears were vaguely reminiscent of Walkman headphones. Later, much later, Tice would even think of a fitting nickname—the Talkman—because wearing it guaranteed you would talk. Right now, he was too scared to think about anything.

"So they turned on the juice," he said. "And what that did was drive your jaw together with violent force. All your muscles contract. My nose went to my chest and it felt like a little lightning bolt hitting me right in the forehead. And there was a flash, and again it was momentarily in contact. [Just] a second on, and everything contracts in your body. And I started spitting out pieces of teeth."

They continued jolting him with short bursts, just one or two seconds each—not enough to kill, but enough to terrify and torment. Tice felt the last reserves of strength draining from his body. His knee throbbed and his jaw ached. Each surge of electricity brought fresh agony, and soon he lost count of how many shocks he received. Perhaps ten, maybe twelve. They paused to ask him more questions. He struggled to form the words to answer. They asked once more if he would make a videotape.

He slurred out a no.

"Finally, he gets mad," Tice remembered. "He says, 'No one knows you are here. We're going to kill you. Right now.' The guard on my right, who had been striking me with a pistol butt, I assume it was a pistol butt, I could hear the unmistakable sound of the slide being drawn back and a round being chambered. He pressed the gun up against my temple.

"I thought to myself, 'Okay, now's not the time to be scared, because it is too late to be scared.' So I was getting angry now. Believe it or not, anger just welled up inside of me. And I just pushed my head back against the gun to let him know that I was mad. And he didn't like that at all. He just hauled off and pulled the gun back and just struck me across the side of my face as hard as he could with the flat of the gun. And I fell off the chair."

They gathered him up and sat him on the little metal stool, and reattached the Talkman to his head. He had nothing left, no more strength to resist. His prison clothes were soaked with sweat and urine. The interrogator repeated the pledge that Tice could include a personal message to his wife and children. At this moment, nothing in all the world seemed more important than letting his family know he was still alive. He willed his swollen jaw open.

"Okay, I'll make the tape."

~ ❧ ~

Baghdad Biltmore
February 23, 1991
1930 Local

Time had no meaning here. Solitary confinement fused the hours into a single, continuous period, with no difference between day and night. The prisoners had no contact with each other and no news about the war, except the lies told by their captors. During David Eberly's most recent interrogation, he had been informed that 70,000 American troops were dead, and so was President Bush.

One fact each prisoner knew for certain was that the airstrikes on Baghdad had diminished. Early in the war, they heard a steady cadence of thuds and booms as targets were struck all across the city. More recently they heard only silence. For that reason, the sudden shrill of jet engines roused them from their blankets. Each prisoner gazed upward and listened. An air-raid siren wailed in the distance. The corridor filled with footsteps as the guards abandoned their posts.

Inside his cell, Eberly felt a queasy sensation. He pressed his back against the wall and curled up, pulling his blanket tight. The Biltmore shuddered as a 2,000-pound bomb struck its south end. Eberly heard shattering glass, falling ceiling tiles, and the clank of metal. A gray cloud of smoke and dust invaded the cell, choking him.

"I pulled my legs tighter and buried my face between my knees as the building swayed with loud cracking noises," he said. "I could hear and feel concrete crumbling and imagined that any second the ceiling was going to collapse on me or the floor was going to drop out from below. In the hallway, there was screaming: 'Get us out of here! Hey! Can anybody hear? Let us out!'"[2]

The building calmed, and the prisoners once more heard the air-raid siren, along with sounds of a city under attack—barking dogs and people shouting on the street. Marine pilot Michael Berryman wondered if the bomb was a prelude to a daring rescue mission, with Delta Force operators storming the building to liberate them.

"In the silence, we all started yelling out our names," Berryman said. "We just wanted to let everybody around us know who was there. It was our only accountability process at that point."[3]

Amid the shouted names, he heard television correspondent Bob Simon identify himself. For an instant, Berryman marveled that CBS News had managed to embed a camera crew with Delta Force, to provide live rescue coverage. Then Simon called out his cell number and Berryman's heart plunged. Thirty seconds later, he knew this was purely a bombing raid, and that no one in Riyadh realized they were here.

"Somebody yells, 'Incoming!' and you start to hear a click-click, click-click, click-click," Berryman remembered. "Those clicks were the fins of that laser-guided bomb making its corrections down the laser beam. And you know that if the bomb is close enough that you can hear the fins making their corrections, it's going to be close."

The north end of the building reared up and collapsed, sending another shock wave through the Biltmore. Walls buckled and steel doors blew away from their frames, ushering in torrents of flying debris. Remarkably, nobody was killed or even seriously injured. But the Nighthawks still had two more bombs to drop. Soon Berryman again heard the ominous clicking of fins.

"That third bomb was headed right toward the center of the building," he said. "It would have killed every one of us. Well, it went right over the top of the building and landed out in the parking lot and exploded. When it exploded, there was this huge fireball that came back into the rooms where the glass had been blown out. It was just the most eerie thing I had ever seen because the flame came in and then sucked itself out just as quick."

The fourth and final bomb plunged down an elevator shaft, detonating in the basement. The Intelligence Service headquarters was a fractured ruin, yet somehow the second-floor central corridor still stood. Both F-117s vanished into the night, and soon the siren faded. A final silence descended over the Biltmore. Some prisoners ventured into the hallway, picking gingerly across piles of rubble, but within a few minutes the guards returned and rounded them up.

The shouting, shoving guards led everyone down a shattered stairway and outside into a moonlit courtyard. Eventually a khaki school bus rumbled up and groaned to a halt. The bus had no seats so they sat on the floor. Anyone caught whispering or lifting his eyes to the windows received a sharp blow to the head. An hour later, the bus pulled through the gates of Abu Ghraib prison, where the group was off-loaded and herded into cramped holding cells.

The F-117 attack was another misstep in the air campaign, caused by another intelligence failure. Riyadh had identified three possible POW detention sites in Baghdad, none of which were the Biltmore. Only an errant smart bomb had spared their lives.

The experience of being bombed was truly terrifying, worse even than being shot down, but it did bring some unexpected benefits. At Abu Ghraib, they were under the charge of the Iraqi army, not the Intelligence Service. Savage interrogations became a thing of the past, and the daily food ration increased slightly. In the holding cells, before being separated again, the prisoners memorized the names of their cellmates. No longer did they need to worry about Saddam playing games after the war, releasing some prisoners and denying knowledge of others. Now they could account for one another, ensuring that nobody was left behind.

CHAPTER 25

Close Calls

ANY SUSTAINED AIR CAMPAIGN WAS SURE TO HAVE UNWANTED BY-products: shootdowns, crashes, POWs, death. Thousands of people were using dangerous machines in pursuit of difficult goals. The sheer number of variables invited chaos, and this campaign in particular featured some strange and outlandish events.

The first incident was a nearly tragic case of friendly fire that occurred on the opening night of the war. A trio of B-52Gs were departing Iraq after a low-level bomb run as their F-4G Wild Weasel protectors continued hunting SAM batteries from high overhead. One of the Weasels acquired an Iraqi radar and fired a HARM missile, which came off clean and sprinted for its target. The subsequent chain of events was never definitively established, but the prevailing theory holds that the HARM became distracted by a B-52 tail gun's fire-control radar. The missile lost its Iraqi target and instead followed the new emissions to their source, tearing away the gun turret and eight feet of fuselage.

The gunner was spared since he operated the turret remotely, and the pilots managed to keep their wounded bomber aloft long enough for an emergency landing at Jeddah. The plane eventually would be repaired and returned to service, but with a new nickname stenciled on its side: *In HARM's Way*.

Four days later, an F-16 pilot endured a self-inflicted shootdown. Colonel Jon Ball was attacking a target on the northern Kuwaiti coastline in what seemed like a normal bomb run. Ball hit the pickle button and felt the Mark-84s fall away, but shortly afterward he was rocked by a heavy explosion. His Viper suffered massive damage and began nosing for the ground. Ball coaxed the dying airplane to the Persian Gulf and stayed with it until he was several miles out to sea, hoping to get beyond the reach of Iraqi gunboats before ejecting.

Ground defenses around the target area were fairly thick, so the initial assumption was that Ball had been hit by an undetected missile or AAA burst. But other pilots in the flight weren't so sure. The explosion left behind an enormous brown cloud, far different from the typical SAM or artillery blast. Later, camera footage from a trailing aircraft would reveal that Ball had been the victim of his own 2,000-pound bomb. The Mark-84 detonated just four seconds after release, triggered by a faulty fuse.

Ball was director of operations for the 614th Lucky Devils, the same squadron that had lost two F-16s over Baghdad during the Package Q strike. Now the Lucky Devils feared the loss of yet another pilot, but they soon learned that Ball was a guest of the U.S. Navy. An SH-60B Seahawk helicopter from the guided-missile frigate USS *Nicholas* picked him up shortly after ejection, and he was back with his squadron by the end of the day.

Crews who service and maintain military aircraft face potentially deadly hazards on a daily basis. In the early morning hours of February 20, an experienced navy petty officer named J. D. Bridges vanished from the flight deck of the USS *Theodore Roosevelt*. Bridges had stepped too close to the screaming jet engine of an A-6 Intruder as the plane prepared for launch. He was sucked inside, and a bright flash lit the deck as the engine jammed and seized. The entire accident occurred within two seconds.

Bridges had been training a new deckhand on securing aircraft to the catapult. He was leaning forward to check the trainee's work when the port engine sucked him into its air intake passage. The engine was at full throttle, generating twice the force of a tornado. While the Intruder pilot had not seen Bridges disappear into the long, narrow inlet, he sensed a problem and shut down the engines. Witnesses paused for an instant, stunned, unwilling to imagine what the spinning steel blades had done to their crewmate.

They were even more stunned a few seconds later, when Bridges wriggled from the inlet and crumpled onto the deck. His helmet, gloves, and goggles were gone, and his shirt hung in shreds, but none of his injuries were life-threatening.

Investigators determined that after Bridges was sucked into the intake, his shoulder became wedged against the engine's nose cone. The cone shattered his collarbone but kept him from being pulled into the razor-sharp blades just beyond. His helmet left his head and smashed into the blades, causing the engine jam that saved his life. Bridges remembers the horror of being inside the intake, feeling the air being sucked from his lungs, until the engine powered down and he could push himself free. Video of his accident would become a staple of flight deck safety films.

<hr />

Southeast Iraq
100 Miles from Saudi Border
February 17, 1991

Captain Scott "Spike" Thomas and Lt. Eric "Neck" Dodson had been looking forward to this mission, for it was a rare treat to fly into combat with your best friend. They had launched as the trailing pair of Benji flight, a four-ship tasked with patrolling the Euphrates River. After the four F-16s met up with a tanker and topped off their fuel, the Benji flight lead cut loose Thomas and Dodson as their own two-ship element, maximizing coverage of the river.

Their mission was simple. During the past month, Iraqi supply lines had dwindled as F-111s and other precision bombers systematically destroyed concrete bridges over the Euphrates. Iraqi engineers, desperate to resupply their starving army, were working nonstop to reopen the lines with pontoon bridges. Thomas and Dodson would bomb any of the temporary spans they found.

Heavy clouds and thunderstorms blanketed the area, forcing Thomas to contemplate aborting the mission. But as they neared the river the clouds peeled away, offering decent skies for bridge hunting. They found plenty.

The pontoon bridges were juicy targets, and they took turns making easy, relaxed runs. Nobody was shooting at them, and the few radar warnings they received were distant and benign. They pickled off the last of their bombs and turned for Saudi Arabia, still carrying enough fuel to skip the tankers. Thomas began to climb with Dodson about a mile off his wing. His plan was to take them above the thunderstorms that stood in their way to the south. He was passing through 32,000 feet when the aircraft made an unfamiliar sound, jarring and metallic.

"I can only describe it as similar to the noise of your car's transmission falling out from beneath and hitting the freeway pavement," he recalled. "The sound was distinct, and the accompanying deceleration grabbed my attention immediately."[1]

The loss of airspeed told Thomas his engine was dying, but when he scanned his instruments, all the readings were green. "The engine was still turning and burning, but it just wouldn't put out thrust," he said. He informed AWACS of the problem, called his wingman in closer for a visual inspection, and jettisoned his external tanks to reduce drag.

As Dodson moved in to take a look, AWACS vectored a flight of F-15s to cover their six o'clock. Dodson could see no signs of an impact, but the airplane definitely had a problem. He inquired about the fuel reading, and Thomas said he was at 4,600 pounds, more than half a tank.

"You are leaking tons of fluid and it looks like gas," Dodson reported.

When the trouble began ten minutes before, Thomas believed he could hold the jet together long enough for an emergency landing at the nearest friendly airstrip. Now he was forced to consider punching out as soon as they crossed the border. He mused that at least his friend would have a front-row view of an actual ejection.

"Is this all the airspeed you can get?" Dodson asked.

"That's it, man. I can dump the nose, but I really don't want to. I want to keep this wind going for me."

AWACS advised that the border was still fifty-five miles away, and Thomas began to wonder if he might need to eject sooner. The idea of coming down inside Iraqi territory chilled him. He'd seen the POW tapes on television, and he could tell those guys had been tortured. He tried not to think about it and busied himself by getting ready for the ejection, which now seemed inevitable. He still hoped it might not happen until they reached the friendly side of the border.

"I prepared the cockpit by clearing out everything strapped to my legs and near the seat," he remembered. "Water bottles got stuffed in my pockets, helmet bag, maps and checklists set aside. I tightened my harness straps and cinched down my helmet, ready to take the ride of a lifetime."

At forty miles out, Dodson came on the radio with some more bad news: "Well, it looks like you've got sparks and shit coming out of your engine now."

Thomas accepted the fact he wasn't going to make it to Saudi Arabia. AWACS notified the search-and-rescue command post at King Khalid Military City. Moments later, wisps of smoke entered the cockpit and Dodson radioed that the shower of sparks had evolved into a full-blown fire. Thomas replied that he was getting out.

"I instinctively moved my feet to the rudder pedals, back of my head to the headrest, elbows in, reached for the handle and pulled," he said. "All I saw was red as the ejection seat rocket motor exploded to life. Other pilots who have taken an ACES II ejection seat ride have experienced time compression, and felt the seat riding up the rails into the wind. Not me. I felt no time between the initial blast and flying through the air on my back. The free-stream wind caught the lip of my helmet, threatening to rip it off."

The chute popped open at 12,000 feet and Thomas took in the view. He saw his tumbling canopy and ejection seat, and the abandoned, nose-down Viper trailed by a fifty-foot tongue of flame. They all vanished into the cloud cover, leaving him alone in the wind and swirling snowflakes.

Soon the clouds swallowed him too, not letting go until about three thousand feet, when a rocky, desolate landscape appeared and stretched all the way to the horizon. The only sign of human activity was a cluster of black dots, which he assumed to be old campfires. Thomas worried about breaking a leg or twisting an ankle, but the landing was smooth. His only injury was a gash to his chin from the ejection, which dribbled blood onto his neck and chest.

"I heard tones and ringing in my ears," he said. "I was in a lonely place, for a while anyway. Out of the clouds comes Neck, hauling ass below the weather to help me out. He scouted the area, exposing himself to the threat of anti-aircraft artillery and surface-to-air missiles."

Dodson reported the area clear. He would orbit as long as his fuel permitted, but they stayed off the radio in case the Iraqis were trying to triangulate. Thomas knew his rescuers would wait until dark, which was still more than an hour away. He inventoried his supplies, and when distant rumblings told him a storm was coming, he propped up the inflated life raft for some shelter. Soon fat raindrops were drumming against the raft as heavy gusts tried to wrench it from his grasp. The storm passed quickly, leaving a starry sky in its wake. He wondered where his rescuers were.

Thomas didn't realize it at the time, but he was a hunted man. Two groups of Iraqi soldiers were scouring the area in trucks, and the inbound CSAR teams called in a flight of F-15E Strike Eagles to deal with the nearest group. Thomas heard the muffled growl of jet engines and assumed it was a patrol that had relieved his wingman. He had no idea the Strike Eagles were preventing his capture.

The sound he most longed to hear was that of rotor blades. Huddled beneath the life raft trying to stay warm, he thought of the television show *M*A*S*H*, a favorite from his youth. In that show, the thrum of approaching choppers was an ominous, foreboding sound, but to him it would mean safety and freedom. Soon he heard helicopters approaching from the south. He grabbed his helmet and radio and leapt from beneath the raft. Two low-flying silhouettes appeared just a few hundred yards away.

"Benji Fifty-Three is up! I'm on your left! Turn left," he radioed, but the Blackhawks continued northeast. "You passed me up! You passed me!"

The helicopter crews never heard his transmissions. Ongoing problems with the survival radios would persist until the end of the war. Thomas pulled out his strobe and activated it, and they circled back. The first Blackhawk roared directly overhead and kept going, but the second hovered and settled just twenty yards away. Thomas waited on a knee, fighting the urge to run to it. His training told him to stay put and let the rescuers come get him, but after several long minutes he was ready to disregard the training. He stood and took a step toward the chopper, and at that instant something grabbed him from behind. He turned to find himself staring into a pair of night-vision goggles.

"Sir, are you okay?" asked the crewman from the other Blackhawk.

"Yes, I'm Benji Fifty-Three. Let's get the hell out of here!"

The trip home was uneventful, except for an SA-7 that had been launched in their direction but landed well short. Search-and-rescue during Desert Storm would be deemed less than satisfactory, largely due to factors beyond the control of the rescue teams, including bad radios and a muddled chain of command. Yet this night's mission had been flawless, and at King Khalid Military City the CSAR crews celebrated and posed for pictures with Scott Thomas and Eric Dodson.

* * *

With the kickoff of the ground war roughly a week away, coalition airpower focused almost exclusively on Saddam's front-line troops and their formidable defenses. Iraqi combat engineers had constructed steep sand berms, oil-filled fire trenches, and sprawling minefields to funnel coalition troops into narrow kill zones.

F-111 Aardvarks and other precision bombers knocked out artillery emplacements that were zeroed in on the kill zones. A-10 Warthogs experimented with methods for burning the fire trenches, while F-117 Nighthawks destroyed pipelines and pumping stations to prevent the trenches from being refilled. Marine jets flung napalm and other incendiary weapons on troop formations in southern Kuwait.

MC-130 Combat Talons dropped 15,000-pound "daisy cutter" bombs in an attempt to clear minefields. The daisy cutter, officially the BLU-82 ammonium nitrate bomb, was one of the largest conventional weapons in history, and it was originally used to create instant landing zones in the jungles of Vietnam. The size of a small car, the bomb rested on a cargo pallet that MC-130 crews simply slid down the ramp. Riyadh hoped daisy cutters would detonate all mines within their 5,000-foot blast radius, but no reliable evidence emerged to support the theory. The bombs did succeed in terrorizing Iraqi troops, and in causing some coalition soldiers to think a tactical nuclear weapon had just been detonated.

In Riyadh, Iraqi troop strength and morale remained a fierce point of debate. Everyone involved with the air campaign—from the Black Hole team to the pilots who observed with their own eyes—believed the Iraqi army was on the verge of collapse. But American intelligence analysts warned ground commanders to expect heavy resistance. To put the matter to rest, Schwarzkopf authorized a series of forays into Kuwait and Iraq.

The experience of the 101st Airborne Division was telling. On the afternoon of February 21, a scouting party of Apache gunships probed forty miles into Iraq and discovered a bunker complex sitting along the division's planned invasion route. The Apaches swarmed the complex, firing rockets and chain guns, until a psychological operations team arrived and shouted surrender instructions over a loudspeaker. By dusk more than 400 Iraqis, including the battalion commander, were being herded aboard twin-rotor Chinooks.

The Bush administration gave Saddam one final opportunity to avoid a ground war. Iraqi forces would need to begin an immediate and unconditional retreat from Kuwait, and complete their withdrawal within a week. The ultimatum was not a free pass—the Pentagon estimated that a one-week deadline would force the Iraqis to abandon at least half of their remaining combat equipment. Saddam responded by torching more wellheads. If the world would not let him keep Kuwait, he was going to leave it a cinder.

AIRPOWER IN THE
GROUND WAR

CHAPTER 26

Left Hook

THE COALITION GROUND PLAN EVOLVED OVER TIME. ORIGINALLY, SCHWARZ-kopf's staff proposed an unimaginative thrust into the Iraqi defenses in southern Kuwait, a bloody, head-on assault that would have delighted Saddam. As additional American and allied troops flowed to the Gulf, more options became available, and the plan grew increasingly sophisticated.

Saddam's expectations for the coalition ground attack were clear. He anticipated an amphibious landing on Kuwait's beaches by the 17,000 U.S. Marines sitting aboard ships in the Persian Gulf. Inland, Saddam expected an armored attack along the Wadi al-Batin, a river valley that formed Kuwait's western border. Accordingly, Iraqi divisions took up entrenched positions along the Kuwaiti coastline and the Wadi al-Batin.

While Saddam's suspicions of an amphibious assault were initially correct, Riyadh later abandoned the idea as too risky. Yet all those marines sequestered at sea still made an impact—their mere presence was enough to hold six Iraqi divisions pinned to the beach. The marines staged a series of landing exercises to keep the ruse alive. Inland, coalition troops conducted probes and feints into the Wadi al-Batin, reinforcing Saddam's assumption for that route.

Throughout the thirty-eight-day air campaign, Iraqi forces kept watch over the coast and wadi, vigilant for attacks that would never come. Meanwhile, in Saudi Arabia, a mammoth column crept far to the west, planning to outflank them.

Schwarzkopf's "left hook" strategy sent 250,000 soldiers—along with their tanks, armored personnel carriers, and wheeled vehicles—deep into the Saudi desert. They waited until the air war began to reduce the chances of being observed and then journeyed hundreds of miles into forbidding wasteland. The clandestine westward expedition carried enough food, ammunition, and supplies for sixty days—an enormous logistical feat. But now, as the ground war was finally getting underway, a critical timing problem threatened to undermine the left hook.

The marines in eastern Saudi Arabia attacked first, just as planned. In the early hours of February 24, after one final B-52 strike to soften the Iraqi front lines, marine armor started cutting into the defenses of southern Kuwait. The attack was a diversion. As the marines slogged along, methodically clearing lanes through minefields, Saddam and his generals would conclude the main assault was underway. The next day, G+1, with all eyes still locked on Kuwait, Schwarzkopf would throw his left hook into western Iraq.

The plan's timing assumed a slow marine advance, hindered by obstacles and heavy fire, but it wasn't playing out that way. The marines were pushing through minefields with only light resistance, speeding so deeply into enemy territory that Schwarzkopf worried about a counterattack on their flank. So far the Iraqis showed little interest in fighting—more than 8,000 starving conscripts had surrendered already—but if some second-echelon units rallied, it could mean trouble.

Conversely, the marine juggernaut might trigger a panicked stampede back to Iraq. In that case, Kuwait would be liberated before Schwarzkopf's left hook had a chance to land on the Republican Guard. A rare opportunity to stabilize the region would be lost if Saddam's best divisions survived to threaten his neighbors another day.

The solution to both scenarios was the same. Schwarzkopf instructed his army commanders to move up their timetable. Rather than waiting for G+1, they would attack now, as soon as possible.

Saudi Frontier
February 24, 1991 (G-Day)
0300 Local

Four ground-hugging helicopters of the 101st Airborne plodded through smothering fog as they crossed into Iraq. Leading the group was Lt. Col.

Richard Cody, the same man who had led Task Force Normandy against two early warning radar stations almost six weeks earlier. Cody's Apaches had kicked off the air war by opening a radar-free corridor for the fighter-bombers. Now he was once more inside western Iraq, but the current mission was not going as smoothly. His advance element was dropping a string of radio beacons, marking the trail for what would be the largest helicopter assault in history. But the nearly impenetrable fog bank slowed their work.

Cody got a call that an OH-58 Kiowa had crashed near the border, and another helicopter was hopelessly lost in the murk. He turned his Apache around and set down near the crash site. Remarkably, both crewmen had survived. Cody radioed division headquarters that the assault would need to be delayed until the fog lifted, or they could expect more crashes.

The hours passed slowly, and the bank showed no sign of retreat. A brigade of troops loitered in their assembly areas, awaiting the order to board the helicopters. Dawn broke, brightening the gloom only slightly. By 0700 they could wait no longer, and the turbine whine of Blackhawks, Hueys, and Chinooks filled the assembly areas. Soon they were in the air, some barely ten feet from the sand, sweeping forward in waves toward their objective: a desolate plain some ninety miles inside Iraq. Objective Cobra would be a forward operating base, an oasis of fuel and supplies for staging further advances.

The Apaches went in first to attack the only real threat, a dug-in battalion just north of the objective. The gunships were organized into six-ship companies, with staggered firepower designed to keep constant pressure on the enemy.

"Companies normally operate in two teams," explained Lt. Col. William Bryan, who commanded an attack-helicopter battalion in the 101st. "The light team of two Apaches will usually be the first to engage, covered by the heavy team of three or four helicopters. Then the heavy team will take up the fight. In Europe we're taught to mask, to use the terrain as cover from behind which we launch attacks. In the desert, you couldn't hide."[1]

As the Apaches kept up a steady fire, the first wave of transport helicopters rolled in, disgorging troops and combat equipment, including

105mm howitzers. By 0830 artillery shells were falling on the Iraqi position, and the skirmish ended shortly afterward with 300 POWs. Now
Cobra's construction began in earnest. Heavy-lift helicopters ferried in
rubber bladders of fuel and dropped off pallets of ammo and rations. Their
rotors churned up a choking sandstorm, but by mid-afternoon the forward base was up and running.

The Apaches paused long enough to refuel and rearm, and then they
were gone. The division's next objective, Highway 8, was a Euphrates Valley artery that connected Baghdad with Basra. A brigade of paratroopers
would be choppered in to sever that artery, but first the gunships needed
to open a path. They thundered north toward the highway, encountering
only the occasional Iraqi convoy. "Once they saw the armed helicopters
appear, they would get out of their vehicles and take cover," Bryan said.
"We engaged the vehicles, destroyed them."

By nightfall the Apaches had cleared the way to Landing Zone Sand,
just twenty-five miles from Highway 8. The next morning a flock of Chinooks hauled in Humvees outfitted with TOW missile launchers, and
scores of Blackhawks delivered troops who trundled off to establish the
roadblock. Almost instantly, American soldiers stood within 150 miles of
Baghdad. The heliborne incursion of the 101st, which came to be known
as the "Lightning of Desert Storm," dropped a barrier between the capital
and its engaged army.

Burqan Oil Field, Central Kuwait
February 25, 1991 (G+1)
0753 Local

Schwarzkopf's concern about the vulnerable marine flank was prescient.
During the overnight hours, documents found in an overrun Iraqi command bunker revealed plans for a heavy counterattack, to be launched out
of the Burqan Oil Field. If true, Iraqi tanks were massing inside the oil
field at this very moment. Greasy black smoke from burning wellheads
made aerial reconnaissance impossible, so the marines decided to lob in
some artillery shells and see what happened.

From his command post barely a mile away, Maj. Gen. Mike Myatt listened as the barrage thundered inside the sprawling, smoke-obscured oil complex. His command post (CP) tent had been placed near the field the previous night, before news emerged of the Iraqi plan. Now, as the artillery shells continued to fall, Myatt and his staff saw distant movement. A ragged line of vehicles dashed from the black cloud. The intel had been accurate; the tanks were there. But as a formation of T-55s headed straight for his tent, Myatt realized he had stirred a hornet's nest. The CP guard, a company of LAV-25 light armored vehicles, opened fire. Suddenly the commander of 1st Marine Division found himself inside a raging battle.

The CP radios howled with reports of other units under fire. Two full mechanized brigades—roughly two hundred and fifty vehicles—had been hiding inside the oil field. The Iraqis were still preparing their counterattack when the artillery barrage flushed them into hurried action. Their advance was sloppy, the shooting inaccurate, but their sheer numbers jeopardized the marine right flank. Iraqi tanks drew within 400 yards of Myatt's command post.

"Send all the Cobras you can," a staff officer yelled into the radio, his voice barely audible over machine-gun chatter. To the south, at an airstrip nicknamed Lonesome Dove, the Cobra gunships lifted off.

When the Marine Corps found a good weapon, they stuck with it. Such was the case with the AH-1 Cobra, the world's first dedicated helicopter gunship, which had been in marine service since 1969. Bell Helicopter originally built the Cobra with a single engine for the army, but marine versions had twin engines as backup over water. The newest variant, the AH-1W SuperCobra, or Whiskey Cobra, featured significantly upgraded engines and weapons. Each slender, two-seat helicopter now en route bristled with eight guided missiles, fourteen rockets, and a three-barreled Gatling gun under the nose.

Marine LAV crews and riflemen beat back the initial rush, but after regrouping, the Iraqis were game for another try. When the Whiskey Cobras arrived, enemy vehicles were once again closing on the command post. The helicopters swept ahead of the LAVs, engaging tanks and armored personnel carriers with TOW missiles. They gradually fell back as they fired to keep the advancing targets at optimum range. When the TOWs were gone, they toggled over to laser-guided Hellfire missiles. The Cobras were not yet equipped with onboard laser targeting, so a forward air controller on the ground used his laser designator to illuminate targets.

The Iraqis kept coming, despite a trail of disabled vehicles in their wake, and the Cobras continued falling back as they fired. Soon they were hovering directly over the command post, their 20mm Gatling guns blazing. As a river of spent shell casings poured onto the tent, Myatt turned to his operations director and shouted above the din, "You picked a good spot for the CP!"[2]

Once more the Iraqis wavered and retreated, and this time for good. By noon they had vanished behind the oil field's dark curtain. Elsewhere, marine M-60 tanks and Cobras mopped up remnants of the failed advance. Across the battlefield more than 100 Iraqi vehicles burned, with bodies sprinkled around them in clusters. Marine ground losses had been light, but an OV-10 Bronco observation plane was lost to a shoulder-fired missile. The spotter in the back seat died instantly, while his pilot survived and was captured. A Harrier jet also went down, but the pilot parachuted to safety.

The battle of Burqan Oil Field turned out to be little more than a speed bump for the marines. In its aftermath Al Jaber Air Base fell, and the liberation of Kuwait City appeared inevitable. Marine ground forces likely would have held the flank without air support, but suffered far greater casualties. Helicopter gunships, buzzing the battlefield like deadly locust, proved a decisive factor. "When the Whiskey Cobras came in, it was a slaughter," said one observer. "The Iraqi counterattack got nowhere."[3]

CHAPTER 27

Twenty-Three Tanks

ON G-DAY, WARTHOG DRIVER CAPTAIN ERIC "FISH" SALOMONSON AND his wingman, Lt. John "Karl" Marks, flew three missions, spending just enough time on the ground to rearm and refuel. When they at last landed in the darkness, sweat-soaked and weary, nothing sounded better than a hot meal and a few hours of sleep. But with the ground war at full motion, Warthog firepower was in high demand. By 0400 of G+1, they were suiting up for another day of flying.

The squadron schedulers showed mercy, assigning them alert duty for the morning rather than sending them out on a mission. Salomonson told Marks they would get the jets cocked and ready and then hopefully snooze until a call came for their services. They strode through the brisk night air toward their planes. Even at this hour, the air base was in frenzied activity, with aircraft taking off and landing, and aircraft taxiing to the fuel pits, service bays, and arming stations. Squat tractors towed around pallets of bombs like passenger luggage at a commercial airport. The machinery of the air campaign reached a new gear when the ground war began, and it would continue without interruption until the war was finished.

Salomonson and Marks talked with their crew chiefs and then turned to the preflight procedures. Shortly before 0500, the base siren wailed its now-familiar Scud alarm. A month earlier they might have scrambled for shelter and pulled on bulky chemical warfare suits, but too many false alarms made them complacent. They ignored the siren and finished their preflight. No missiles fell, but minutes later came an order to launch. There would be no catnap.

They took off and headed for coordinates in southern Iraq. An operator aboard an EC-130 Airborne Battlefield Command and Control Center explained that a Republican Guard column had been spotted moving south. Their orders were to engage the column and destroy as many vehicles as possible. Shortly after crossing the border, they made radio contact with a pair of Hog drivers from another squadron who were on their way home after working the night shift. These two had discovered the convoy, and they were pleased to know that someone was following up.

"They said they had popped the first and the last tank in the column to bottle them up, and that there should be plenty of targets left," Salomonson remembered.[1]

A gray dawn was blooming as they reached the target area and checked in with the local forward air controller (FAC). The FAC advised them there were no friendlies in the area, and the ground defenses were minimal. "You guys can just go in there and start shooting," he said.[2]

Demolished tank hulks still smoldered on the road from the original attack. The Iraqis knew more "circling buzzards," as they called the hated A-10s, would soon appear, so they broke formation and scattered. Some tanks simply hunkered near the roadside, while others had made a mad dash for nearby revetments. Those who ran didn't realize their fatal mistake—the revved engines glowed white on infrared.

Salomonson could scarcely believe his good fortune. "I immediately rolled in, and the tanks were beautiful hot targets against a cool background," he said. "It had just quit raining and the ground was muddy."

"You could see where they had left the road by the churned-up tank tracks, and right at the end of each set of tracks there was a tank," Marks noted.[3]

"They were very easy to lock up and we just kept rolling in, in a shooter-cover attack," Salomonson said. "It was an A-10 pilot's dream, an air-to-mud pilot's dream, to have twenty-five or thirty operational Soviet tanks that had just been running."

Each A-10 carried four infrared Mavericks and a full load of 30mm ammunition, an ideal loadout for the situation. Iron "dumb" bombs would have merely weighed them down. As flight lead, Salomonson took the first run while his wingman stayed in high cover.

Salomonson picked a roadside tank, fired a Maverick, and pulled off. From overhead, Marks could see the missile track to its target and burst into a perfect orb of crimson and orange. The tank's turret popped off and somersaulted through the air. The pilots switched their positions and Marks had his first opportunity to shoot. Ten minutes later, six tanks were ablaze, each shattered by a missile impact.

The untouched tanks sat still and quiet, leading Salomonson and Marks to believe they were abandoned. Their attack altitude was too high to see figures on the ground, but they could imagine panicked crews scurrying away. They decided to make a few passes using the seven-barrel GAU-8/A Avenger autocannon. For Hog drivers, a live-fire gun run was the ultimate rush. In an age of automated weapons, strafing felt like a lost art, a throwback to previous generations of fighter pilots.

"You feel the jet rumble under your seat, and you see the bullets hit the tank and chew it up," Salomonson said.

"You'll see flashes from the armor-piercing depleted-uranium rounds, and you'll see metal from the tank splashing up in a molten spray," Marks added. "It's a little bit tougher to get them to burn with the gun, but if you hit them with enough rounds, usually ten or fifteen seconds, maybe even a minute later, you'll see the ammunition cooking off."

They strafed and shredded two tanks—bringing the total to eight—and made a few final passes before turning south for fuel and ammo. "We damaged quite a few more with the gun," Marks said, "but we only claimed those that were burning and exploding when we left as confirmed kills."

Rather than returning to base, they landed at a forward operating location and awaited further orders. It was only midmorning but they'd already scored more kills than most A-10 pilots would get in a career. Salomonson and Marks could spend the rest of the war on the ground and still feel satisfied about their contribution.

They were barely down the ladder when an operations officer ran up with news about the battle developing around Burqan Oil Field. So far the marines were holding the line, but they needed airpower north of the field to ensure no Iraqi reinforcements came from Kuwait City. "Get saddled up again! Go!" the ops officer yelled.

The last sortie had been a cakewalk, hardly different from a visit to the practice range. This new mission would carry them into the thick of battle, with plenty of SAMs and antiaircraft fire. Friendly forces would be in close proximity, forcing the pilots to sort through the chaos to avoid fratricide. As they flew east, another complication emerged—a low-hanging cloud deck. Their attack runs would need to be made at low altitude, increasing the risk from ground fire.

Kuwait looked like a surreal Hollywood backdrop, a post-apocalyptic nightmare. Flaming oil gushers stretched skyward, their orange torches bathing the desert in an eerie glow. Iraqi sand berms and oil trenches shared the moonscape with blackened bomb craters. The smoky overcast imposed a constant state of twilight, and a soft rain underscored the gloom.

Salomonson and Marks made contact with a controller who was busy trying to organize the rescue of a downed Harrier pilot. They offered to help but the controller said they were needed up north, where Iraqi tanks had been spotted along the highway out of Kuwait City. They flew north and checked in with a Marine FastFAC in an F/A-18 Hornet who was working the area. The AAA along the highway was some of the thickest they'd ever seen, and the FAC warned them to be careful. A second Harrier was hit just before they arrived and had barely limped back to base.

They circled the area, asking questions and trying to get their bearings. The tanks had pulled off the road and were nestled inside prepared revetments. Thick ropes of tracers whipsawed through the sky. Salomonson continued to grill the FAC for details, and after a few minutes the marine became impatient. "Look, are you guys coming in or not?" he demanded.

"Of course, when you say something like that to two Hog drivers, it's like a slap in the face, so we went in," Marks commented.[4]

They used the same shooter-cover technique as before, but with more urgency—the cover man rolled in on his target as soon as the shooter pulled off. Both pilots were experienced flight leads yet were frequently paired to fly together. The familiarity brought a smooth rhythm that required little verbal communication. They kept a constant eye on the AAA, jinking whenever it drew too close. Within twenty minutes, six more Mavericks had found their marks. When they switched to gun runs, the short-tempered FAC became an unabashed A-10 believer.

"The marines were pretty impressed with the aircraft and the job we did," Marks said. "They're used to working with some of the fast-movers, who can't carry nearly the ordnance and can't stay on station as long as we can. I guess they couldn't believe we still had anything left to shoot, especially after we shot all the missiles and kept coming back in, shooting more tanks with the gun."

Armor-piercing rounds destroyed two more tanks, bringing the day's total up to sixteen. Finally, they turned for Saudi Arabia, but they promised the marines they'd return for another round.

Less than two hours later, they were back for their final mission of the day. Typically, pilots were limited to one or two sorties before a mandatory rest period, but wartime brought exceptions. Today they were looking at a minimum of twelve hours in the cockpit. By now, the threat to the marine right flank had passed, and any Iraqi hopes of slipping reinforcements into the oil field had long evaporated. Salomonson and Marks chose a fresh stretch of tank-lined highway and began pounding targets. The AAA was less intense here, and they bagged six more tanks without difficulty.

They moved about four miles up the road and found ten more vehicles in revetments. Their ammo and daylight were both running short, but culling a few tanks from this group would be a nice way to finish the day. They were feeling bold and daring, aware that today's achievement would earn them a place in the air force history books. Whether from overconfidence or fatigue, or both, they didn't notice the antiaircraft emplacements protecting these tanks.

"I rolled in and shot one with a Maverick," Marks remembered. "It blew up immediately, and as I pulled off I looked back. There must have been a couple of gun pits at that particular spot in the road, because they just completely opened up on me. I had puffs at and above my altitude, just all around."

He maneuvered and thought about Salomonson, who would be coming in right behind him. "I started yelling, 'Fish, come off! Come off! Heavy flak!'"

"I was rolling in with the gun, just about ready to squeeze," Salomonson said. He heard the frantic radio call and broke off his attack.

The close call yanked them back to reality. They were in a combat zone with waning fuel and ammunition. The marines didn't need them anymore, and it was nearly dark. There was no need to blemish this record-setting day by bringing home a damaged airplane, or not coming home at all. "We decided we'd had enough fun, so we just came on back," Salomonson said.

A crowd gathered when they landed, and press pool cameramen shot video of them adding their twenty-three tanks to the squadron tally board. Reporters tossed out questions about how it felt, and how they planned to celebrate, but they declined to gloat. Any A-10 pilot could have done the same, they stated. The best reward was knowing they had helped the guys on the ground, and so on.

A veteran reporter finally chiseled through the public relations façade. "Take us into the cockpit" for an attack run, he said. The two young aviators stood before the cameras, describing each step with an almost clinical detachment. But when it came to lining up the target in the gunsight and squeezing the trigger, they could no longer hide their emotions. With beaming eyes and barely suppressed grins, they spoke about the roar of each quick burst, followed by telltale "sparkles" on the target, indicating their aim had been true.

According to legend, the A-10's design team consulted an unlikely source: retired Luftwaffe colonel Hans-Ulrich Rudel, who destroyed 519 Soviet tanks during his service on the Eastern Front. The story holds that Rudel's advice helped shape the Warthog into the ultimate tank killer. Rudel was dead by the time Salomonson and Marks scored their twenty-three kills. Otherwise, he likely would have been grinning too.

CHAPTER 28

Missiles and Misfortune

SCUDS WERE ONCE AGAIN A PROBLEM. IRAQI MISSILE CREWS HID IN THE western desert, threatening cities in Israel and Saudi Arabia. The war's first week had been the worst, when a total of thirty-three missiles rained down, but patrolling A-10s and F-15Es halved that number the following week. When Schwarzkopf permitted small groups of commandos to prowl the desert and call in airstrikes, the missile launches plummeted to a paltry four per week. But more recently the numbers had begun climbing again, and nobody understood why.

American and British special operations teams were still roaming the expanse in dune buggies and dirt bikes, checking culverts and underpasses where the missile crews liked to hide. Saddam deployed mobile infantry to hunt the teams, leading to some high-speed chases and last-minute helicopter extractions. Coalition warplanes occasionally aided in an escape, such as on the night of February 13, when heliborne Iraqi troops were chasing an American squad. AWACS diverted a pair of Strike Eagles bound for Al Qaim, the operator explaining that three Iraqi helicopters were offloading troops near a friendly position.

"There was no doubt in our minds from the radio transmission from AWACS that we had to get there in a hurry," said F-15E pilot captain Tim Bennett.[1] He and his wingman throttled toward the coordinates. At about fifty miles out, Bennett's backseater, Capt. Dan Bakke, picked up the spinning helicopter rotors on his radar. As far as he could tell, they were still on the ground. The pilot and his weapons officer talked it over and decided to drop a laser-guided bomb, unless the choppers took off, in which case they would shoot AIM-9 missiles.

"Our main goal was to get something on them fast, to let them know we are there," Bennett said. "Finally, we break out of the weather at about three thousand feet—it was not good weather that night. Just as soon as we break out, the AAA starts coming up. We're about twenty miles from the contacts, and then, at around fifteen miles, Dan's got them in the targeting pod."

"It's infrared, and the helicopters are hot, and the rotors look like discs," Bakke explained. "I'm doing the laser, putting it on the white spot, waiting. We released the bomb about six miles away and it has over thirty seconds time of flight."

"About ten seconds after the bomb comes off, I start seeing an air-speed readout on the radar," said Bennett. "I'm thinking, 'This thing is moving. Go back into air-to-air and bring up an AIM-9.'"

"What in fact happened, according to the guys on the ground, is that the helicopter was at eight hundred to a thousand feet when the bomb impacted," Bakke said. "It hit just forward of the center of the rotors, right in the cockpit. And I guess, if you've ever seen a James Bond movie where the helicopter—the model they film—just vaporizes and disappears, that is exactly what happened."

Their wingman had been flying cover overhead. Bennett now called him down and told him to place six bombs on the site of the fireball, to kill any Iraqi soldiers who had disembarked. Within minutes, the threat to the American ground team had been completely eliminated.

Despite the efforts of the Special Forces, weekly Scud counts continued to rebound. In Riyadh, a realization set in that the problem might not be solvable. The desert was too large, with too many hiding spots. Black Hole strategy switched from destroying Scuds to simply deterring launches. Strike Eagles patrolled suspected launch zones nightly, dropping an unguided bomb every thirty minutes. The F-15E crews considered this new mission ludicrous, but Buster Glosson hoped an Iraqi missile crew might see one of the blasts and decide to scrub their launch for the night.

To Glosson and other Vietnam veterans, the Scud problem was vaguely familiar: small groups, hidden in the terrain, periodically emerging for a quick attack and then vanishing once more. Glosson advised Schwarzkopf that the only option left was to call in the B-52s and carpet bomb the launch zones. Schwarzkopf wanted no part of that Vietnam-era tactic. For now, they would continue to hope the wildly inaccurate Scuds didn't hit anything important.

— ⁓ —

Dhahran, Saudi Arabia
February 25, 1991 (G+1)
2042 Local

The plaintive howl of air-raid sirens stretched across the city, a sound that once terrified residents but now merely annoyed them. Ten minutes earlier, American early warning satellites had picked up the plume of a Scud launch in southern Iraq. Data pointed to Dhahran as the target, so the city went on alert. Many people decided against going to the shelters. By now, they perceived the Scuds as almost comical, while the Patriot antimissile batteries guarding the city were deemed invincible. Neither reputation reflected the truth.

The crew that fired this particular missile likely aimed for Dhahran Air Base, a high-value military target, but, like all Scud crews, they would settle for anything of value. The air base hosted two Patriot batteries, Alpha and Bravo, which had sufficient range to protect the entire city and its suburbs. At this particular moment, Bravo's radar happened to be down for maintenance, meaning Alpha battery would need to handle the inbound Scud alone, normally a manageable task. However, presently Alpha's tracking system was suffering from a hidden software glitch.

The error caused a timing delay of just one-third of a second, which—in the world of hypersonic missiles—was a lifetime. Alpha battery's broken tracking system never spotted the forty-foot ballistic nightmare bearing down on Dhahran, and never launched a missile to intercept it.

Dhahran Air Base was spared, as the Scud missed it by a full three miles, landing instead in the suburbs of Al Khobar. The warhead unleashed its explosive fury on a long metal warehouse tucked behind a shopping center. Typically, the loss would have been limited to pallets of consumer goods, but the influx of coalition troops had meant converting the warehouse into temporary housing. Long rows of cots accommodated nearly 130 soldiers.

The 14th Quartermaster Detachment was a reserve unit from western Pennsylvania that had been activated in January and deployed to Saudi Arabia just six days ago. Despite their recent arrival, these citizen-soldiers shared the widespread indifference toward Scuds. They ignored the howling sirens, particularly since they could do little else. The strip mall had no air-raid shelter, so their orders were to shelter in place. Card games and conversations continued, as other soldiers passed the time by snoozing or writing letters home.

The warehouse interior became an instant hell as the missile plunged through the roof and gouged a twelve-foot crater in the concrete floor. A shock wave flung twisted metal, flaming cots, and torn bodies more than 100 feet in every direction. Bloody survivors crawled from a spreading blaze that seemed bent on consuming them. They dragged unconscious friends, many missing an arm or leg, into the dark parking lot. As fire engulfed the structure, ammunition from personal weapons began cooking off.

America's single worst loss of the Gulf War occurred not on the battlefront, but in an upscale Saudi district some 200 miles from the fighting. The death toll of twenty-eight could have been far worse, considering the grievous injuries to many survivors. Until now, Americans had come to regard Desert Storm as a nearly bloodless war, an impression that military briefers nurtured and cultivated. That myth became another Scud casualty.

The Patriot missile's aura of invincibility was also gone, and postwar analysis would further discredit it. Iraqi Scuds were modified from the original Soviet design to achieve greater range, and, as a result, they tended to break apart during descent. The missile's fragmentation ruined any hope of accuracy, but it also created an unintended benefit: a falling debris field that camouflaged the warhead from interceptors. Of Patriot's forty-one credited kills during the war, few if any actually involved destruction of the warhead. When it came to Scud attacks, the coalition had been lucky, in all instances except one.

～

Objective Steel, Southern Iraq
February 26, 1991 (G+2)
1502 Local

British armored forces, operating as part of Schwarzkopf's massive left hook, were streaking across the Iraqi desert toward Kuwait. Most Iraqi troops they encountered were already dead, the shredded victims of artillery or airstrikes. Those still living offered token resistance before throwing down their weapons and surrendering. The Brits paused long enough to assign escorts for a trip to the nearest detention camp, and then they continued their drive eastward.

A line of lightly armored Warrior fighting vehicles, belonging to the Royal Regiment of Fusiliers, covered the British flank. The Warriors now spotted an Iraqi column in the distance and radioed in a request for air support to destroy it. A pair of A-10s responded to the call.

Communications were less than ideal. A British air liaison officer on the ground described the situation to an American FastFAC in an F-16, who then relayed the information to the Hog drivers. The undulating desert offered few useful landmarks, so the three parties came to rely on a burning tank hulk as a point of reference.

The A-10 flight lead spotted a column from 15,000 feet and dropped down to 8,000 for a closer look. Peering through binoculars he saw tracked, sand-colored vehicles bearing no inverted V markings or fluorescent panels used by the coalition. The smoldering tank sat roughly where he expected it to be. He rolled in, as his wingman stayed high in cover, and fired a Maverick missile, scoring a hit. They swapped positions, and four minutes later the wingman fired his Maverick, also with success.

A frantic call came across the radio to cease fire immediately, as two Warrior fighting vehicles had been struck. Somehow they had mistaken the British column for the Iraqis. Nine young soldiers were dead and eleven wounded. The distraught pilots could offer no explanation, but insisted they had been told that no friendlies were within six miles of the burning tank.

Investigators determined there had been at least two tank hulks in the area, and the Warthogs had keyed off the wrong one. A postwar study found that the coalition's markings for friendly vehicles were effective only to 5,000 feet. Beyond that, a pilot would never see them.

CHAPTER 29

Waning Hours

CAPTAIN BILL ANDREWS CONSIDERED HIMSELF FORTUNATE TO BE SITting in the cockpit of an F-16, even if at the moment people were trying to kill him. Getting here had been a struggle, as the competition for fighters was always fierce. Most aspiring fighter pilots eventually opted for bombers or transports, but Andrews had refused to settle.

His first flying assignment was as an instructor pilot in the T-37 Tweet, teaching new students the same skills he himself had just mastered. Then came a four-year stint flying the EF-111 Raven, a career upgrade that still fell short of his ultimate goal. His persistence was rewarded in 1988 with an F-16 assignment, and two years later he found himself in the Persian Gulf. His first combat experience, as part of a forty-ship raid on an Iraqi airfield, was the culmination of a decade's work.

Now he was supporting the ground war, flying sorties that were more challenging and intense. The sky teemed with aircraft, increasing the chances of a midair collision. Iraqi divisions that hadn't already surrendered were now in full retreat, and their air defense units were popping up in random and unexpected places. Currently, Andrews and his wingman were thirty miles northwest of Basra, bombing a Republican Guard division, and the AAA fire was some of the worst they'd seen yet.

They dove in at a forty-five-degree angle, pickling off their bombs at about ten thousand feet, and then pulled into a high-G recovery. Andrews was turning for the egress route when an infrared-guided missile slammed into the rear of his airplane. He knew it was a heat-seeker because there had been no warning tones, only the sudden, violent impact.

"It was like I was sitting at a stop sign and someone rear-ended me," he said. "I knew that in the next couple of seconds I had to get my hands from being pinned against the canopy down to the ejection handle."[1]

He reached the handle, and seconds later he was hanging beneath an open parachute, drifting through a low cloud deck. He checked for his survival radio and felt it tucked snugly in his vest. Pulling out the radio now would be risky since he might drop it, but with Republican Guard troops waiting below, this might be his only chance to let someone know he was alive. Andrews gingerly slid the radio free. He established contact with other members of his flight, who were weaving through the clouds and AAA searching for him.

A hard landing fractured his leg, but that was the least of his concerns. Republican Guard troops were shooting at him from a distance. Bullets buzzed past and kicked up dirt all around him, so he tossed down the radio and raised his arms in surrender. The Iraqis stopped shooting. They climbed from their foxholes and began a cautious approach, their AK-47s raised and ready to fire.

As he sat there, waiting for his captors to arrive, Andrews contemplated his situation. The soldiers he had been bombing just a few minutes earlier now controlled his fate. Long ago, as a cadet at the Air Force Academy, he heard Vietnam POWs describe their captivity. The chilling stories stayed with him, and he realized he was about to endure a similar experience.

An F-16 swooped in below the cloud deck, and as it passed Andrews saw a SAM leap into the air in pursuit. If it was an infrared tracker, like the one that tagged him, the pilot would have no warning. Andrews reached out and grabbed his radio. "Break right with flares!" he yelled. The plane turned hard right and spat a stream of glowing orbs.

"He put out flares and decoyed the missile so he got away, which was great," Andrews explained. "I threw down the radio after I said that. The guys with AK-47s just kind of swept by me and shot the radio, which was right next to my hand."[2]

Rumaila Oil Field, Southeast Iraq
February 27, 1991 (G+3)
1530 Local

The liberation of Kuwait was nearly complete. Outside Kuwait City, impatient marines waited along the roadside with orders to let Arab forces liberate the capital. To the west, American armor had slammed into the Tawakalna Division and obliterated it. The remaining Republican Guard divisions now dashed for Basra, hoping to escape the same fate.

Helicopters of the 101st Airborne had established a new forward operating base, called Viper, located due west of the Rumaila Oil Field. Shortly after Bill Andrews went down on the far side of the oil field, a request came in to Viper for a rescue attempt. An 101st operations officer took down the details and then radioed a battalion search-and-rescue helicopter. Typically, the Black Hawk trailed the fighting, ready to dash forward if an Apache or Kiowa went down.

"Bengal One-Five, do you have Doc Cornum on board?" the ops officer inquired.[3]

"Bengal One-Five, roger."

"Do you have her stuff on board?"

"Yeah," the pilot replied.

"Do you have gas?"

"We just left the FARP," he said, referring to the division's forward arming and refueling point.

The ops officer explained that an F-16 pilot was down inside Republican Guard territory, and they were being tasked to go get him. The rescue chopper wasn't going in alone. A pair of Apache gunships would escort them to Andrews's coordinates and hold off any nearby Iraqis while the Black Hawk's team of Pathfinders established a perimeter on the ground. Then the battalion flight surgeon, Maj. Rhonda Cornum, could go to work.

In the rear of the helicopter, Cornum listened to the conversation on her helmet's radio headset. The thirteen-year army veteran was here by choice; she could have stayed in Fort Rucker, Alabama, but the battalion commander asked her to deploy. Although small in stature—she weighed just 110 pounds—Cornum commanded more respect than any other physician on base. As the Black Hawk lifted off, she checked her gear and developed a game plan.

"I planned to jump off with one of the Pathfinders to see if Andrews's leg was so bad that we'd need to splint it on the ground before we put him on a stretcher, or whether I could wait to work on him in the aircraft," she remembered. "I knew he was conscious because he was in radio contact, but we still had to move fast to get him on board. We couldn't leave him in the desert long, and the entire crew was vulnerable while we were on the ground."

They picked up speed, skimming the desert at 130 knots. Soon their Apache escorts arrived, one on each flank, and Cornum listened as AWACS directed the trio toward their destination.

"I remember crossing over a convoy and seeing American vehicles with inverted Vs painted on the sides and tops," she said. "We waved to the troops bundled up in their bulky chemical gear, and they waved back at us. The air was filled with smoke and soot from oil fires."

She heard the pilots debate using their night-vision goggles, even though it was only midafternoon, and she watched the swiveling heads of the door gunners as they scanned the bleak desert landscape.

"About forty-five seconds after we passed over the last American vehicle, and without any warning, green tracers began streaking up at us from the ground, while I heard the crack-crack of weapons firing," she said. "Sergeant Ortiz, the lead Pathfinder, took my head and slammed it to the floor, and in a second all three Pathfinders instinctively were half lying on me with their weapons ready."

Both door gunners opened up, filling the cabin with acrid smoke and brass shell casings. The Iraqis were scoring plenty of hits—she felt bullets biting into the airframe's metal skin. Next came the heavy boom of exploding AAA rounds. The bursts were getting closer, louder. "We're taking fire," a pilot told AWACS. The helicopter banked hard left. They were aborting the rescue attempt.

An antiaircraft round struck the tail boom, severing it. The Black Hawk's turbine engines screamed in protest.

"We're going in!" the pilot shouted.

"I took hold of something on the door frame and felt the aircraft shuddering," Cornum recalled. "We were still banked to the left when the left nose hit the sand, flattening, and then twenty thousand pounds of aircraft went end over end in a ball of flying metal and gear and spinning rotors. Everything went black."

Cornum awoke pinned beneath the wreckage. It was dark and still and quiet. Feelings of peace and serenity swept over her, followed by an almost irresistible urge to sleep. She nearly succumbed before glancing to the left and seeing a small yellow flame, like a candle. Her thoughts turned to broken fuel lines and the agony of burning to death.

She couldn't move her arms, so she kicked with her legs, digging a depression in the sand. Cornum pulled her body through the depression with a boot heel and wriggled free of the crash. She emerged to find four or five Iraqi soldiers standing over her. Unlike the POWs she had treated, these men looked well fed, with clean weapons and crisp uniforms.

"They had a professional way about them, and I recognized them as members of the Republican Guard. One of them, without saying anything, reached down and grabbed my right arm," she said. His tugging caused an unbearable pain. She screamed, and began to realize the extent of her injuries. "My arm was broken between the shoulder and the elbow, but it wasn't a displaced fracture. At least not until the Iraqi pulled apart the pieces of bone."

Both arms were broken, and a bullet had pierced her right shoulder. Of the seven others aboard, only two survived. Both pilots were dead. The armored Apaches managed to withdraw with heavy damage. They reported the rescue chopper down, likely with all hands lost—it was difficult to imagine anyone surviving that impact. Yet when a search party reached the crash site, they found only five bodies. There was no sign of Doc Cornum or the two crewmen.

* * *

The Iraqi evacuation of Kuwait City began on the evening of February 25, when Saddam announced the withdrawal of all forces due to "special circumstances." Soon after, U.S. Navy A-6 Intruders and J-STARS ground-surveillance aircraft confirmed a mass and panicked exodus. Iraqi tanks and armored personnel carriers were heading north toward Basra, part of an enormous convoy that included commandeered luxury cars and public buses. The invaders were leaving, and taking as much of Kuwait as they could drive or carry. Stolen vehicles brimmed with electronics, jewelry, artwork, and household furnishings. Six months earlier, Iraq's army rolled triumphantly down Highway 80, and now they fled via the same route.

Buster Glosson called the F-15E wing commander at Al Kharj and told him to launch a dozen precision bombers immediately. The Strike Eagles were already fully engaged, their commander explained. The only crews on the ground had just entered a long-overdue rest period. Glosson said to wake them up and get them flying. He needed all-weather aircraft.

Groggy Strike Eagle crews left Al Kharj in makeshift flights of two and four, essentially planning the attack along the way. "There was a huge thunderstorm just south of Basra and north of Kuwait City," one flight lead noted.[4] "It was right over the main drag where those guys were running north. At first, I thought I could skirt the west edge of it, then turn in from the north. But when we got up there, I could see that there was no way that could be done. So I said, 'Okay, we're going in,' and boom, we turned right and went into the worst thunderstorm I have ever seen in my life."

Webbed lightning flashed continually and heavy turbulence rattled the cockpit. Rain sheeted so thickly that the plane's targeting radar couldn't reach the ground. Yet through it all, they could see a shimmering river of headlights that stretched for miles across all six lanes. It looked like rush hour in a major American city. The Iraqi convoy spilled onto a secondary highway that ran along the coast. A pair of Strike Eagles pushed north to a spot where the two roads intersected.

"We figured we would bottle them up at this intersection," a weapon systems officer explained. "We rolled in on the first pass, dropped three bombs, saw them hit, saw a couple of secondary explosions, then lots of AAA started coming up. This was like going after a cornered animal. They were pissed and the AAA got really heavy."

As both highways descended into hopeless gridlock, the F-15Es rolled in, carving chunks from the traffic jam with cluster bombs. The thunderstorm moved out to sea, permitting other strike aircraft to participate in the turkey shoot. USS *Ranger* crept closer to shore so her Intruders could forgo the tankers and fly directly to the highway. Deck crews went into overdrive, rearming the planes with any available ordnance just to get them back in the air. Daylight brought A-10 Warthogs to the Highway of Death, as the media had begun to call it, and the deep burp of their strafing runs could be heard until sundown.

American aircraft hammered the stalled convoy for two full days and nights, destroying more than 1,400 vehicles. Most occupants ran into the desert when the airstrikes began, but at least 300 charred corpses remained. Some reporters claimed the death toll was actually in the thousands, and Highway of Death stories began to dominate the news coverage. In Washington, the Bush administration faced a problematic question: When should a rout end? Kuwait was free, and intelligence reports suggested the Republican Guard was nearly dismantled. The pre-war objectives had been met. Nobody wanted to tarnish the coalition's victory with vengeful slaughter, or even the appearance of it.

As stark television images showed the blackened traffic jam, Colin Powell called Schwarzkopf and said the president wanted a quick, clean end. The two generals had discussed this subject before, but now Powell spoke of a specific time. White House strategists wanted to conclude the ground war precisely 100 hours after it started, which meant a ceasefire at 0800 on February 28, Gulf time.

Schwarzkopf looked at his watch—only six hours away. His top-level commanders, including Chuck Horner, had no objections so Schwarzkopf agreed. The war would end in six hours.

CHAPTER 30

Vague Victory

REPORTS OF THE REPUBLICAN GUARD'S DEMISE WERE PREMATURE. Certainly, the Tawakalna Division was gone, but its death bought time for other divisions to escape to Basra, where they hid their armor in residential neighborhoods. Schwarzkopf told reporters that all but 300 Iraqi tanks had been destroyed, but a postwar CIA study revised that number to 842, nearly half of which were Republican Guard T-72s.

Still, there was no doubt Iraq's army had been thrashed and could no longer play regional bully. Schwarzkopf arranged for a ceasefire conference at Safwan Airfield in southeast Iraq. To attend, Saddam's delegates would need to be granted access to their own air base. When the Iraqi officers arrived, American escorts drove them to the conference tent in Humvees, while A-10s and Apaches orbited in the distance.

The general leading the Iraqi delegation seemed naïve about the scope of his defeat. When he inquired about the number of POWs the coalition held and Schwarzkopf replied 60,000, he blanched. The general turned to an aide and asked in Arabic if this was possible, but the aide only shrugged and said he did not know. The final POW head count actually exceeded 70,000.

Additional Iraqi concerns focused on lost territory, which Schwarzkopf assured them would not be permanent. Unlike Saddam, the coalition had no interest in redrawing Gulf boundaries. The Iraqi general sought permission for helicopter flights over his country, since so many roads and bridges were out. Schwarzkopf agreed, provided that no helicopter approached coalition forces, and he reiterated that any Iraqi fighters or bombers would be shot down. It was a blunder, and one Schwarzkopf would soon deeply regret. In the war's aftermath, Iraqi citizens finally rose up in defiance of the regime as hoped. Saddam responded with unrestrained violence, using helicopter gunships to quash the civilian uprisings.

In Baghdad, the coalition POWs noticed their treatment was improving. Food rations increased as the regime quickly tried to make its prisoners more presentable. Immediately after her capture, Rhonda Cornum received only crude medical care for her broken arms and other wounds. She also endured a guard's sexual assault. When the ceasefire went into effect, Cornum was admitted to Rashid Medical Center, where she received professional care supervised by the chief of orthopedics.

On the morning of March 5, Cornum and her fellow prisoners were doused with cologne and bused to a Baghdad hotel, where they were turned over to the International Red Cross. They showered for the first time in weeks, enjoyed good food, and exchanged stories of torture and deprivation. The following day they boarded a civilian jetliner and were flown to Riyadh under escort from a British Tornado and an American F-15. The POWs would return home celebrated as heroes. America's gratitude extended to all service personnel, who were welcomed back with parades and parties. The ghosts of Vietnam had been exorcised at last.

Victory's euphoria faded quickly. George Bush had assembled a diverse coalition that overcame daunting challenges to achieve its stated goals. But an unstated goal—the ouster of Saddam Hussein—remained unrealized. The dictator survived the war and the internal strife that followed and now sought to crush those factions who dared oppose him. Belatedly, the Bush administration stepped in, establishing no-fly zones in northern and southern Iraq to protect the Kurdish and Shia populations, respectively.

The no-fly zones meant the air war would continue indefinitely. American and allied pilots patrolled the zones, shooting down the occasional Iraqi fighter, and engaging air defense batteries that harassed them almost daily. In April 1994, a flight of F-15Cs patrolling the northern zone misidentified a pair of army Black Hawk helicopters, which were ferrying an international team to meet with Kurdish representatives. AWACS failed to correct the error and the Eagles destroyed both helicopters with missiles, killing all twenty-six aboard.

Consequences of Desert Storm rippled outward in unimaginable ways. The original deployment of U.S. troops to Saudi Arabia—and their continued presence after the war—was viewed by Islamic fundamentalists as a desecration of sacred soil. One wealthy and influential Saudi radical, who spent much of the 1980s fighting the Soviet occupation of Afghanistan, needed a new enemy to rally his followers. Osama bin Laden used the U.S. military presence to focus his newly formed Al Qaeda on the United States.

* * *

For years, military analysts studied the forty-three-day air campaign, trying to determine if Desert Storm represented a new era in aerial warfare. Airpower, it seemed, had been more decisive in the Gulf War than in any other conflict in American history. From stealthy F-117 Nighthawks releasing precision-guided munitions, to the brutish A-10 Warthog with its tank-shredding cannon, coalition warplanes clearly had made a difference. The analysts tried to quantify airpower's contribution to defeating Iraq.

The most exhaustive study, the five-volume *Gulf War Air Power Survey*, was commissioned by the secretary of the air force and directed by Johns Hopkins University. The survey concluded that airpower paved the way to a swift victory by coalition ground forces. A 1994 study by RAND Corporation entitled *A League of Airmen* largely supported this finding, but it too was paid for by the air force, leaving a lingering question of bias.

The U.S. General Accounting Office (GAO; now Government Accountability Office) released an objective evaluation of the air campaign in 1997. GAO findings dampened some of the earlier enthusiasm about precision weapons. Analysts noted that the F-117's bombing accuracy never exceeded 60 percent, well below the original air force estimate of 80 percent. Tomahawk cruise missiles fell well short of the 98 percent accuracy initially claimed by the navy, although investigators decided to keep classified the Tomahawk success rate they calculated. Despite the downgrades, GAO authors noted that precision weapons were still vastly superior to unguided bombs.

"The air campaign, which incurred minimal casualties while effecting the collapse of the Iraqis' ability to resist, helped liberate Kuwait and elicit Iraqi compliance with U.N. resolutions," the GAO ultimately concluded.[1]

In 2001 the scholarly journal *International Security* published an article entitled "The Myth of Air Power in the Persian Gulf War and the Future of Warfare," by Daryl G. Press, a professor of government at Dartmouth College. "The evidence from the ground campaign shows that the conventional wisdom about the Gulf War is wrong," Press stated. "Although air power played an important role in the coalition's victory, its role has been exaggerated and misunderstood."[2]

Press argued that coalition aircraft failed to significantly reduce the strength or morale of Iraq's army, and that coalition ground forces would have achieved a lopsided victory even without a protracted air campaign. "At most, 40 percent of Iraqi armored vehicles were neutralized by the air campaign," Press wrote. "But a close look at the ground battles strongly suggests that these vehicles would not have caused many additional coalition casualties had there been no air war." He estimated the increase at "maybe an additional 20–200 dead."

Schwarzkopf and his generals acknowledged after the war that they had overestimated the size and skill of Iraq's army. And there could be no doubt that the air campaign had its shortcomings. While many front-line Iraqi troops were found starving, the rear echelon Republican Guard units remained well fed and supplied, suggesting that airstrikes on Iraqi supply lines were less than completely effective. Horner and Glosson also noted that Iraqi communications remained functional, largely due to a backup network of underground cables.

Regardless, an outright dismissal of the air campaign's effect on the ground war is difficult to fathom. No ground commander in history would decline the opportunity to have enemy strength reduced by 40 percent. Just as important was the air campaign's psychological impact on Iraqi forces. During the ground war, there were documented instances of Iraqi units surrendering to scout helicopters and tank crews wriggling from their hatches and running away at the sight of coalition aircraft. "In the Iran-Iraq War my tank was my friend," said one captured Iraqi general, "because I could sleep my soldiers in it and keep them safe from Iranian artillery. In this war, my tank was my enemy."[3]

The only bona fide myth of the Gulf War air campaign was that it had been a bloodless affair. Journalists latched onto this notion early in the war, after viewing footage of laser-guided bombs plunging down air ducts. Schwarzkopf and his public affairs staff reinforced the impression of a video game war during their daily press briefings.

"I'm now going to show you a picture of the luckiest man in Iraq," the general told his audience one morning. Gun-camera video rolled of a precision strike on an Iraqi bridge. "Keep your eye on the crosshairs," he said. A truck appeared on the bridge, passing directly through the crosshairs as the aircrew refined their aim. The oblivious truck driver reached the far end while the bomb was in flight. "And now, in his rearview mirror," Schwarzkopf joked as a massive explosion consumed the bridge. Everyone chuckled.

"Great PR footage, a near-sanitary war; even the soldiers don't seem to get killed," remarked one A-6 Intruder pilot. "[My air wing], like most of the combatant outfits in the theater, I am sure, had similar video, with a slightly different end to the story. The video is there, with the crosshairs tracking a group of trucks as they race down a road. The guys in the trucks obviously know that someone is after them, because soon into the footage the trucks abruptly pull over to the side and stop, and their occupants get out and begin running for a nearby ditch.

"Here is where things change. The FLIR [forward-looking infrared] reticle moves off of the stationary trucks, and the crosshairs are now superimposed over the ditch where the Iraqis are trying to hide. Seconds later the ditch blows up, undoubtedly killing all of its cowering inhabitants."[4]

The air campaign killed 10,000 to 12,000 enemy combatants. The Iraqi government claimed that 2,300 civilians died during airstrikes, a number that went uncontested. Civilian casualties are always regrettable, but the care exercised by Desert Storm aviators was unprecedented in the history of air warfare. American and allied warplanes dropped 88,500 tons of bombs in just six weeks. The three-and-a-half-year Rolling Thunder campaign totaled 864,000 tons of bombs, roughly ten times more. Yet despite meticulous efforts to limit North Vietnamese civilian casualties, U.S. estimates put Rolling Thunder's civilian death toll at 182,000, or *seventy-nine times greater* than in Desert Storm.

When the Vietnam War finally ended, a cadre of young officers from all services returned home vowing the mistakes of the past would not be repeated. This group, aided by a Reagan-era surge in defense spending, would lead the U.S. military through a transformation. Desert Storm was proof that their career-long goal had been attained and they could retire satisfied. Within five years, Schwarzkopf, Horner, Glosson, and most of the other Vietnam holdovers were gone.

The next generation of American military leaders would face new challenges—volatile peacekeeping missions in Somalia and the former Yugoslavia, followed by lengthy post-9/11 campaigns in Afghanistan and Iraq. For these men and women, the experience gained from Desert Storm would prove invaluable.

ACKNOWLEDGMENTS

I am grateful to the pilots and other Gulf War veterans who took the time to describe their experiences to me. Every person I interviewed was kind, patient, and forthcoming. I only hope I did their stories justice.

My gratitude extends to those individuals who furnished background information but were not mentioned by name in the final draft. They include Capt. Chuck Maurer (U.S. Army), who as a young 82nd Airborne paratrooper witnessed the devastating effects of airstrikes on Iraqi forces. Lieutenant Colonel Jim Keck (USAF, retired), an electronic warfare expert, told me about: flying in the back seat of an F-4G Wild Weasel, working at the TACC in Riyadh, and sitting in the command chair of an AWACS plane. These details were invaluable.

My sincerest appreciation goes to Col. Ralph Getchell (USAF, retired) and Maj. Emmett Tullia (USAF, retired), who reviewed all or a portion of the manuscript for accuracy, and to Mr. Barry Sparks, a veteran journalist and longtime friend, who offered valuable feedback regarding flow and content. Any errors in this book are my responsibility alone, and unrelated to their generous efforts.

Military history editor Dave Reisch was supportive and encouraging, and I am grateful to him and the entire Stackpole team.

Finally, I would like to acknowledge the more than 600,000 American military members who deployed to the Persian Gulf for Operation Desert Storm. You made it look easy; we know it wasn't.

APPENDIX

Table 1. Iraqi Flight Activity Versus Coalition Kills. Source: *Gulf War Air Power Survey*

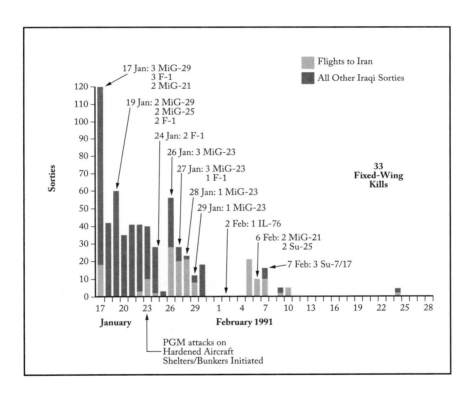

Table 2. Coalition Air Strikes by Day Against Iraqi Targets. Source: *Gulf War Air Power Survey*

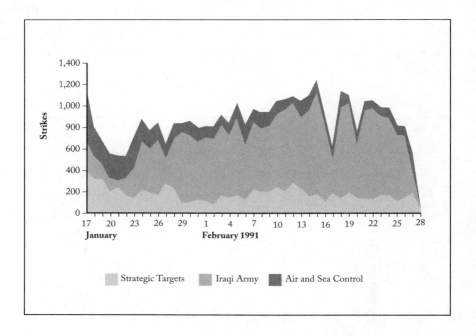

FURTHER READING

Two books from the 1990s remain the best general accounts of the Gulf War, describing the combat by air, land, and sea, as well as the political and diplomatic intrigue surrounding it. Of these two nonfiction narratives, Rick Atkinson's *Crusade: The Untold Story of the Persian Gulf War* (1993) is slightly more entertaining because of Atkinson's eloquence and Pulitzer-winning journalistic flair. But *The Generals' War: The Inside Story of the Conflict in the Gulf* (1995) by Michael R. Gordon and retired U.S. Marine general Bernard E. Trainor also reads well and has the edge in military analysis, particularly with regard to the ground war. These volumes make good companions and can be read together without becoming repetitive.

It Doesn't Take a Hero: The Autobiography of General H. Norman Schwarzkopf (with co-author Peter Petre, 1992) and *Every Man a Tiger: The Gulf War Air Campaign* by Tom Clancy and Chuck Horner (1999) chronicle two long and distinguished military careers that culminated with leadership of Operation Desert Storm. Schwarzkopf and Horner both describe their disillusionment with U.S. practices during the Vietnam War, and their decision to remain in the military and help foster change. Their Gulf War accounts naturally focus on the high-level strategic and logistical challenges they faced while managing the war from Riyadh, which offer a glimpse into the wily chess game Saddam Hussein played with coalition leaders.

For a look at the war from inside the cockpit, turn to William L. Smallwood's twin books *Warthog: Flying the A-10 in the Gulf War* (1993) and *Strike Eagle: Flying the F-15E in the Gulf War* (1994). Smallwood traveled to U.S. Air Force bases around the country, collecting hundreds of interviews from recently returned Hog drivers and Strike Eagle crews. He then wove their individual stories into fast-paced tributes to two highly successful aircraft types. Smallwood steps back and lets these combat veterans describe the missions in their own words, complete with the colorful slang and jargon unique to military aviation.

Several pilots returned home to write their own accounts. Keith Rosenkranz's *Vipers in the Storm: Diary of a Gulf War Fighter Pilot* (1999) features plenty of combat sorties but also offers special insight into the everyday life of an F-16 jock. Details of running through preflight, or the nuances of using a "piddle pack" might not interest the casual reader but will captivate aviation buffs. The U.S. Navy counterpart is *Angles of Attack: An A-6 Intruder Pilot's War* (2002) by Peter Hunt. Before joining the navy and earning his wings, Hunt obtained a history degree from Brown University, and his adept writing shines in this tale of flying the now-retired Intruder and living aboard the now-scrapped *Ranger*.

For reference books, find a copy of *Gulf Air War Debrief* (1991) edited by Stan Morse and printed by London's Aerospace Publishing. For a coffee table book that appeared just a few months after the war, it contains a wealth of useful information accompanied by rich photography and artwork. Finally, the thin but nicely illustrated volumes by Osprey Publishing can also be useful, particularly when researching the contributions of a specific aircraft type.

NOTES

Prologue

1. Quotations and descriptions concerning the Jeff Tice shootdown come from the following sources:

   Mary Jordan, "Pilot Tells Terror of Bailout, 46 Days as a POW," *Washington Post*, March 16, 1991; Keith Rosenkranz, *Vipers in the Storm: Diary of a Gulf War Fighter Pilot* (New York: McGraw-Hill Professional Publishing, 1999), 192–95; F-16 HUD tape of Col. Jerry Nelson, commander of the 401st TFW(P), January 19, 1991; and telephone interviews with Maj. Emmett Tullia (USAF, retired), spring and summer 2015.

Chapter 1: Seeds of Crisis

1. Norman Schwarzkopf and Peter Petre, *It Doesn't Take a Hero: The Autobiography of General H. Norman Schwarzkopf* (New York: Bantam, 1992), 339.
2. Ibid.
3. Michael R. Gordon and Bernard E. Trainor, *The Generals' War: The Inside Story of the Conflict in the Gulf* (New York: Little Brown & Co., 1995), 26.
4. Schwarzkopf and Petre, *Hero*, 340.

Chapter 2: Deployment

1. Quotations in this section are from Schwarzkopf and Petre, *Hero*, 352–53.
2. Stan Morse, ed., *Gulf Air War Debrief* (London: Aerospace Publishing, 1991), 13.
3. William L. Smallwood, *Warthog: Flying the A-10 in the Gulf War* (Dulles, VA: Brassey's Inc., 1993), 25.

Chapter 3: Turbulence

1. Tom Clancy and Chuck Horner, *Every Man a Tiger* (New York: Putnam, 1999), 175.
2. Ibid., 93.
3. John W. Leland and Kathryn A. Wilcoxson, "The Chronological History of the C-5 Galaxy," Office of History, Air Mobility Command, Scott Air Force Base, Illinois, May 2003.
4. E-mail correspondence with Cynthia Borecky Knapp (USAF, retired), September 2015.
5. Telephone interview with Frederick K. Arzt (USAF, retired), September 23, 2015.
6. List of fatalities:

   Maj. John M. Gordon, Aircraft Commander, 68 MAS, Kelly AFB TX

Maj. Richard W. Chase, Pilot, 68 MAS, Kelly AFB TX
Maj. Richard M. Price, Pilot, 68 MAS, Kelly AFB TX
Sr. M.Sgt. Carpio Villarreal Jr., Flight Engineer, 68 MAS, Kelly AFB TX
M.Sgt. Rosendo Herrera, Flight Engineer, 68 MAS, Kelly AFB TX
Tech. Sgt. Daniel G. Perez, Loadmaster, 68 MAS, Kelly AFB TX
S.Sgt. Edward E. Sheffield, Loadmaster, 68 MAS, Kelly AFB TX
Tech. Sgt. Lonty A. Knutson, Crew Chief, 68 MAS, Kelly AFB TX
S.Sgt. Daniel Garza, Crew Chief, 433 OMS, Kelly AFB TX
Capt. Bradley R. Schuldt, Passenger, 7 AD, Ramstein AB GE
M.Sgt. Samuel M. Gardner Jr., Passenger, Det 14, 31 WS, Hahn AB GE
S.Sgt. Marc H. Cleyman, Passenger, Det 14, 31 WS, Hahn AB GE
S.Sgt. Rande J. Hulec, Passenger, Det 2, 31 WS, Ramstein AB GE
7. Gordon and Trainor, *Generals' War*, 84.

Chapter 4: Instant Thunder
1. Quotes and descriptions from the Horner/Warden clash come from the following sources:
   Rick Atkinson, *Crusade: The Untold Story of the Persian Gulf War* (New York: Houghton Mifflin, 1993), 61–63; Clancy and Horner, *Tiger*, 244–49; and Gordon and Trainor, *Generals' War*, 91–94.
2. William L. Smallwood, *Strike Eagle: Flying the F-15E in the Gulf War* (Dulles, VA: Brassey's Inc., 1994), 36.

Chapter 5: Black Hole
1. Buster Glosson, *War with Iraq: Critical Lessons* (Charlotte, NC: Glosson Family Foundation, 2003), 17.
2. Mark Bowden, "The Desert One Debacle," *The Atlantic*, May 2006.
3. Glosson, *Critical Lessons*, 83.
4. Smallwood, *Strike Eagle*, 48.
5. Gordon and Trainor, *Generals' War*, 200.
6. Glosson, *Critical Lessons*, 113.

Chapter 6: Leading Edge
1. Atkinson, *Crusade*, 15.
2. Warren Thompson, *F-117 Stealth Fighter Units of Operation Desert Storm* (Oxford, England: Osprey Publishing, 2007), 28.

Chapter 7: First In
1. Major A. J. C. Lavalle, ed., "The Tale of Two Bridges and The Battle for the Skies Over North Vietnam," Office of Air Force History, Washington, D.C., 1985.
2. Telephone interviews with Col. Ralph Getchell (USAF, retired), summer 2015.
3. Clancy and Horner, *Tiger*, 322.

Chapter 8: Attack of the Machines

1. In most instances, SAM kills are nearly impossible to confirm. A radar may go offline because it has been destroyed, or because the operator has shut it down to avoid destruction.
   Williamson Murray, *Air War in the Persian Gulf* (Mount Pleasant, SC: Nautical & Aviation Publishing Company of America, 1995), 118.
2. See Dogfights television series, "Dogfights of Desert Storm," Season 2, Episode 12, originally aired by History Channel on December 5, 2007.
3. Steve Davies, *F-15C Eagle Units in Combat* (Oxford, England: Osprey Publishing, 2005), 40.

Chapter 9: Bogeys and Bandits

1. Davies, *F-15C Eagle Units*, 36.
2. Morse, *Debrief*, 51.
3. Davies, *F-15C Eagle Units*, 42.
4. Edward Colimore, "Home Supplants Terrain of War," *Philadelphia Inquirer*, March 25, 1991.
5. Morse, *Debrief*, 71.
6. Ibid.

Chapter 10: Luck Runs Out

1. Julia M. Klein, "The First U.S. Casualty: 'A Life-affirming Person,'" *Philadelphia Inquirer*, January 19, 1991.
2. Lon Wagner and Amy Yarsinske, "Scott Speicher—Dead or Alive?" *Virginian-Pilot*, December 30, 2001.
3. Robert Wilcox, *Wings of Fury* (New York: Simon & Schuster, 1997), 276.
4. Spoken by Lt. Cdr. Barry Hull, VFA-81. Quote from Wagner and Yarsinske, "Scott Speicher—Dead or Alive?"
5. Central Intelligence Agency Report, "Unclassified Intelligence Community Assessment of the Lieutenant Commander Speicher Case," March 27, 2001.

Chapter 11: Low Level

1. Morse, *Debrief*, 56.
2. "BBC On This Day—1991: Tornado Down," accessed May 20, 2016, http://news.bbc.co.uk/onthisday/hi/witness/january/17/newsid_2641000/2641621.stm. Also see John Peters and John Nichol, *Tornado Down* (London: Signet, 1993).
3. Atkinson, Crusade, 101.

Chapter 12: Basra Raid

1. Smallwood, *Strike Eagle*, 90.
2. Davies, *F-15C Eagle Units*, 24.

3. For additional quotes and descriptions of this incident, see Smallwood, *Strike Eagle*, 92–102.

Chapter 13: Pain and Suffering

1. Guy Hunter, in a videotaped interview conducted by staff of the National Prisoner of War Museum, Andersonville, Georgia, June 1996.
2. Edward J. Marolda and Robert J. Schneller Jr., *Shield and Sword: The United States Navy and the Persian Gulf War* (Annapolis, MD: Naval Institute Press, 2001), 183.

Chapter 14: Package Q

1. Telephone interviews with Maj. Emmett Tullia (USAF, retired), spring and summer 2015. Additional quotes and descriptions from Maj. Tullia's F-16 HUD tape, January 19, 1991.
2. First Lieutenant Kimberly D. Snow, "20 years later: Former Gulf War POW, current Ohio Air National Guard member remembers captivity," accessed May 22, 2016, http://www.ong.ohio.gov/stories/2011/062011_roberts.html.
3. Rosenkranz, *Vipers in the Storm*, 178.
4. Snow, "20 years later."

Chapter 15: Eagles Go Hunting

1. *Dogfights*, "Dogfights of Desert Storm."
2. Ibid.

Chapter 16: Great Scud Hunt

1. Smallwood, *Warthog*, 92.
2. Ibid.
3. Atkinson, *Crusade*, 125.
4. David Eberly, *Faith Beyond Belief: A Journey to Freedom* (Richmond, VA: Brandylane Publishers, 2002), 10.

Chapter 17: Search and Rescue

1. Eberly, *Faith Beyond Belief*, 15.
2. Darrel D. Whitcomb, *Combat Search and Rescue in Desert Storm* (Maxwell Air Force Base, AL: Air University Press, 2006), 9.
3. Smallwood, *Strike Eagle*, 128.
4. Whitcomb, *Combat Search and Rescue*, 128.
5. Ibid., 129.
6. Captain Michael P. Vriesenga, ed., *From the Line in the Sand: Accounts of USAF Company Grade Officers in Support of Desert Shield/Desert Storm* (Maxwell Air Force Base, AL: Air University Press, 1994), 179.
7. Morse, *Debrief*, 99.
8. Vriesenga, *Line in the Sand*, 182.

9. Guy Gugliotta, "Downed Navy Flier Rescued in Iraq," *Washington Post*, January 22, 1991.
10. Smallwood, *Warthog*, 106.

Chapter 18: Desperation
1. Smallwood, *Strike Eagle*, 132.
2. Whitcomb, *Combat Search and Rescue*, 132.
3. Smallwood, *Strike Eagle*, 133.
4. Whitcomb, *Combat Search and Rescue*, 136.
5. Ibid., 137.
6. Michael C. Berryman, in a videotaped interview conducted by staff of the National Prisoner of War Museum, Andersonville, Georgia, June 1996.

Chapter 19: Bag of Tricks
1. Atkinson, *Crusade*, 187.

Chapter 20: Taking Shelter
1. Warren Thompson, *F-117 Stealth Fighter Units of Operation Desert Storm* (Oxford, England: Osprey Publishing, 2007), 39.
2. Telephone interview with Brig. Gen. Tony Schiavi (USAF, retired), July 31, 2015. Also see: Morse, *Debrief*, 94, and the F-15C HUD tape of Capt. Rhory Draeger, January 26, 1991.

Chapter 21: Khafji
1. The lost crew of Spirit Zero-Three:
   Maj. Paul Weaver
   Capt. Thomas Bland
   Capt. Arthur Galvan
   Capt. William Grimm
   Capt. Dixon Walters
   Sr. M.Sgt. Paul Buege
   Sr. M.Sgt. Jim May
   Tech. Sgt. Robert Hodges
   Tech. Sgt. John Oelschlager
   S.Sgt. John Blessinger
   S.Sgt. Tim Harrison
   S.Sgt. Damon Kanuha
   S.Sgt. Mark Schmauss
   Sgt. Barry Clark

Chapter 22: Preparing the Battlefield
1. Smallwood, *Warthog*, 96.

2. Ibid., 126.
3. Ibid., 138.
4. Reed Karaim, "B-52 Crash in Gulf War was Eerie Repeat," *Philadelphia Inquirer*, August 18, 1991.

Chapter 23: Kill Box
1. Glosson, *Critical Lessons*, 194.
2. Atkinson, *Crusade*, 263.
3. Ibid., 312.
4. Smallwood, *Warthog*, 176.
5. Ibid., 177.

Chapter 24: Missteps
1. PBS *Frontline*, "The Gulf War," accessed June 1, 2016, http://www.pbs.org/wgbh/pages/frontline/gulf/war/3.html.
2. Eberly, *Faith Beyond Belief*, 130.
3. Berryman, National Prisoner of War Museum interview.

Chapter 25: Close Calls
1. Scott Thomas, "Ejecting Out of a Flaming F-16 Over Iraq," *San Antonio Express-News*, May 13, 2011. Thomas's account includes transcribed dialogue from the mission tape that day.

Chapter 26: Left Hook
1. Morse, *Debrief*, 160.
2. Gordon and Trainor, *Generals' War*, 366.
3. Morse, *Debrief*, 168.

Chapter 27: Twenty-Three Tanks
1. Smallwood, *Warthog*, 195.
2. Morse, *Debrief*, 177.
3. Captain Eric Salomonson and Lt. John Marks, videotaped interview conducted by the joint media pool in Saudi Arabia on February 26, 1991, accessed June 2, 2016, http://www.c-span.org/video/?16771-1/a10-fighter-pilots-persian-gulf-war.
4. Smallwood, *Warthog*, 196.

Chapter 28: Missiles and Misfortune
1. Smallwood, *Strike Eagle*, 145.

Chapter 29: Waning Hours

1. Chuck Paone, "'Heritage' speakers offer insights on pride, sacrifice and service," November 3, 2009, accessed June 3, 2016, http://www.afmc.af.mil/news/story .asp?id=123175543.
2. Colonel William F. Andrews, transcribed interview conducted by VMI Cadet Philip Wilkerson on March 15, 2008, accessed June 3, 2016, http://digitalcollections.vmi .edu/cdm/ref/collection/p15821coll13/id/18.
3. Rhonda Cornum and Peter Copeland, *She Went to War: The Rhonda Cornum Story* (Novato, CA: Presidio Press, 1992), 6.
4. Smallwood, *Strike Eagle*, 198.

Chapter 30: Vague Victory

1. U.S. General Accounting Office, "Operation Desert Storm: Evaluation of the Air Campaign," June 1997, 36.
2. See International Security, Fall 2001, Volume 26, Number 2, 5–44.
3. Clancy and Horner, *Tiger*, 478.
4. Peter Hunt, *Angles of Attack: An A-6 Intruder Pilot's War* (New York: Ballentine, 2002), 313.

INDEX